D1281947

Louis Kahn to Anne Tyng

The Rome Letters 1953–1954

Louis Kahn
to Anne Tyng

The Rome Letters 1953–1954

Edited with Commentary by
Anne Griswold Tyng

*To Louis Kahn's children and the grandchildren he never knew
in the hope that they will discover and understand more of him as
a human being.*

*To our daughter Alex and her husband (Lou's great nephew)
Steve and their children Becca and Julian.*

To Sue and her son Gregory.

To Nathaniel.

First published in the United States of America in 1997 by
Rizzoli International Publications, Inc.
300 Park Avenue South, New York, NY 10010

Copyright ©1997 by Rizzoli International Publications, Inc.

All rights reserved. No part of this publication may be reproduced in any manner whatsoever
without permission in writing from Rizzoli International Publications, Inc.

Library of Congress Cataloging-in-Publication Data
Kahn, Louis I., 1901–1974
  Louis Kahn to Anne Tyng : the Rome letters 1953–1954 / edited with
    commentary by Anne Griswold Tyng
      p. cm.
    Includes index.
  ISBN 0–8478–2009–2 (hc). — ISBN 0–8478–2053–X (pbk.)
  1. Kahn, Louis I., 1901–1974—Correspondence. 2. Architects—
United States—Correspondence. 3. Tyng, Anne Griswold, 1920– .
I. Tyng, Anne Griswold, 1920– . II. Title.
NA737.K32A3   1997
720'.92
[B]—dc21   97–15445
                    CIP

Designed by Sisco & Evans
Printed and bound in Singapore

Contents

$5 \times 3'\text{-}9\frac{5}{8} = H.$

Preface

$3 \times 3\text{-}9\frac{5}{8} = H \; of \; Flr$

It is rare indeed when the passionate search in architecture is shared
by two people who are passionate about each other.
Lou Kahn wrote to me in 1954, "I am waiting anxiously for us
to be together again in our own wonderful way of love and work
which again is nothing really but another form of that love.
I believe it can only be that way with a few."
I believe our creative work together deepened our relationship
and the relationship enlarged our creativity. In our years of working together
toward a goal outside ourselves, believing profoundly in each other's abilities
helped us to believe in ourselves.
Although we were born in quite different parts of the globe,
and came from different cultures and religions, we shared
a sense of ourselves and each other that was somehow free of the
perception of those differences as limitations.
The differences only expanded our view of the world
and each other.

—*Anne Griswold Tyng*

Born on a Castled Island in the Baltic

1 Kahn told me that his year of birth was actually 1902, but was incorrectly documented as 1901 by an immigration official when he entered the United States.

2 When I was invited to teach at the Baltic Summer School of Architecture and Planning in Tallinn and Parnü, Estonia, my acceptance was strongly motivated by my desire to visit Lou's birthplace.

In 1901[1] Louis Kahn was born on the castled island of Saaremaa (formerly Ösel) in the Baltic Sea off the coast of Estonia. Roughly the size of Rhode Island, the island is now part of Estonia, although at different times it has belonged to Finland, Sweden, Denmark, Germany, and, most recently, Russia. In the light of the complicated history of his birthplace, Lou understandably described himself as a Finnish Jew since the Finno-Ugric language is still a bond between Estonia, Finland, and Scandinavia. Lou was only five when he immigrated to the United States with his mother, younger sister, and brother, his father having preceded them. At that time the usual access to Saaremaa was by boat from Riga, Latvia. When I visited Saaremaa in 1993 I was able to go by bus from Tallinn, by ferry across the water, continuing by bus to the only town on the island, Kuressaare.[2] Lou's description of the castle on Saaremaa had given it a fairy-tale quality. And there, dominating the town and the island like a fairy tale come true, is the Bishop's Castle, a stronghold now used as a museum. Its tower, built by the 1260s, was incorporated during the period from 1338 to 1381 into the present massive cubic structure with its inner courtyard. Around the castle are angled ramparts featuring a watchtower, all surrounded by a moat. The castle must have been etched in the memory of a boy of five with its impressive scale dominating the small town of almost entirely one- and two-story buildings.

The fourteenth-century Bishop's Castle at Kuressaare on the island of Saaremaa in Estonia provided the young Louis Kahn with an early model of monumentality.

Courtyard and tower of the Bishop's Castle at Kuressaare.

A typical church on the island of Gotland near Tingstäde, an ancient site of a Viking ting *or court (from which the name Tyng is derived).*

This early experience of monumentality was reinforced when Kahn returned to visit his birthplace as an architect of twenty-seven—no wonder Lou was in love with castles. For almost a month, Kahn revisited childhood scenes and while he was there slept on the floor of his great aunt's one-room dwelling. He recalled with relish eating the simple fare of little red potatoes and flat fish.

The island has white cliffs along one side. On a gentler shore a nature preserve has been established. Windmills are strategically placed on soft rises of land near the edges of the island and on promontories to catch the Baltic winds. The wood detailing of the windmills and the more elaborate wood detailing of some of the houses must certainly have caught Lou's eye. The island is dotted with white churches built of dolomite from the local quarry. The Karma church is unusual in having a single row of columns down the central aisle. Even if Lou did not go into the churches, he would not have missed the expression of scale that pervades their architecture. From the top of tower or spire to the main body of the church, the scale steps down to an attached lower roof aligned with the main roof, stepping down again to the roof of a smaller wing. What appears as a miniature door emphasizes human size, linking it by the progression of roofs to the top of the spire. Often the walls have only a few small openings of squares, triangles, or circles. An architectural historian in Tallinn told me that a comparative study has noted similarities between the churches on Saaremaa and those on the neighboring island of Gotland.

On Saaremaa there is a small crater and on my visit to Gotland I had found a similar, somewhat larger crater lake at Tingstäde, an ancient site of a Viking *ting* or court (from which my name Tyng is derived). I wondered if parts of the same meteorite might have landed, creating both craters. Such a possible cosmic connection recalled the fantasy Lou and I had that our remote ancestors had met somewhere in the Baltic. We imagined that my ancestor, a Viking chieftain, had carried off his ancestor, a Laplander princess. Lou reminded me of a Laplander with his pronounced cheekbones and the upward tilt of his eyes.

A comparative study has noted similarities between the churches on Saaremaa and those on the neighboring island of Gotland.

Louis Kahn's father and mother, Leopold Kahn and Bertha Mendelsohn Kahn, c. 1900.

Lou's father, Leopold Kahn, from Estonia, met his mother, Bertha Mendelsohn, in the Baltic port of Riga while on leave from the Russian army in which he served as paymaster. On leaving the army Leopold lived with Bertha on Saaremaa where he was a scribe for residents of the castle. Lou once told me that his great aunt's family had owned a resort hotel on Saaremaa. Family lore has it that Bertha Mendelsohn was related to the musician Felix Mendelssohn. My research suggests the connection may be through one of Felix Mendelssohn's cousins, married to a young woman whose family owned a string of hotels. One hotel on the Baltic in Germany was where the Mendelsohn family stayed en masse. Bertha played the harp and was familiar with the works of Goethe and Schiller, a cultural background that suggests she came from a well-to-do family. Both Leopold and Bertha came from large families of six or so siblings.

When I met Lou's parents, I felt an immediate fondness for them. His mother reminded me of my own mother in her warm universality and positive attitude. To a degree Kahn resembled his mother—they both had blue eyes and wavy sandy hair. He seemed to have inherited her philosophic nature as well as a good dose of his father's humor. His father was full of jokes and, although a somewhat flirtatious romantic, I understand he could be quite stern.

Louis Kahn's fascination with the light of glowing coals almost cost him his life. When he was three, he shoveled coal into his pinafore apron. Flames seared his face and the palms of his hands with which he instinctively shielded his eyes. Because of the severe pain and the prolonged suffering without proper treatment, his father at first thought it might be better if he died, but his mother was determined that he live. The fact that he lived of course made him more precious to his parents, and Lou himself must have unconsciously experienced a triumph or transcendence in having survived. This traumatic event recalls the archetypal story of the infant Moses who was tested with hot

coals. Perhaps a memory of the infant Moses' ordeal reinforced his parents' belief that Lou was destined for greatness. His father, who at times worked as a stained glass artist and whose graceful script made him a valuable scribe, encouraged his son to draw. One of Lou's memories as a small child is of his father, with Lou's hand in his, tracing the patterns made by icicles on the window of the house. Lou's early fascination with light through the frozen patterns of icicles and the glowing colors of hot coals reappears in the powerful treatment of light in his architecture.

Louis Kahn's passport photo, 1928.

On arriving in the United States, the Kahn family settled in the Northern Liberties area of Philadelphia. They were extremely poor and moved seventeen times in two years within the same neighborhood because they could not afford to pay the rent. At school he would slip in with the crowd of children hoping to escape notice, but some of them called him "scarface." In time, having his drawings on the blackboard, which the teacher frequently saved, gave him a sense of worth, especially since he was sent home with stars pasted all over his hand and arm. He was chosen from his school to attend, one day a week, the Public Industrial Art School, established by a Quaker, J. Liberty Tadd. Tadd thought so highly of Lou's drawing ability that he had him teach older students how to draw animals at the zoo. When he noticed that Lou had holes in his shoes, he gave him three dollars to buy new ones. Lou bought a pair of sneakers for a dollar and gave the rest to his mother. He also managed to earn money painting signs in the windows of the neighborhood stores. For several years Lou won Wanamaker prizes for his drawings. Later at the Graphic Sketch Club (founded by Samuel Fleischer and now called the Fleischer Art Memorial)—a twenty-block walk from his home—Kahn took weekend art classes and one day found a room, open for a meeting, with a grand piano in it. He could play almost anything by ear and so impressed Samuel Fleischer's sister, Helen, who had come to the meeting, that she insisted on giving him a grand piano. There was no room for both his bed and a piano in the apartment, so Lou then slept on the piano. While at the prestigious Central High School, he was awarded prizes for his drawings from the Pennsylvania Academy of the Fine Arts. He also earned money in a somewhat questionable way by making drawings for less gifted students, with a deliberate ink blot here and there, hoping to disguise his work. William F.

Gray, the teacher of the course on architectural history who inspired Lou to become an architect, may have turned a blind eye to this enterprise. Perhaps in those days it was possible for Lou to restrain the unmistakable vitality of his line. He was so convinced that architecture was his life's work that he passed up the scholarship he was offered at the Pennsylvania Academy of the Fine Arts. Lou's attraction to architecture must have been the fascination of extending his artistic abilities into the three-dimensional creation of spaces to contain and shape light and to evoke a sense of monumentality.

While at the architecture school of the University of Pennsylvania, Kahn earned money by playing the piano for silent films in a neighborhood movie theater. He was due at his job before the end of the Saturday football games, which he particularly enjoyed watching. He would stay at the game as long as possible, and then, of course, he had to run all the way to the theater, often imagining he was running with the football. One Saturday, in a narrow alley he tried to jump from one curb to the other, fell and hit his head on the curb. When he came to, he found he could not see, so he sat there deciding that he would have to be a musician after all. Fortunately, after what seemed to be half an hour, his sight returned. When the theater decided to install an organ, Lou was told he would have to find another job. Lou quickly assured them that he could play the organ, and in a day he learned the basics from a friend so he could continue playing for the theater.

After graduation Lou worked for two years in the office of Philadelphia's City Architect, John Molitor. He was responsible for designing temporary buildings for the Sesquicentennial International Exhibition in a style reminiscent of the work of his professor at Penn, Paul Philippe Cret. It was unusual for an architect just beginning his career to have an opportunity to design monumental buildings, even though they were put up and taken down within a year's time, much like stage sets. In retrospect, Lou was not too satisfied with his designs and commented with a smile that it was probably a good thing that they were taken down. He then worked for another two years with William H. Lee on buildings for Temple University, saving money for a year's travel in Europe.

His travels started in England in May 1928, passing through the Netherlands, Denmark, Sweden, and Finland before visiting Estonia. He spent almost a month from the middle of July to the middle of August visiting his birthplace on the island of Saaremaa. From there he went through Lithuania and Latvia to Germany, Czechoslovakia, and Austria, arriving in Italy in the beginning of October and staying there five months. The sketches he made during those months illustrate his special delight in Italy—the Amalfi coast, Sorrento,

Drawing from Kahn's article
"Monumentality," published
in 1944 in New Architecture
and City Planning.

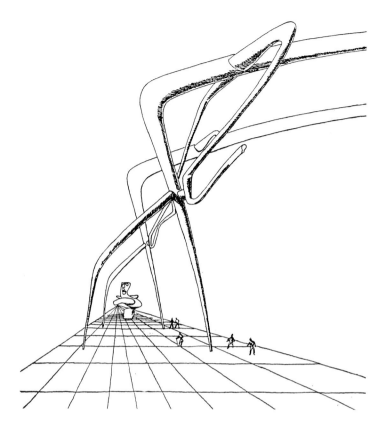

16

3 Louis Kahn Letter to Anne
Tyng, 22 November 1953.

Capri, Pompeii, and Paestum. Lou later wrote me of his enthusiasm: "The Mediterranean is full of wonder and beauty. The parts I saw around Italy I shall never forget. Try very hard to take a squint at Positano, Capri, Amalfi and if possible Paestum and even more south."[3] He visited Switzerland and France before sailing home from England on 12 April 1929.

The Great Depression was imminent and Lou was lucky to find work with his former professor Paul Cret for a year and then with Zantzinger and Borie for two years before being out of work. Once unemployed, he joined with other architects in the same situation and formed the Architectural Research Group. During the next four years without a steady job, Lou in a sense reeducated himself, plunging into the problems of public housing, structural systems, prefabrication, and planning studies. In 1935 Lou obtained his architectural registration and joined with Alfred Kastner in Washington to work on the Jersey Homesteads—low-cost housing with a cooperative factory and a cooperative farm supported by the International Ladies' Garment Workers Union and endorsed by Albert Einstein, then at Princeton University. Although part of the project was built, it was never fully realized due to cost, funding problems, and suspicions that it might have something to do with communism. Lou worked on a number of unbuilt projects, many of which were exhibited locally and, in 1944, at the Museum of Modern Art in New York.

George Howe in Washington recommended Lou for several housing projects that did not get beyond the design phase due to lack of funding. Lou wrote to me of the time he said to Howe, "Let's associate and George said OK. We agreed to split even, only I said he must get $2000.00 more because he had everything in the way of an office—supplies, girl, overhead etc. and then how, according to George, it all turned out that he owed me $2000.00."[4] George Howe and Louis Kahn were associated on the Pine Ford Acres Housing in Middletown, Pennsylvania, as well as Pennypack Woods in Philadelphia. In the first case five hundred housing units were built and one thousand units in the second. Other housing projects included Carver Court in Caln Township, Pennsylvania, and Lily Ponds Houses and Stanton Road Dwellings, both in Washington, D.C. Howe and Kahn were joined by Oscar Stonorov to form one of the teams to work on the Willow Run housing for workers at Ford's airplane factory in Michigan. In 1942 Howe left the partnership to take the job of supervising architect of the Public Buildings Administration in Washington and the firm became Stonorov and Kahn. They continued work on housing projects and became well known as a progressive architectural firm, with work published in *Architectural Forum* and exhibited at the Museum of Modern Art.

One indication of Lou's future potential can be found in his article "Monumentality."[5] In it he proposes a synthesis of structural innovation with monumentality inspired by Gothic forms. The forms are still only sculpturally conceived without a basis of technical means and without knowledge of geometry that could build the monumentality up with proportional increments. The spirit is there in his vision of the future, but he was not yet free of the concept of "style." He had not found the essence of archetypal geometry that transcends his early empathy for monumentality in Saaremaa's castle and in Beaux-Arts scale. Lou's understanding of that geometric essence gave power to his later work in its achievement of a truly new, yet timeless, monumentality.

4 Louis Kahn Letter to Anne Tyng, 9 February 1954.

5 Paul Zucker, ed., *New Architecture and City Planning* (Philosophical Library: New York, 1944).

17

Born on a Mountain in China

I was born in 1920 on the other side of the world in Kuling in the Lushan mountains of Kiangsi, China, the fourth of five children of Episcopal missionary parents, both of whom were from the Boston area. My birthplace was discovered by Dr. E. S. Little who was looking for a place free from the oppressive heat, humidity, and rampant epidemics of the plains. He processed deeds through unwitting local authorities for an uninhabited valley with its fresh-flowing streams high in the mountains. He appropriately named the place Kuling (cooling). Amid threats of anti-foreign violence, the serious matter of foreigners occupying Chinese territory came to the attention of the dowager empress. Ultimately, through the efforts of a member of parliament and friend of Dr. Little, a ninety-nine year lease was packaged with financial aid the empress had requested of England. Just a decade after Kuling was established, my parents made it our summer home.

My father was an intense Episcopal clergyman with a quick temper. After graduating from Harvard College Phi Beta Kappa in three years at the age of nineteen in 1905, he considered devoting himself to political reform. While working on his master's degree, he suffered a nervous breakdown and moved to Washington near Puget Sound to work in lumbering as a means of recovery. After two years he was advised by a congregational minister friend that the lumber business required someone who wore a smaller hat and bigger shoes than he, and that he should return to Boston to decide what to do with

"Lion's Leap" at Kuling,
Anne Tyng's birthplace, located
in the Lushan mountains of
Kiangsi, China.

Anne Tyng's parents, Ethel and Walworth Tyng, in Kuling, 1912.

Anne Tyng, 3, at front, with her mother and her sister Mary, 10, and brothers John, 8, and Billy, 4.

his life. For a year he studied law at Harvard while completing his master's degree, but in 1908 he felt called to the ministry after reading the diary of his great grandfather, one of several generations of passionate clergy.

My father went to the Episcopal Theological Seminary in Cambridge, Massachusetts, graduating in 1911. While there he took part in the Sunday services in Newburyport, where the local minister introduced him to my mother, Ethel Atkinson Arens, a student at Radcliffe, class of 1911. My parents immediately fell in love. In fact my father heard a voice that said, "This is your future wife." My father admired my mother's musical ability since his own mother was musically talented. My mother played the violin and later had us children all take piano and violin lessons and play together in a family group. On graduation she was offered a job as head of the economics department at Mills College in California, but my father lured her away from academia. Before he left for the mission field in China he proposed to her. That same year her mother died and my father returned to marry her, taking her back with him to China.

As a young child I was horrified to hear that girl babies were drowned by poor families since only sons could worship their ancestors. Although I was assured by my parents that "we don't do that," there were many uneasy reminders that boys were indeed more valued than girls. My brother Bill had to take special Latin classes before going off to boarding school in the United States, whereas I was allowed to take Latin with Bill if I wished but only if I could keep up with him. My parents believed education was more important for boys who had to support their wives. I didn't mind the idea of being supported, but I objected to being called "my unworthy interior," the expression of a polite Chinese man for his wife. I felt I would rather be worthy if it meant supporting myself out in the world.

My love of architecture was engendered early in life by my father. In Changsha in Hunan province where my father was stationed, I loved watching him supervise the building of the school and church for the mission. I was even more fascinated during the construction of our house in Changsha that my father designed. It was built of bricks that he had rescued from the demolished city wall, and the interior paneling was red oak salvaged from the ruins of a temple. Dinner-table conversations often revolved around his enthusiastic descriptions of the building progress. My father also designed our cottage in Kuling built of local granite.

Since I was born in our Kuling house, every summer was a reminder of where I began, giving a sense of birth and renewal when we burst out of the confines of our walled and locked winter compound in Changsha to ride the train

Walworth Tyng supervising the building of a mission at Changsha in Hunan, China.

to Wuhan, take the riverboat down the Yangtze River, and climb up the five-mile mountain trail to Kuling to explore its valleys, mountains, and streams. Part of the magic of Kuling was that we went everywhere on foot—the only vehicle on the mountain was our cook's bicycle. We were always in touch with the earth and water as we explored and skipped rocks up and down the mountain streams. For many years we had no electricity, using kerosene lamps for light, until the nearby Kuling American School hooked us up to their generator in return for using our house as a faculty residence and a temporary assembly hall.

As we became older, our stay on the mountains was extended through the winter at the Kuling American School except for a six-week break at Christmas to allow time for travel home. In 1926 in the middle of the school year, classes were canceled because of the Communist uprising. On Christmas break in Changsha, the hotbed of Communism and birthplace of Chairman Mao, we were keenly aware of strong anti-foreign feeling. The American Consul's son and my brother Billy, then seven, staged their own parade around the tennis court shouting in Chinese the familiar slogan heard on the streets: "Down with American Imperialism."

As a result of the increasing unrest, all five of us children, my mother, our cook Wu Sz Fu, and his wife fled in the middle of the night with a minimum of luggage, boarding a freight car on a siding away from the railroad station.

In the crowded car we were to stay absolutely quiet, which was extremely dif-ficult with several babies and no place to sleep. Before dawn we were attached to a train that took us to the Changsha station where mobs were attempting to board even freight cars, hanging onto the sides and climbing onto the roof. My father had come to the station to watch surreptitiously our departure and noticed that crowds approaching our car would turn away. He edged closer to discover that the doors were pasted with paper strips marked "danger explosives." We reached Wuhan safely and were lucky to find passage on a freighter headed downriver to Shanghai. Passing between opposing armies on either side of the river, we were ordered immediately to leave the officer's cabin we were occupying and go to the bridge protected with sandbags. When it was safe to return to the cabin, we found spent shells in the wall just level with the bunk where my two-year-old brother Franklin had been snatched up from his nap. My father later joined us in Shanghai before we all left for a two-year extended furlough in the United States.

In 1929 we began our return to China by driving across the country to California in a 1927 Studebaker, a seven seater with two folding seats, plush upholstery, curtains, and flower vases. It had outside running boards, solid wheel hubs, a spare wheel on the side, and an outside baggage rack on the back. We camped out along the way, visiting the Petrified Forest, the Grand Canyon, Bryce Canyon, Yellowstone, and Yosemite. In California no one wanted to buy our car, and since freight was inexpensive, we took the car to Shanghai where it saw many years of use as a minibus.

Back in Kuling, in my first year of boarding school at the age of nine, I sur-vived an aching homesickness by getting involved in my first architectural venture. I joined with other students to build an igloo in the first big snow. We packed the snow in a wooden box to make icy blocks which we corbelled gently into a dome high enough for all of us kids to stand in. I was not satisfied and insisted we build another one high enough for our 6'4" headmaster to stand in. We had to find things to stand on to reach high enough but I remember vividly the sense of achievement since I was the smallest boarder at the school. The following spring I persuaded some friends to help me build a "secret" clubhouse in a bamboo grove on a hill beside the recreation field. It was a circular hut made by bending down the flexible bamboo tree-tops to fit between opposing trunks and weaving them together with smaller branches to form a shelter.

Walworth Tyng with the 1927 Studebaker that was sold on the Tyngs' arrival in Shanghai where it was used as a minibus for many years.

In the summer of 1930 fighting erupted between competing warlords in the Kuling area and the whole school, somewhat reduced in number, moved to Shanghai. We boarded with our headmaster in the French quarter and attended the Shanghai American School for a year. Although it was a very big, strange city, I remember bicycling my way across the city by myself to visit the Duff family from Kuling.

We were back at school in Kuling the following year before going back to the United States in 1933. Our parents went back to China for the last time in 1935. On furloughs in the United States, we lived wherever my father might serve in a church, generally in New England or New York. As a result of these frequent moves we developed an adaptive resilience.

Having been around the world at four and across the Pacific at six, nine, and thirteen, I again circled the globe at sixteen after graduation from boarding school in the United States. I spent an entire year and a summer traveling with my sister Mary before going to college. We spent the summer in Kuling rediscovering childhood haunts that seemed smaller in scale than we remembered. Japan was at war with China, and Mary and I were staying with our parents in Changsha when the Japanese dropped a bomb in our garden, making a big hole but luckily without any injuries or damage to the house. Although the Japanese were bombing trains to Hong Kong by then, their "Christmas present to the world" was to allow one train to go through without being bombed. Mary and I were still able to leave China safely on that last train to Hong Kong. It was two years later before my parents finally escaped from China through the last loophole between Japanese occupied territory, often by primitive transportation and with little more than the clothes on their backs.

Finding Identity in Time and Space

I came to Cambridge at the age of eighteen after spending twelve years in China. At Radcliffe I majored in fine arts, and in one of my classes at the Boston Museum of Fine Arts I was startled to see a portrait of an Ann Tyng by John Singleton Copley. This namesake helped extend my identity beyond my transient upbringing and deeper in time to my New England roots. In my junior year I was excited to discover that I might study architecture and I managed to take a summer architecture studio. The idea of creating three-dimensional form for human use galvanized something in me that I had not imagined was there. As my father might have said, I felt "called to architecture." For me it was an expanding threshold of identity in space. Every design articulated an aspect of who I was and who I might become. I discovered through our studio critic Professor Henry Frost that I might get credit in my senior year at Radcliffe for taking architectural design at the Smith Graduate School of Architecture and Landscape Architecture (previously called the Cambridge School) which he founded and directed specifically for women students. We all adored him, and it was undoubtedly due to his efforts and to World War II that Harvard opened its doors to women architects.

Anne Tyng rowing on the Charles River in Cambridge, 1943, during her first year of architecture school at Harvard.

Family reunion at Uncle Griswold Tyng's house in Jamaica Plain, Massachusetts, 1938. Clockwise from bottom left: Franklin, 14; Mary, 25; Bill, 19; Anne, 18; and John, 23.

When I graduated from Radcliffe in 1942, I felt the joy of somehow being in the right place at the right time when women were first permitted to study architecture at Harvard. In my first year, against all advice, I took the equivalent of seven courses—first- and second-year structure simultaneously with statics at the Engineering School along with the second-year design studio. I had not taken any undergraduate math and up to midyear I was close to flunking second-year structure. I felt doomed when I was confronted with an exam question on the cut-off point for plate girders. Luckily we were allowed reference books, and in sheer desperation I found a very long formula that I thought might just do with a few substitutions. I cringed when our professor, known for his sarcasm and his ominous conviction that women would lower academic standards, announced we would "now look at Miss Tyng's solution." Instead of the scathing comments I expected, my solution turned out to be a valid one, although not the graphic method we had been taught. He thereupon timed both methods on the blackboard and found them equal. He later told me that Radcliffe women had a tougher mentality than other women and I finished the course with an A.

The creative challenge of architecture opened up a whole new world for me. I was intensely drawn to the combination of science and art, of the pragmatic and the aesthetic, of rigorous facts and intuitive leaps. The missionary zeal of the Bauhaus-influenced faculty at Harvard matched my own newly awakened fervor.

It was a stimulating environment with an international mix of students and an equal number of men and women, a balance that shifted to a much smaller ratio of women to men after World War II. There were also a few mature students adding another dynamic to the school. William Wurster was studying regional planning before becoming dean at M.I.T. His wife Catherine Bauer lectured on housing and they rode their bicycles together around Cambridge. Philip Johnson, having been curator at the Museum of Modern Art in New York as well as having written his book *The International Style: Architecture Since 1922* with Henry-Russell Hitchcock, was also a student. He built a glass house for himself in Cambridge for his thesis and of course for giving parties. Philip also acted as a critic to other students. For me his criticisms lightened up my heavy conscientiousness and helped me develop a degree of objectivity. There were many lively juries during which he kept the faculty on their toes. Richard Hudnut was the dean, Walter Gropius was chairman of architecture, and his Bauhaus colleague Marcel Breuer was a professor as well as a partner with Gropius in their practice. Faculty and students mixed at parties—at

Philip's house in Cambridge, Breuer's house in Lincoln, and at a party for Gropius's sixtieth birthday.

While at Harvard, in addition to the design of various building types, I also designed and built a full-size Morris chair using a solid wood frame on a plywood base. For my thesis, I. M. Pei helped me draw trees. He and his wife Eileen, a landscape student, both made delicately beautiful drawings.

Upon graduation, I spent my first year of work in New York employed in several temporary jobs—working for Konrad Wachsmann making perspectives of his prefabricated Panel House, for industrial designers Van Doren, Knowland, and Schladermundt, and for Knoll Design Associates. The more established firms in New York where I had applied told me that they did not hire women architects in a tone and manner that implied it was improper and outrageous to expect any consideration. I decided to join my parents and work in Philadelphia.

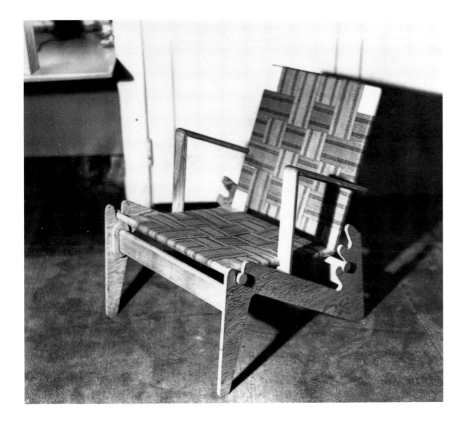

Modified Morris chair designed and built by Tyng while at Harvard University.

27

Professional and Private Lives

Anne Tyng, 1944, at right.

age 24

In 1945 the office of Stonorov and Kahn was in the space they had shared with George Howe in the old *Evening Bulletin* building in Philadelphia, at the corner of Filbert and Juniper streets diagonally across from City Hall. I first came there to have lunch with my friend Betty Ware Carlhian who had worked in their office for a year and was planning to return to Harvard to finish work toward her architecture degree. By chance both Oscar Stonorov and Lou Kahn were in the office when I reached their ninth top floor unfinished loft space. I had hardly been introduced before they asked if I would take my friend's place and work for them. Since I had heard they were a progressive firm known for low-cost housing projects, I promptly accepted. The space was not well insulated and was not air-conditioned. Occasionally we were subjected to ammonia fumes when the *Bulletin* presses were being cleaned on the floor below. On the elevator at eight-thirty in the morning I was almost overpowered by the smell of Stonorov's cigar. These were minor complaints in the light of a stimulating and informal office atmosphere. Everyone, including Oscar and Lou, was on a first-name basis. Although I was the only woman architect in the office, I was encouraged to take part in all phases of the work: client conferences, surveying, design, structure, detailing, specifications, and field supervision of the building process. I felt my work was valued, but when I solved a problem that Fred Savage, the office manager, had said was "impossible," I was shocked to hear him then say that I could "think like a man."

Louis Kahn, c. 1950.

Oscar Stonorov was primarily an entrepreneur, while Louis Kahn was primarily the architect/designer. Oscar was a great bluffer and quick to seize opportunities. He was bald, slightly heavy, and confident in his ability and charm. In contrast, Lou was extremely shy because of the scars on his face from his childhood burn, but the scars seemed to me to be part of a natural charisma. His wavy mop of reddish sandy hair was prematurely graying and his blue eyes, which tilted impishly upward at the sides, seemed to be on fire from within, compelling me to look beyond the scars. On swelteringly hot summer weekend charettes when Lou occasionally worked shirtless, it was hard not to notice how unusually broad his lightly freckled shoulders were in proportion to his slim hips. I had never met anyone remotely like him. He generated a profound energy—in his resilient walk, in the lively lines of his drawings, and in his ideas which seemed to take shape as he drew and talked.

Oscar and Lou seemed to be vying for my attention as the only woman architect in the office. Oscar put me to work surveying a piece of property he owned and designing two prefabricated steel house prototypes for the site. He liked to think of himself as a gentleman farmer and suggested I design some cow stalls. While waving his arms in a sweeping gesture at the cow stalls in the barn, he stepped backward into a post hole. He wasn't hurt, and I managed to stifle my laughter. In contrast to Oscar, Lou could joke and laugh at himself, although at the same time he was extremely intense. In spite of his modesty Lou had an aura of primacy like a king without a kingdom. If he wanted a kingdom I would help him.

Lou was forty-four and I was twenty-five when we met. By then I was reasonably comfortable with my American identity, although I had not lost my resilient sense of adventure from traveling and having lived half my life in China. However, I was naive in expecting men to have the same standards as my brothers in regard to marital fidelity. I soon became aware that Lou's interest in me was unusually intense and it included a powerful physical attraction that I immediately realized was mutual. I found it difficult to believe that he was happily married and at the same time so intensely interested in another woman.

Lou and I worked together on a solar house for Libbey-Owens-Ford Glass Company. They wanted forty-eight architects from forty-eight states with forty-eight designs—no firms or partners. Oscar was maneuvering for credit as the architect, but Lou was actually the design architect without any input from Oscar. Our scheme had a long north-facing, almost blank brick wall, with east and west glazed walls angled toward southeast and southwest to join the south-facing glazed wall. The plan provided optimal southern exposure with all three glazed walls oriented to receive solar energy from morning to

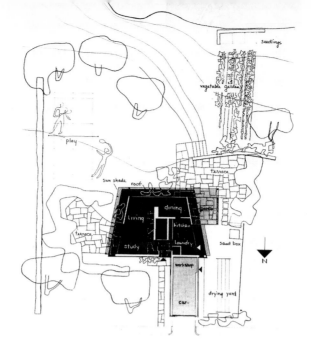

evening. Oscar then had someone in the office draw up a similar scheme but with the long blank wall facing south and three glazed walls oriented toward the north without sun. Eventually they both sent telegrams agreeing that "their" design must be credited to both Stonorov and Kahn.

The office projects gave me a valuable breadth of architectural experience: a remodeled carriage house for an artist and photographer couple; a Pocono camp main building; Unity House, for the International Ladies' Garment Workers Union; a shoe store; a playground for the Western Home for orphaned children; the Triangle Area Redevelopment Plan. Surveying for the Triangle Area Redevelopment Plan—an exterior survey of the condition and use from building to building and block to block of the area from Market Street to the Benjamin Franklin Parkway and from City Hall to the Schuylkill River—was an extensive job on which David Wisdom and I worked together. The opportunity for the Triangle Area Redevelopment came about when the so-called Chinese Wall elevated railroad tracks were demolished along with the old Suburban Station building. With the removal of the Chinese Wall came the opportunity for a dramatic change in the character of a large area of Philadelphia. I worked with Lou on the design of proposed new structures—office buildings, apartment buildings, low-rise housing, and a school—to fit in with the existing buildings that were to remain after redevelopment. Of course we didn't really design the buildings but only determined shapes and sizes that were convincingly recognizable for their scale and function.

It was during this work that Lou was surprised to receive telephone calls from people Oscar had lined up to work on an exhibit Lou had not heard of. It became clear that they had called Lou because they preferred working with him rather than with Oscar. Lou and I discovered that the head of Gimbel's was sponsoring an exhibit to celebrate the Greater Philadelphia Movement, and Oscar had secretly set up a separate office at Gimbel's Department Store without informing Lou. The tour de force of this exhibit was to be a model of the central area of Philadelphia in which the entire Triangle Area would be mechanically turned upside down, changing from existing to proposed views. Oscar had intended to use our Triangle Area Redevelopment Plan as the basis of this model. In spite of Oscar's blatantly unethical conduct, Lou and I and others in the office continued working with the model-maker for the exhibit. By 1947 Oscar's high-handed disregard toward his partnership with Lou, combined with the fact that Lou had received a commission from the Philadelphia Psychiatric Hospital based on his earlier work for the institution, brought about Lou's move to set up his own practice.

When Lou split with Stonorov in 1947, David Wisdom and I joined him at 1728 Spruce Street. The building was the residence and office of Robert Montgomery Brown, who became a partner with George Howe on the new *Bulletin* Building at Thirtieth Street. We shared the same secretary, Alma Farrow, who had been with us in the old *Bulletin* Building. We also shared our second-floor, one-room office with the structural and mechanical engineers Cronheim and Weger. With the responsibility of his own office,

Tyng and Kahn at 1728 Spruce Street, where Kahn established his first independent practice in 1947.

Lou worked with more intensity and for longer hours. I had moved into town as my enthusiasm for architecture and for Lou far outweighed the social lures of the Main Line. I was also interested in working on my own projects in my spare time, and Lou encouraged me to work in the office. Lou and I had established a stimulating personal and working relationship which became more strongly collaborative in his independent practice. We were both workaholics: in fact, work had become a kind of passionate play. We were able to bring out each other's creativity, building on each other's ideas. There were exciting overlaps and differences in our approach to architecture. Lou made visionary sketches and I built models as a step toward more tangible realizations of building concepts that might embody his visions. My giving structural body to his visions became an energizing connective force between us. We also had fun humming Bach, Haydn, and Mozart to keep us alert on long, late charettes. Lou's creative use of language intrigued and stimulated me. Lou was a true poet in always wanting to use words in a fresh yet profound way, not just for the words themselves but also to express another way of looking at different aspects of architecture.

During the three years on Spruce Street, Lou and I worked together on six houses. Three of these were built—the Roche house, the Weiss house, and the Genel house—while the Hooper, Ehle, and Tompkins houses never went beyond the design stage. Working on the Weiss house was the most fun— the Weisses were such wonderful clients. Perhaps because they had no children the house was, in a sense, their "baby." It was convenient for Lou to have me drive him to the site, since he did not own a car or have a driver's license, so I had the opportunity of participating in the entire construction process. Lou and I went to the quarry to find just the right color of stone—warm but not too rusty or too pink. We also found a very large, long, and slightly curved stone that could be used for a garden seat which the Weisses loved and used with the outdoor fireplace. I helped Lou paint a mural next to the living room fireplace using motifs from the Pennsylvania Dutch countryside in black and white patterned squares based on Lou's concept of giant "pointillism." A black and white pattern to represent the Weiss's dalmation was tucked into the lower right-hand corner of the mural. The house received the Philadelphia chapter of the American Institute of Architects' gold medal and is still carefully maintained by the Weisses.

During the construction of the Weiss house, Lou went to Israel for two months as a housing consultant, and I was faced with the design of leader pans for the butterfly roof. Since the roof on the bedroom end was already cantilevered on the sides, it could not be cantilevered on the end, and the leader pan had to reach in over the thick stone wall under the window to catch the

The Lenore and Morton Weiss house, East Norristown Township, Pennsylvania, completed in 1950, for which Kahn received a gold medal from the Philadelpia chapter of the American Institute of Architects.

Kahn and Tyng with Lenore Weiss (left) and her mother and stepfather during a picnic at the construction site for the Weiss house.

Bedroom end of the Weiss house.

*Detail of the Weiss house
showing triangular leader pan
designed by Tyng.*

Kahn, Tyng, and Lenore Weiss during construction of the Weiss house.

rainwater. I designed a triangular leader pan two feet on a side that reached out over the stone wall like a large hand. I was able to turn the triangular leader pan so that it caught the water from the cantilever and at the same time the water from the low point of the main roof. The contractor was unenthusiastic but could see that it worked. I was terrified that Lou would hate it because I had not seen anything like it myself. But when Lou returned he was pleased because it worked in both scale and shape.

Although Dave Wisdom usually worked with Lou on the Radbill Building of the Philadelphia Psychiatric Hospital, I also helped whenever necessary. On that building I suggested a much larger triangle as a drive-through entrance canopy, and Lou lightened the effect of the three supports by using less bulky double columns that made the canopy seem to float.

I think that for Lou and me loving each other and working together became integrated and took on a life of its own. I felt strongly that loving Lou should be an asset and not a liability in our work together. That meant a healthy degree of autonomy with no possessiveness or special prerogatives. Lou later wrote, "I don't believe that we ever took each other for granted. That is rare and living."[6] I tried to maintain a professional attitude in the office so as not to take advantage of our personal relationship.

6 Louis Kahn Letter to Anne Tyng, 7 January 1954.

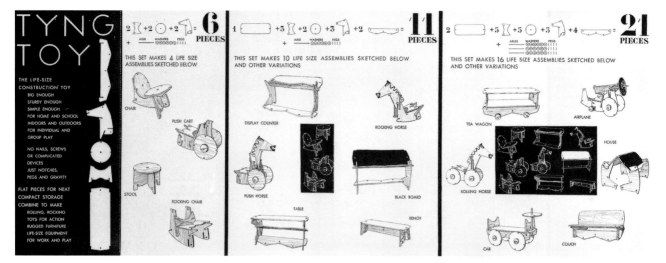

38

*Brochure and promotional
photograph for Tyng Toy,
designed by Tyng and patented
in 1949.*

During 1948 I was studying for my architectural registration exams and Lou helped me on history, a subject that had not been emphasized at Harvard. I was the only woman to take the exams in 1949. In addition to the written exam for state registration, an oral exam was required for national certification. In Harrisburg one of the three reviewers was so against the idea of a woman architect that he refused to speak to me and actually sat apart and turned himself away so that he wouldn't have to look at me. Their questions dealt primarily with on-site supervision of the building process. Any misgivings were apparently resolved because I passed.

My first independent spare-time project was the design of a plywood construction toy with five different shapes: a bilateral butterfly shape, a circle, an elongated piece, a "spiral" form, and a large rectangle. In retrospect I can see that those five shapes correlate with the essence of geometric symmetries—bilateral, rotational, helical, and spiral—that underlie my later theory of cycles in creativity. Those five shapes could be put together to create child-size furniture: stool, chair, bench, table/desk, and easel. They could also fit together to make rocking and rolling toys: rocking chair, rocking horse, push-cart, wagon, car, and airplane. The toy was exhibited in museums in the United States and abroad and widely published, including a spread on the women's page of the *New York Times*. Lou helped me with the brochure layout and Robert Montgomery Brown allowed me to make the first full-size set in his basement using his power tools. I gave a set to Lou's daughter, Sue. It was called Tyng Toy and patented in 1949.

Another independent project was an elementary school that I worked on from 1949 to 1951, published in the Philadelphia chapter of the American Institute of Architects yearbook of 1952. Both Bucky Fuller and Robert Le Ricolais had used tetrahedron/octahedron geometry, but only in a single layer truss. Since supports for such trusses had been apparently thought of as different structures, I was concerned with the problem of how to support such a truss in a way that would be part of the geometry. From three points of support I "grew" the geometry vertically in wider triangulated layers to create three "columns," extending and widening the geometry horizontally from each column in three layers that diminished to two wider layers and finally to one layer at the center where, at its widest, the structure originating from each of the three points of support meet to complete a large triangular roof structure. The three points of support occurred on the exterior of the truncated triangular building containing three classrooms. Each building was conceived as a cluster of three trees with tapering branches meeting in a canopy. While the classroom spaces were not contained within the trussed structure, they were harbored by the three "trees." In this way the

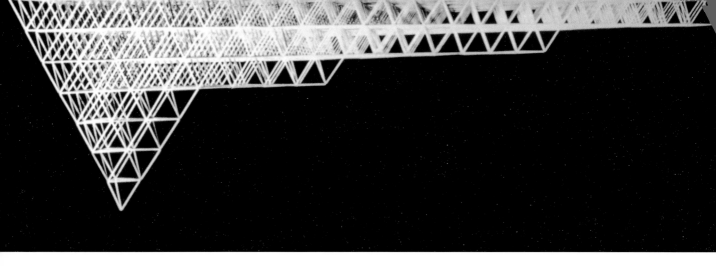

The model (opposite) and elevation (above) for a proposed elementary school in Bucks County, Pennsylvania, in design 1949–51 (unbuilt), demonstrate Tyng's solution to the problem of supporting a triangulated truss in a way that would remain part of the structural geometry.

geometry formed its own support. Lou's daughter, Sue, then eleven years old, was a great help on the model, and Lou drew some animals to put on a board in the classroom. I believe Lou admired the transparency of its structure; perhaps it struck a chord with his earlier concepts drawn for his article on "Monumentality," suggesting an incremental, technically feasible geometric means for the realization of his visionary images.

The model of the elementary school was built at our new office at Twentieth and Walnut streets. During the time we were there, from 1950 to 1962, Lou's most significant seminal works were produced. The three offices for his independent practice increased in space and in numbers of employees, and each office characterized a different phase of his work and development that I like to think of as "exploratory," "seminal," and "flowering." At 1728 Spruce Street we had explored the play of sloping roofs; modular ordering of openings and structure; and the geometry of triangular leader pans, triangular fireplace, and triangular canopy. Here we developed hipped roofs, hollow ceilings, hollow columns, three-dimensional space frames, clustering and wrapping of hierarchical spaces, concepts for clerestory lighting of large central spaces, and the extension of "servant" space concepts for hollow ceilings to hollow mechanical and ventilating "columns"/towers. At Kahn's last office at Fifteenth and Walnut streets the flowering of many earlier concepts occurred in bolder expression. Shadow joints between materials expanded to

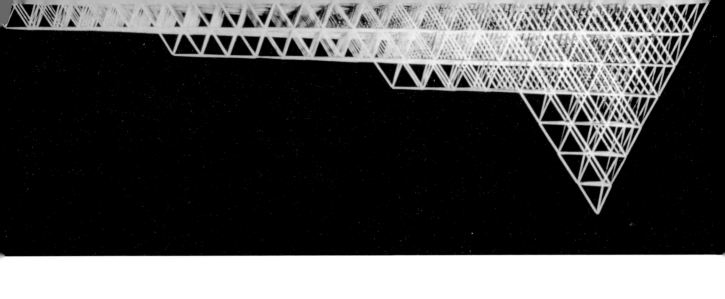

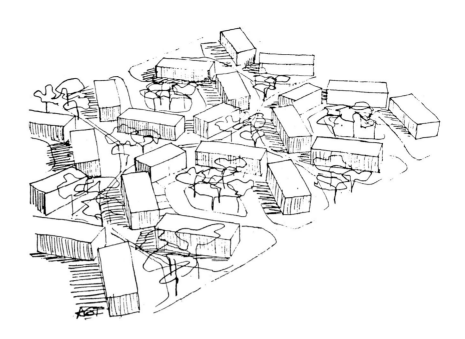

Tyng's sketch for her clustered
hexagonal cul-de-sac scheme
designed for the City Planning
Commission Row House Studies
was applied by Kahn and
Tyng to a site in northeast
Philadelphia.

42

light joints in the cycloid vault for the Kimbell Art Museum; the "squaring of the circle" concept for the Unitarian Church became the "cubing of the sphere" at Exeter; and hollow structural columns proposed for Bryn Mawr evolved into monumental cylinders for shading and ventilating at Dacca.

At Twentieth and Walnut streets we had extended the concept of served and servant spaces to planning concepts in "docks" and parking towers, in hierarchical principles of movement for existing streets, and in separation and interlocking of pedestrian and vehicular movements to enhance both. Along with these concepts, Lou developed a powerful imagery for the city as a living organism. In our studies for the Philadelphia City Planning Commission, with Lou as consultant architect and Louis McAllister, Kenneth Day, and me as associated consultant architects, we developed a "green" walkway system for the southwest Temple University area. At about the same time, our consultant group was commissioned to do row-house studies for the Philadelphia City Planning Commission. The clustered hexagonal cul-de-sac scheme I designed was applied to a site in the northeast including a proposed elementary school and shopping center. I carried the concept further within another hierarchy of scale for a proposed New Town in Bucks County. Lou, along with McAllister and Day, were then commissioned by the Philadelphia Housing Authority to build the first phase of the Mill Creek Housing. This work stimulated a rich mix of theory and practice.

In addition to commissioned work on housing and planning, we worked on
traffic studies. Lou spoke poetically to me of expressways as rivers, through-
streets as canals, and cul-de-sac parking streets as docks. I responded that we
should apply the ideas to Philadelphia and made a drawing applying the cul-
de-sac dock to a four-block area including Sansom Street where many parking
garages already existed. I also proposed a hexagonal system that required no
traffic lights. This unpaid spare-time project became the "Traffic Studies" for
Philadelphia.[7] I had joined with other architects and planners including Martin
Meyerson, Blanche Lemco, Louis Dolbear, and Barclay Jones in a Young
Planners Group. As our first public event we decided to invite Lou to speak
about planning and hold the event in the spectacular boardroom of the
Philadelphia Savings Fund Society tower. Lou was extremely apprehensive
about speaking because his previous attempt during the Depression ended in
disaster when his carefully prepared slides were turned upside down. Lou
insisted on returning the audience's admission money when he was too
unnerved to continue. For the PSFS talk Lou and I made many drawings for
slides, and I promised to make absolutely sure that they would be right side
up. All he had to do was talk about the slides. He finally agreed. The talk,
well-publicized and well-attended, was a big success and marked a significant
moment in his own development toward greater confidence in articulating his
ideas and signaled greater recognition in his career.

7 Louis I. Kahn, "Toward
a Plan for Midtown
Philadelphia," *Perspecta:
The Yale Architectural
Journal* 2 (1953).

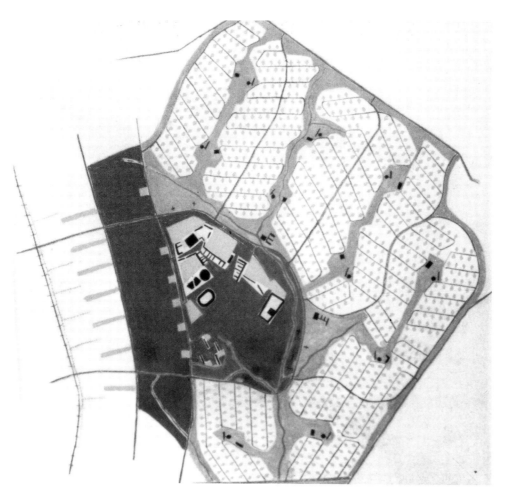

Cul-de-sac scheme for proposed
New Town, Bucks County,
Pennsylvania, 1952.

During the early studies for Mill Creek Housing, Lou was invited to the American Academy in Rome as resident architect for three months. I was left in charge to hold my own with Day and McAllister while he was out of the country. Each of us worked on different schemes, all of them presented to the Housing Authority. All but efficiency apartments were required to have cross-ventilation, so I developed a plan with scissor stairs near either end of the corridor. Each stair contained a fire stair and a private stair, one over or under the other. The private stair connected living/kitchen areas to bedroom areas on another level, providing cross-ventilation through the building. Since it was difficult to understand in drawings, I made a model differentiating each apartment with its stair connection in its own color. Public stair landings occurred on alternate sides of the building from floor to floor, as did the corridors, but they were always connected by a central elevator space. After I had shown my scheme to Day and McAllister, Day asked me to "draft up" his scheme for him, explaining to me verbally what sounded a lot like the scheme I had already designed. Of course I told him there was no point in drawing the same scheme again, so it was not really a surprise to me when, at our meeting with the Housing Authority, Kenneth Day sat on my housing model, apparently by accident.

When Lou returned from Rome, he developed the concept of three square towers with all corner apartments. Each apartment had its own balcony, which he justified as necessary for bracing between the exterior columns. Of course the square towers were consistent with the "quad" houses, with four corner houses in square plan. The quads were houses with more than two bedrooms, each with their own outdoor spaces on the ground.

The Mill Creek Redevelopment Plan for the Philadelphia City Planning Commission (published in booklet form in 1953) included an area from Forty-fourth to Fifty-second streets and from Lancaster to Haverford avenues. This time the associate consultants were McAllister, Day and me, although the work was done by our office. We reduced through traffic by developing an interlocking vehicular and pedestrian system in which each movement facilitated and enhanced the other. While maintaining the pattern of existing streets and access to all existing houses, we changed alternate streets into pedestrian "green fingers" and, perpendicular to them, looped streets, accessed from the parallel streets that alternated with the green fingers. The green fingers reached out from the larger pedestrian way created by closing a wider street as a community green. This greenway provided continuous pedestrian access to existing and proposed shopping areas, schools, and churches, with vehicular access to these functions on parallel streets. These proposals demonstrated that it was not necessary to wipe out existing street patterns as Le Corbusier had proposed for Paris; rather, by simply modifying the use of existing streets, a more effective movement at all scales and speeds could be developed.

From 1951 to 1953 I was working with Lou on the Yale University Art Gallery and in my spare time designing a house for my parents on the Eastern Shore in Maryland. Although historians have speculated on the influence of Bucky Fuller and Robert Le Ricolais on the Yale Art Gallery ceiling and on our City Tower project (1952–57), Lou and Bucky did not really communicate since they spoke such different creative languages. Bucky had worked with pure geometric forms but not with geometry as an underlying principle for a variety of tangible architectural expressions. As Patricia Cummings Loud has carefully documented in *The Art Museums of Louis I. Kahn*, Bucky did not go to Yale as visiting critic until after the decision had been made to use the octet geometry as the basis of the Gallery ceiling. (Bucky later told me that I knew how to make geometry into architecture and suggested we work together on a mosque before I left for an International Congress of Women Architects in Iran in 1976.) Another factor is that triangulated geometry is difficult if not impossible to visualize in the mind's eye, but Lou had my model of the elementary school (1951) right under his nose. In fact he tried threading pencil-size ducts through it in various ways to see if it would work as a hollowed out "servant space." Since the Yale Art Gallery was Kahn's first prestigious building, he was nervous and his first schemes indicate a conventional structure. I asked Lou, "Why bother to build it if you don't use an innovative structure?"

Robert Le Ricolais's letter to Lou in April 1953, referred to by David G. De Long as a possible influence on our City Tower,[8] was written after we had sent drawings and photographs to be published in *Perspecta 2*. By that time I had already designed my parents house as a total space frame structure hollowed out for living like a bee's honeycomb, and construction was far enough along for the building to receive an American Institute of Architects award from the Philadelphia chapter in May 1953. Le Ricolais and Fuller had only used space frames as spanning structure in flat trusses or domes in a single layer. In both our tower and in my parents' house the consistent geometry was not only hollowed out for living and work space but was also expressed in several different scales within each building. Vincent Scully

Yale University Art Gallery, tetrahedral formwork for ceiling.

8 David G. De Long, *Louis Kahn: In the Realm of Architecture* (New York: Rizzoli, 1991), p. 56.

The "prismlike triangle" referred to in fig. 412 of *Louis Kahn: In the Realm of Architecture* was not a basis for the proposed City Tower. Our earliest scheme was triangular with curved sides (See Yale *Perspecta 2*) and built up of small articulated elements. The prismlike triangle might be considered an abstraction of what we were already working on. The Tower was conceived genetically rather than from a super-imposed abstraction.

Triangular stairwell within a cylinder at Yale University Art Gallery, 1953.

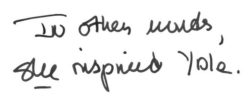

In other words, she inspired Yale.

Letter from cartoonist Bob Osborn congratulating Kahn on the success of the Yale University Art Gallery.

1º nov 53

dear Lou :
That's a
building!
Its a work
of art — one
feels that
keenly.
Our sincere
regards to you.
Bob Osborn

Every time
I think
of that building
it makes
me happy;
its that
Clear

48   Ceiling of the Yale University
Art Gallery, at right.

has suggested that Lou saw in the pyramids the basis for the Yale Art Gallery ceiling. A solid mass, square-based pyramid has very little relation to a triangular-based space frame. Lou of course loved the massiveness of concrete, but in the gallery ceiling he was creating voids and slabs rather than a solid mass. I helped design and made a model of the triangular stair in a cylindrical stairwell—I found the protective wire fabric for the railings on an expedition to a conveyor belt factory in northeast Philadelphia. The spiraling weave of light wire is almost dematerialized, yet it is amazingly strong. (I still use a sample of it as a stair railing in my own house.)

For my parents' house (concurrent with the design of the Yale Art Gallery), my father had requested a pitched roof, considered old-fashioned and senti-mental by students of the Bauhaus "box." But when I found I could use the geometry of the elementary school with the squares of the octahedrons in the horizontal plane for a "squared" plan and the triangles in the sloping roof plane for a pitched roof, I was only too happy to fulfill his wishes. I was even more delighted when I found I could use the geometry as a continuous and consistent system for the whole house. Lou was interested in what I was doing and responded positively to the idea of making the house of one con-tinuous geometry. At the smallest scale, the ridge ties made half-octahedrons, and the eave bracing made tetrahedrons. Larger tetrahedrons made dormer windows, sunshades, and trellises; and the largest tetrahedron occurred on the projecting eave ends of the house. It was not only structurally strong— the engineer Nathan Cronheim said its strength was so obvious there was no point in calculating the loads—but also, if one joint weakened, the load would simply go to other joints. He was right. The house survived the 150-mile-per-hour winds of Hurricane Hazel a year after its completion, in spite of

For the design of her parents' house on Maryland's Eastern Shore, Tyng applied the triangular geometry of the Bucks County elementary school proposal to create the first built completely triangulated architecture with living space hollowed out within the structure.

the fact that the roof rafters were only three-by-fours on seven-foot centers. I had made a model of my parents' house at one and a half inches to the foot, an unusually large scale that showed every joint in scale with standard lumber sizes. The local contractor seemed challenged by the model to prove that he could build it. I don't believe either the contractor or my parents realized how unusual it was. It was, as far as I know, the first built totally triangulated architecture with living space hollowed out within the structure. My parents loved the house, and the local watermen referred to it as "the ship."

In the elementary school I had made the geometry "grow" thicker and then "grow" its own supporting column, a concept Lou explored in several different ways while I was in Rome: in his 1954 "postmortem" versions of the Yale Art Gallery where the columns "contract" and "expand"; in his proposed market building with clustered columns; in the Adath Jeshurun Synagogue where the columns become rooms; and in his "bell bottom" tower where the building itself tapers from a broad base. In my parents' house the geometry was both its total structure and its enclosure. The geometry was also transformed from an elusive gossamer network into a profoundly familiar archetypal form of shelter perceived as ship, ark, or house.

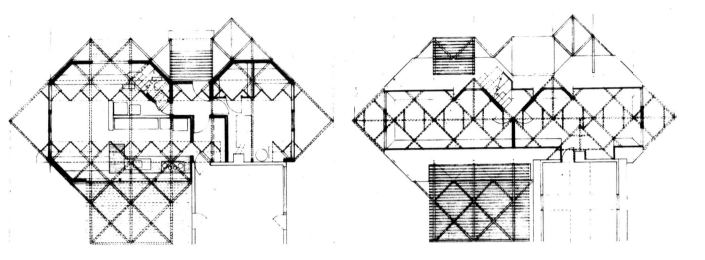

Floor plans, Walworth Tyng residence

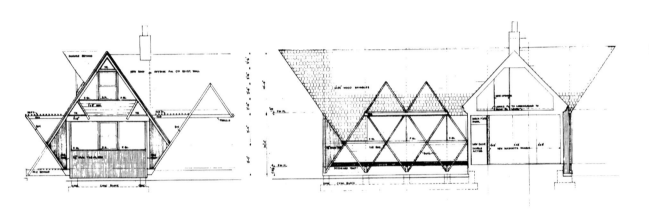

South elevation

East elevation

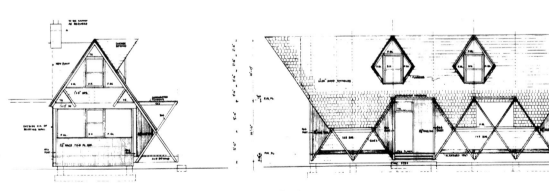

North elevation

West elevation

52

Ethel and Walworth Tyng house
seen from Brannock Bay.

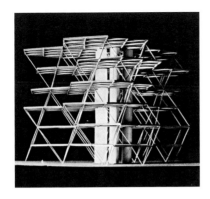

The *Perspecta 2* article shows our proposed City Tower still in a formative stage. Having designed a totally triangulated space frame as a house, I felt that the next exciting challenge would be to explore the same geometry in a tower structure. I made this first crude model with triangles in plan on my own time, hoping to interest Lou in developing the idea further. Lou's extraordinary ability to draw and express the imagery of the space-frame tower made him impatient with the more time-consuming process of figuring out specific geometric relations. My own interest lay in the rigor of a three-dimensional "reading" of how geometry comes together, its genetic tendency, and how and where that tendency can lead to variations. The model was then a necessary tool for developing tangible solutions. Of course the city tower was an "extracurricular" project, and I felt guilty taking up his and my time working on it when Lou was struggling to establish his practice. But at the same time I felt that such a project would help to establish him as a strongly innovative architect. Lou later wrote to me, "There are I believe few people who really understand the importance to architecture of the space frame. As you say no one has tackled the multi-story space idea."[9]

I was determined to help Lou in every way possible to realize his full potential, but at the same time I also felt concern about my own future. I was then thirty-two, and had worked and been in a relationship with him for seven years. It was challenging to play the role of muse to Lou, but the muse is a shadow figure, an empty vessel only existing to gestate and bring forth visible form identified as the man's creation. Such a limited relationship satisfied only a part of me. Another part—my own identity—was struggling for existence and growth. Growth could have been the challenging reality of marriage or forging my own identity outside our relationship.

Tyng made this preliminary model, above left, of the space-frame tower, which Kahn then sketched to reveal its expressive qualities (above right).

The final proposal for the City Tower project, opposite, applied Kahn's and Tyng's work on space-frame geometry to a higher tower structure.

9 Louis Kahn Letter to Anne Tyng, 5 July 1954.

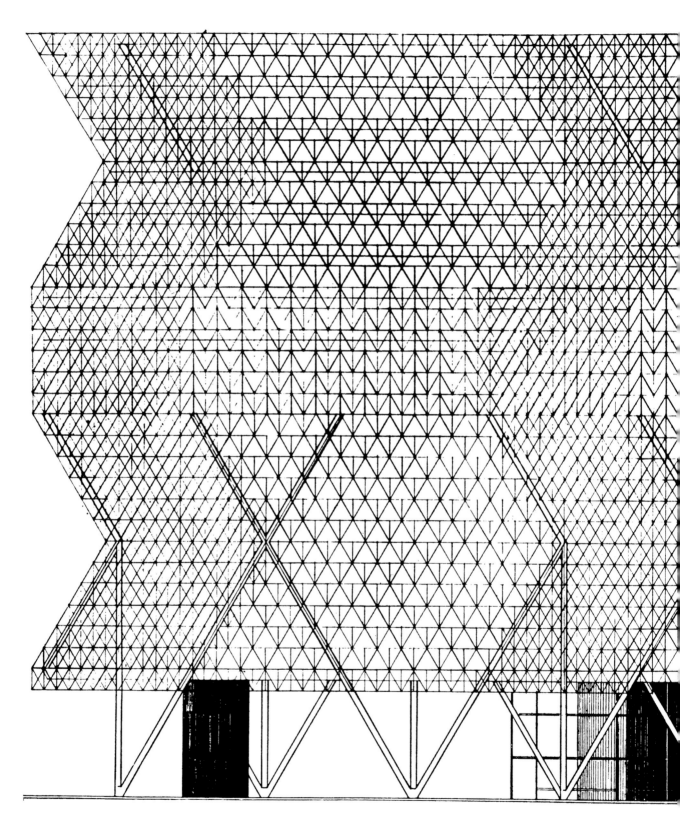

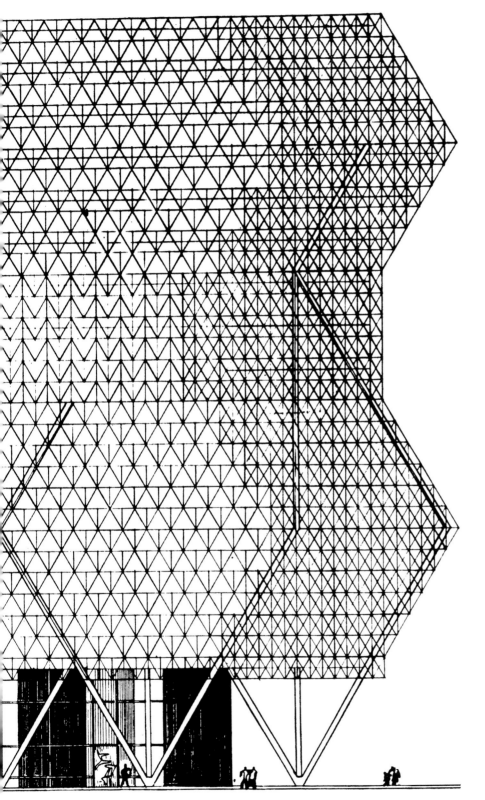

Elevation of preliminary version of proposed City Tower by Tyng.

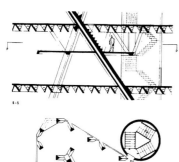

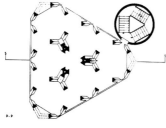

Plan and section of the "Hollow Capital" in the final proposal for the City Tower project.

In the fall of 1952 I applied for a Fulbright to study with Pier Luigi Nervi in Italy. I managed in the midst of various charettes to take an evening course in Italian to fulfill the Fulbright requirement. In the spring of 1953 at the Philadelphia chapter of the American Institute of Architects, I exhibited the model and photographs of my parents' house which was to be completed that fall. Although incomplete buildings were not eligible for an award, the jury composed of Philip Johnson, Edward Stone, Sr., and Edouard Catalano gave it an honorable mention award citing its "ingenious structural system." Lou also received an award for the Radbill Building of the Philadelphia Psychiatric Hospital, but not the gold medal which I believe it deserved.

Almost simultaneously I was offered an alternate Fulbright for Finland or West Germany and I received the shocking news that I was pregnant. The Fulbright ceased to be an option because at that time an unmarried and pregnant woman would not be considered a shining example of the American professional. I knew Lou well enough to realize that he was too poor to get a divorce, and since he often expressed the fact that he hated lawyers he was unlikely to be willing to go through the whole miserable process. I remember going through the days in a kind of haze wondering what to do about the situation while continuing site visits to New Haven and Maryland and working in the office. I tried discussing the problem with Lou, who offered no suggestions. If he didn't want to deal with something, he simply clammed up.

I finally decided the best thing to do was to go to Rome anyway. My brother Bill had married an Italian and was living there. Although Bill, a year-and-a-half older than I, had always been protective toward me when we were children, those days were long past and I was concerned about what kind of reception I might get. It is hard for people now to understand the attitudes that existed then. I don't believe Lou himself had much of a clue about what I was up against. After one of my site visits to my parents' house in Maryland, I drove on to Savannah, Georgia, where my father had taken charge of a church for the summer. I discussed furnishings for their house with them and told them I was planning to go to Italy. Only Lou and the doctor knew I was pregnant, and I could not tell my parents yet for my own peace of mind. I needed all my energy for coping with the situation. The collective projection onto unmarried mothers was that they were, at the very least, "delinquent" or "sinful." I was not about to accept such archaic pronouncements. Having our baby in Rome might be positive, graceful, and even romantic for our love child.

The autumn of 1953 marked a turning point in Lou's life and work. Until then he had been known as a progressive architect principally for his work on low-cost housing projects. But now his most prestigious building to date, the Yale University Art Gallery, was about to open simultaneously with the publication of Yale's *Perspecta* 2, featuring our planning work and our early version of the proposed City Tower (on both of which I was credited as a principal architect). Our exploration of fundamental geometric forms had opened up to him a whole new world of three-dimensional possibilities, and once he was in touch with these possibilities there was no turning back. Recent discoveries had revealed the geometry of the bonding of atoms and molecules that had evolved over millenia. This natural geometry was a resource for architecture that preexisted concepts of "style," and a scaleless principle that transcended the conflict between the lavish scale in Lou's Beaux-Arts training and the pragmatic minimal-scale, low-cost housing of the International Style. The new-found authority he derived from the "beginnings" of form gave him a non-arbitrary basis for his convictions about architecture. Geometry was an archetypal source for both monumentality and structural innovation. It embodied naturally evolved structural principles as pure essences and as the basis of infinite variations. It was a breakthrough that started the flow of concepts and ideas between us, both philosophic and tangible, that he built on for the rest of his life. Lou wrote of our sense of breakthrough, ". . . very few indeed understand the modern potentialities in the same way we do."[10]

While Louis Kahn began to experience well-deserved recognition for his work, I was the sole passenger on a freighter that was heaving through rough seas on its way to Rome. I felt confident that concepts and buildings Lou and I had developed together were significant achievements for bringing him the fame that he longed for, but on a personal level I had never felt more alone, uncertain, and filled with misgivings. Having Lou's baby was not the breaking-away I was thinking of when I applied for a Fulbright.

During the following year, our letters were a vital link for us. They tell from Lou's point of view a crucial part of the story of our relationship—of love, work, and growth—of resistance to change and the necessity for change.

geometry brought Kahn out of the Bauhaus Straight jacket

✳ ✳

10 Louis Kahn Letter to Anne Tyng, 10 July 1954.

✳

Letters from Louis Kahn to Anne Tyng:
November 1953–December 1954

"As I sat down, I said, 'I must now write to Anny—I can see her
as though she sits beside me.'"

21 July 1954

"I read your letters quickly at first, more slowly over some tea and again
before going to bed at Timothy Dwight. The train is another favorite
again and now I shall wait a few days and read it again before putting it away.
So it is with people who mean something to each other, and with those
one loves there is no end and the beginning is far before
the beginning of life altogether."

9 February 1954

"Tonight I shall continue to work alone—alone I can be with you too
and I can do much better work when I dream about what you would go for."

27 February 1954

61

"I must build one of the great buildings of the time . . . . You must help me build
this particular building. I doubt if I can do it without you."

29–31 May 1954

"But your suggestions are a constant stimulus and inspiration
and I know that circumstances will lead our minds together.... News of Alex
and you I wait for with warm anxiety, I have kept all your letters and
have hid them away but I am sure in a quite obvious place. I am going to
read them all over again."

3 September 1954

"I actually believe it is you who gave me my present confidence in my art, but that
is really mutual because I think you the really unusual talent."

30 November 1954

"I am not going to pretend to be anything but blue and uninteresting
to myself. My only hope is that everything and everybody I love will be happy
together again in my mind and actually."

10 December 1954

CABLEGRAM

Recieved on board: S/S Flying Spray
October 31, 1953 at 1910 GMT

TO *ANNE TYNG (SS FLYING SPRAY) WSUQ*

FM *(WCC CHATHAM)*

*Bon Voyage

I love you

Lou

62

8 November 1953

Dearest Anne,

J. Maxwell Fassett, Tyng
family lawyer and friend

Isbransen, a shipping
company

It was so frustrating with Fassett et al and the Isbransen people. It was strong with quiet drama. I wanted to hold you before you boarded. The Barge left too soon But you looked happy and good to me as you disappeared from view. New York was empty without you. I left for Philadelphia immediately.

Yale University Art Gallery
opened on November 6,
1954. George B. H.
Macomber Company was
the contractor; A. Whitney
Griswold was the president
of the university.

José Luis Sert, professor of
architecture and chairman of
the department, Graduate
School of Design, Harvard
University

The opening of the Gallery was on Friday. I made my little speech—half of which I forgot— turning the key which I received from Macomber over to President Griswold. The praise of the building was high. The various deans of the Universities including Sert were most praiseful. The lay loved it. I tell you the reception of the Architecture was without reservation wonderful to feel. It was a miserable day the snow and wind was a complete surprise. Seeing the Building from the outside was impossible. In spite of the weather the entire first floor was jammed.

I had not a moment to myself from Saturday morning the 31st to the 6th of the opening. The exhibit of the building as it progressed during study was a headache— the result (the show) is rather mediocre. But I tell you the building can take anything—it is truly strong. Every moment of my enjoyment I share with you I see you everywhere as the one who really gave me the courage to see it thru.

Uris Brothers, New York
developers of Penn Center
for which Kahn worked on
studies (1951–58)

Saturday 7th I had a meeting in New York—Uris Brothers asked the committee to look over their buildings—you remember. Well—when I got there I found that the meeting was called off on account of the weather. The snow had piled up quite a bit. No one let me know. I took the next train back. I told you about the snow of the opening. I forgot a detail. After dinner of the president of the University I accepted several invitations for the evening. I never got to them—on the way a car had to help so many stranded cars stuck in the snow—that after pushing them and pushing ourselves it was too late to go anywhere. It was something like that night at "Containers."

Container Corporation in
Manayunk, a suburb of
Philadelphia, where Kahn
and Tyng were caught in
heavy snow

*Perspecta, The Yale Archi-
tectural Journal* 2 (1953)
included "Toward a Plan for
Midtown Philadelphia" by
Louis I. Kahn

Today Sunday—I tried to find out if I could telephone you in Bordeaux—assuming that you arrived today—but no answer from the Isbransen office, so had to give up the idea. Did you get Perspecta *in Bordeaux. I am so anxious to hear all the dope about your trip— the captain and the mates. Anne dear excuse my belated writing—I miss you. Excuse the short note—more coming soon.*

Love Lou

11 November 1953

CABLEGRAM

L T ANNE TYNG

        AMERICAN EXPRESS PARIS. . .

SENT TELEGRAM PERSPECTA BORDEAUX LETTERS ROME AFTER YOUR WONDER-
FUL LETTERS PERSPECTA PARIS LOVE

        LOU

13 November 1953

64

Dearest Anne

I love you

*The dedication ceremony came off OK. I forgot some of my lines but I improvised a much
better statement (not cricket because all set up in English Formalities) understandable to
all and called the Macombers Master Builders which they are. Mr. Macomber (the old man)
was pleased as punch and kept mentioning his appreciation all evening.*

I am back to school working with Johnson on a collaborative. 2 Problems 1—a new sign   Philip Johnson
*for the Museum of Modern Art involving what architectural changes necessary for
the idea. 2—a poster board for the new Gallery at Yale. The thing is a bit stupid because
collaboration amongst the graphic art's section the painters and the architects is somewhat
cloudy. However that is Yale—no system—all freedom—(DON'T WORRY I know
I'm gabbing but I'm really thinking of you.)*

I hope you received the cable in Bordeaux and the Perspecta *I mailed by air to the American
Express Bordeaux. Please let me know how many copies you should like to have.*

*I am very lonesome writing this note in the office—no one around. I look forward to going
to Yale Sunday night and staying there longer than usual.*

The building was a wonderful success. I am including the letter from Osborn to give the general impression of opinion. But my enjoyment is faint without your sharing it Anne you had so much to do with its success everything in fact. Your encouragement your fight your conviction and faith in me did more than any of the physical efforts or knowledge or even ability. Ability is after all dead without the other ingredients borne of spirit. I have received my letters of praise but so far not from those who count except from Philip Goodwin who writes ". . . In my opinion it in no way clashes with the adjoining building and it carries out in a superb manner the practical and useful purposes wanted . . . I take back what I said about . . . Let me congratulate you again after the long struggle which this building required. It is a big step in advance for a sound working machine for the department of the University and a fine thing to look at for the man on the street."

(I really appreciate this letter a great deal coming especially from a very bitter man (a position I would hate to be in myself) who was almost damagingly critical). Fritz Gutheim (biography of F. L. W.) said that the building is a work of art and the best academic building in the U.S.

I know you care to know that I am feeling OK. I admit I feel lost though. Now I seem to want to make plans to blow up the place. (Please restrain me this last idea is not practical.)

Before I started this little letter I attended the Mayor's Meeting. Penn Center is worse than before. I am invited to a ground breaking ceremony for the first building. The ceremony is no bluff but how can they with no plans! This pen is terrible I can't make good e's and d's—

I am bursting with anxiety about your trip and what you have already seen of Europe. I sent nothing to Paris because I didn't know how long you would stay there and if you changed your mind about going to Paris because of the position of Bordeaux in relation to your objective—Rome.

I hope you are feeling fine and full of hope. I love you Anne

Lou

Bob Osborn, cartoonist who often worked on *Perspecta* and a friend of Kahn

Philip Goodwin, architect for an earlier proposal for the Yale University Art Gallery; also architect, with Edward Durrell Stone, of original Museum of Modern Art

Fritz Gutheim, architctural historian and biographer of Frank Lloyd Wright

The Redevelopment Plan for Midtown Philadelphia, known as Penn Center, and sometimes referred to by Kahn as "PC"

After the ship docked in Antwerp, Tyng went to Paris to visit Edith Schreiber, a friend from architecture school, and her husband, Roger Aujame, who was working for Le Corbusier.

Dearest Anne

Your wonderful letters came I must have read them five times. Trying to guess where you are is like hitting a moving body. It's easy for you—New Haven—me? First you said you were stopping at Bordeaux which you were to reach in 10 days—you had the choice of either Bordeaux or La Pallice in 12 days—

> *I sent* Perspecta *to Bordeaux*
> *I sent a Telegram to Bordeaux*
> *I sent letters to Rome (figuring that your choice of Bordeaux may make you skip Paris)*

Well anyway I figured all wrong

I hope you get this letter in Paris. Now I am again guessing that probably there is no American Express in Nice maybe you'll stay longer in Paris and so am banking on this last.

You will know from my letters that the Gallery went off wonderfully. The comments are most gratifying.

Zepp Clauss, Jane and a few from Z. Cl's office took a special trip to go over Gallery. Zepp called me on Sunday 15th and said it was the finest modern building he has ever seen believes it will cause a sensation. He spent Fri and Sat (I was not there—in Phila) and expects to go back. I didn't feel that there was so much variety to absorb but he (and I am sure he is honest) was ecstatic. He also called the Perspecta *publication terrific! Then Jane got on the phone to reiterate what Zepp had said. They went to Philip Johnson's after Yale visit. Phil does not like ceiling for some reason he is not clear about and Zepp thinks he (Johnson) believes I copied his steel sections for the window frames. I kind of think Zepp also believes I did, which is of course completely ridiculous. I believe mine are better and besides where did he get the idea from and who owns steel. Well . . . silly.*

Alfred "Zepp" Clauss and his wife, Jane Clauss, both architects and friends of Kahn

Today—George Howe and Vincent Scully were talking about the Perspecta *article. George expressed himself in that regard thusly—"I think the street article begins a new era in urban planning it makes complete sense" Scully in concurring made some historical analogies. again—"The space frame building is another great contribution to Architecture. I think Lou and Anne will hear more from others about it." "The Whole* Perspecta *book should put the Arch. Magazines to shame."*

George Howe, with whom Kahn was associated in 1941–42, chairman of the architecture department at Yale University until 1954

Vincent Scully, noted professor of art history at Yale University

Darling Anne I do hope you are in good spirits and that you take heart in my love for you. I feel the same emptiness which I know I must counter with diligent work.

It looks like I am going to get that New York house to do 'Mayer'. Mayer is coming to Phila this Friday to look over Weiss and Genel. Unfortunately he comes the day of the Penn Center Meeting. But I am sure the Weisses will receive us during the day.

As soon as I sign the commission I will send you the plot plan and the conditions. Maybe we can design it together. In any case I know enough about the conditions—large L.R.—may include D. alcove, large kitchen (with breakfast area)—laundry—storage— 4 bed rooms 4 baths and study. Son (now entering law school) may live with them after marriage (I believe a hope on the part of his mother) then of course the art collection and the books are part of the problem. They are purchasing a 3 acre plot on Long Island and I don't have a map but roughly I remember what I drew on the other side of this sheet.

Now Anne have a good time and let me know about money problems. I could send you a bill with each letter which would build up your dollar reserve which I know will do you the best financial good. By-By Honey, will write very soon again.

With all my love

Lou

22 November 1953

Dearest Anne

I wrote the 2nd page of this letter in the office before boarding train for New Haven. You will notice that Dear Ole Harvard came thru as I predicted. You will notice that Clasby and Co. 'Beat the Bulldog Badly.' I bought a pen in the station which you notice writes with the usual difficulty for me. Also the train is juggling badly. If you are now having wine with your meals as I suspect you are please take the first sip with a thought for me. I think of this since I am in the diner having ordered my supper which I expect will be meager and expensive.

You might send a postcard to the office and one to Sue (also to the office if you like). Everyone inquires about you. I informed everyone of your voyages so far. I received a letter from Princeton asking me to participate in a closed conference on "Education and Architecture." Five Deans and Six Architects have been asked including Doug Haskell as Editor. It will be fun to air views on the double barreled subject and I feel quite prepared to talk as well as listen. I am curious about the thoughts of Sert, Saarinen, Skidmore, Abramovitz and the others invited on the subject. The date is Fri. and Saturday Dec. 11, 12.

*Mr. Mayer of New York was down to look at the Weiss and Genel Houses. He brought
with him Mr. Blitz (his assistant and fall guy) and a Mr. Lomez a 'know it all' connoisseur
collector of Chinese art, that later tore into things he saw in a clever but I know half baked
manner. I did allow him to say his piece. They all liked the Genel house very much and
thought it was far superior to the Weiss house and I do agree in many ways that they
showed good judgment. I hope I don't lose the opportunity to do the house and working
with you on it would be real fun and delight. There is of course no indication that
I will not do it.*

*I have been following my old routine of answering and making calls during the day
and working or thinking at night. I have spent more time in New Haven than usual—
partly because of the [Gallery] and partly because I have not the same incentive to come
back to Philadelphia. Pen and I are now putting the finishing touches to Mill Creek
Redevelopment. I have just finished with him on the proposed controls which we have
made more complicated (or rather more flexible for the planner) than the
previous controls.*

Penrose Spohn, an architect
in Kahn's office

*Thanksgiving holidays would ordinarily keep me in Philadelphia. But I am leaving for
Yale tonight because of your mail which I figure by now I can expect there. I want so much
to hear from you honey—you have hardly an idea how much. Will I hear from Antwerp?
Paris? Did you receive* Perspecta? *Is it too early to hear? Anyway I'll find out when
I get to the 2nd floor of the Art Gallery tonight. I shall stay a day and come back for the
Tuesday groundbreaking. The First Building of Penn Center is having its ground-
breaking ceremony. I must attend. I know they don't have the foundation designed yet.
But when I asked the question (you remember) again I was told that it is so standard that
digging now in absence of them is perfectly in order. Just think how low Architecture
has gotten down. We Anne, you and I, are going to show them the way! The other day
I asked our committee and the design committee of Howe's when does architecture begin?
I said that I honestly believe that Mr. Dowling could design an office building without
an architect. He gets the best mechanical and structural engineers to put up the frame and
the mechanical. The elevator people will make a complete set of drawings on the core.
The space dimensions according to these developers are known (either 72' or 90' how long
is a matter of the lot). All Dowling has to decide is whether the windows are horizontal
or vertical and the color of the marble in the lobby and he has a complete and competent
building. He also argues that it is functional which it is as much as most people mean
when they say functional viz.: easy maintenance. So Mr. Architect when or where does
architecture begin? I dare say few Architects could answer and if they did they would say
what about proportions? To the developer proportions are not worth 8 1/2 %.*

68

Dowling, New York devel-
oper involved in Penn
Center

I have never written so much in my life to anyone. I am on my third page which I can fill really with as much love as you have made the pages of your wonderful letters alive with it. I never saw any part of the Riviera and it must certainly be delightful. The Mediterranean is full of wonder and beauty. The parts I saw around Italy I shall never forget. Try very hard to take a squint at Positano, Capri, Amalfi and if possible Paestum and even more south. By all means see Sicily—for me too for I have missed seeing that place but I hope to soon. It would be wonderful indeed seeing it with you. Dearest Anne—keep well and take in all you can. We are approaching New York and I know that if I mail it here it will speed up your getting this letter, so I close with love, will write soon again—something is bound to turn up to write about.

Love, Lou

2 December 1953

Dearest Anny

Received your letter about our problems about having to tell your brother and sister-in-law and about the money problems we are going to have and about the humiliation you must go thru—identity etc. etc. I love your letters, Anny, every word of them—these words however, seem strange and unknown and make my head swim with anxiety and worry. I know it is best that one is not caught withholding such matters from one you live with. How far it will go with your brother and especially how far with your sister-in-law is any body's guess. I hate to have your mother and father think little of you. We must work these things out our way and in a way which becomes the trust we have in each other and in the faith we have in each other's way of sensing what is wrong and right. All I know is that I love you and I love you with sincerity although mixed for the moment with insecurity and maybe also with little humor.

Tyng visited Nervi in his office and showed him *Perspecta 2* with the proposed City Tower. He became quite excited, exclaiming "*mi piace, mi piace*" (I like it, I like it). He then showed Tyng a parking garage he had designed with exterior triangulated truss in concrete, explaining that it was only two-dimensional, in contrast to the three-dimensional City Tower.

What you write about Nervi is really fun and I am all for the idea of working together on the space frame—that is to continue to work on our ideas. What I am interested in now is the development of the column joints (of the City Hall Building type) of intersection with floor construction. In general I believe we know all we need to know for the moment about floors (The idea I see more clearly about floors is that [it] is in every way an expanded slab). The connection and the nature of the column I believe we know but too little. I should like right off that you work for me (really use) (at the usual rate—no special out of country rate) on this problem and send me your time. If you have to go to Milan to find out more please do and again we can work things out I am sure. I have thought recently that there could be an open star-like capital (as the Greek) which may be the shear

69

head transition (capital is the shear head expression) to the column and that the column may express its bending (L/R) in a graphic way. All of which only enhances the whole works.

[sketches with notes]

I am sure you will be delighted to read what the New York Herald Tribune *(Fritz Gutheim) said about the building and about me. It is really a tribute to you as well because your faith in me far exceeds even his remarks and my faith in you made me take your advice and courage which led to some of the things I did. One thing I know you're my girl.*

Fritz Gutheim wrote a piece on the Yale University Art Gallery for the *New York Herald Tribune.*

I am still quite run down physically I don't take care of myself at all. It's difficult for me to live a standard life I hate it and resist it. I am working with greater diligence and getting certain things done. The Mill Creek Redevelopment Report for the [Philadelphia City Planning Commission] for instance is complete at least in text. I will send you the complete work as soon as finished. I have heard nothing from Mayer (New York) Roberts (Philadelphia) Durham (North Carolina)—am just waiting. I will send a copy of the Tribune *article.* The New York Times *also had a piece about the building in their Art Section of the Sunday papers it was not very complimentary in fact I think it was damaging. Fortunately the person who wrote it is no judge of architecture. The* Tribune *thing did not come to my attention until after I had read the* New York Times. *I was sure delighted to have that awful feeling of failure dispelled at least strongly enough to feel relaxed about the whole thing.*

Roberts, unknown to Tyng

Durham, unknown to Tyng

Aline Locheim (later Saarinen), critic for the *New York Times*

70

My best regards to your people but if they treat you in some god damned Victorian manner I shall positively hate them.

With all my love

Lou

Dear Anny, I am going to slip you a ten or so every letter so you don't have to be so tight about things. We'll work the money problem out O.K. don't worry honey.

Fri 18 Dec. 53

1

Dearest Bruce,

Last Monday I looked in your mail at Yale — Tuesday the same — it was not there. I had to leave Tuesday night for Philadelphia — And due again during the Xmas holiday period for the wind up meeting of the Zoo but I hope you found time to write to me and that I have a letter greeting me. Your mother has written me several times she most warmly invites me to stay over at the new house — which I intend to do — also reminds me very coyly about the mural left undone until I make it a reality. Hers really a very lovingly sweet letter — short — but good. She also reminds me that there is room enough even if Bill comes with the family.

Last week end 9-12-13th was the Princeton meeting on education. I believe I already wrote you who was there. Everybody appeared. I discussed my "design" theses but added another area of design influence — the nature of the space. This latter as you will see I believe helps the picture a lot. This is how the "nature of the space" came about. —— I am giving a problem at Yale. A Theatre we called in (a plot to us) people acquainted with the various sides of a activity

1. A Theatre layout man — he told us about acoustical lines, sight lines, lobby requirements, the house itself, the stage, the stage house etc.

2. An actor — he told us of the problem of reaching the audience but what was more important that many plays fare badly because of the limitation of the proscenium. the actor is [informed] the people are outside looking in etc etc.

3. An Author — the same story here as the actor

4. An electrical planner: he wanted to be able to change the atmosphere of the [whole] by electrical devices. Suddenly the place must become red or black with a pin point of light on a man (Hamlet) a blaze of light, a star like pins for over all sight etc.

5. The mechanical planner: The Renaissance ushered like welcomed the best and all of the machinery we can now build The Theatre was then alive with creative impulses and means of illusion

This was also discussed as that Television is producing a new crop of actors with need to T.V. stage. He predicts and shows the trend that acting is back to stay but once more room to work in.

71

Anny honey! I am long winded but I must write it all out. I am trying to really act as though I was talking to you and I only wish you were interrupting me with your stimulating reactions and enthusiasm and your wonderful suggestions – but here goes again.

I realized by all these unsatisfied desires ideas and pent up energies that the present Theatre is dead. That the students now [following] the instructions of the past consultant are just modifying known shapes enough to save ones self respect. Enumerable architects, some from best, are still just modifying while too long lost is life. The nature of the space of the Rennaissance Theatre no longer can [now] induce the exchange between the actor and the author. Romance is an illusion has changed is character. Startling exploits of man in flying then space, and now the flying carpet, Arabian Tales, the legend hardly appeals as much. We need a new [kind] of space acting one of a different nature one that will come to life again to give birth to much wanted expressions which the author will feed the actor and the actor the author. Exterior shapes must wait until 'the nature of the space' unfolds. and before 'order' can be evolved or created.

Now that is the reason why I have difficulty explaining now to you. The bases from which order could be derived was absent!
Now that I can play with the electric like a pianist on a key board with lights hidden in avenues of the construction — Now that I must remind a room of echoes as well as a room of single words or syllables —
Now that I always enter the Theatre at first on one side and after intermission from an entirely different side of the House from the [lobby] (I will mechanically mould the seat banks into an entirely different looking Play Room).
— I have the bases from which an order can be chosen (like the gallery really — it had to satisfy the nature of the space)

nature of the — order — design
space

The genius works without separation but he must in these at times of so many unsolved problems use separation. And the student and the teacher who must understand the student can profitably make the separation. And also I believe that the puzzle of who or who is not a designer can maybe be discovered and all wasted effort consequently.

After every page I must pause to tell you how very very much I love you Anny dear. Not having heard from you is very lonely indeed. I wanted also to read the words of delight that you must have already written about the Herald Tribune editorial. You know I sent a copy of Perspecta to home (Fritz Gutheim) and he wrote back that he thought that our article was really inspired and that he intends to send a copy just to `Urbanistica`. I believe the University already sent a copy to _____ and also to the American Academy in Rome. Do you need more, please tell me will be glad to send them along.

From each other.

Perspecta   now on with my `design` explanation

How the nature of space touches many buildings to day. For instance the first Uris building of Penn Center is in the main going to be occupied by only 4 large companies. Think of it! how right we are about broad, spaces — how foolish economy wise are these narrow column clustered corridor like spaces feet. I saw the Lever Building — it is dead — it looks like something made in Hoboken in one piece and picked up, put in place in one piece vertically (The name Whitman, chocolate rubbed off) in Manhattan. The same is true of the school with its spine corridor and little spaces shapes attached some with a laminated arch system on a 40' span and a lolly column beam system for the 30' span. (We often spoke about this point). The same is true of the house and I believe a good example to bring out the point is the

☐ K.L.
☐ ← 1 unit → ☐ ← DE, (the pieces preparation to discover the
☐ ← 2 unit   nature of the space before placing them
LR   next to each other).

and so on —

Now order
Order I believe is mostly structure. The structure idea backing embodying the needs of air, light, quiet, noise, makes the structure grow into a life of fibers enveloping the space so that its nature can be felt. This the seed the integration from which Design can work

design

is the changing adjusting (choosing?)(throwing away?) to
                    maybe not?
meet circumstantial conditions.

Though the creative mind combines design with order and space, not the repetition happens less obviously it is akin to what happens in feeling and Thinking

Feeling is our great well of consciousness, Thinking is a satellite, a meteor, meant not to be shot from feeling and never to return. It must return to the field of feeling to take meaning in depth. But some people always separate feeling from thinking and build their solution around Thinking only.

> feeling will *always* remain the source made effective for creativity by the adventures of Thinking brough home again.

That is why the creative mind cannot accept the separation categorically of the notion space – order – design and still fully so. because feeling embraces all at once intuitively, BUT the intuition needs help to activate and direct is field to a single objective at times (To build a building) we must know – Therefore we must separate – in order to feel with greater creative effect.

now.

To satisfy then the creative purists let us say $\left(\begin{smallmatrix} N \\ S \end{smallmatrix}\right) \!-\! \odot \!-\! P = 1$

Then **2** in our book means the premise that everything we consider in a building is constructed or Built-up not (like the loose building) a monolith. We must then employ every means of simulation to building, — drawn from the bottom up work our steps built on paper is he built in the field

then **3** is the aethletic expression of this construction and the greater ever constant effort to express its spirit in its knuckles, joints. That a building is not a miracle it is a struggle and the struggle expressed will be noble then restraint one time by an aspiration another as the artist chooses,

Pardon Anny I cannot go on really as you know I can when am wound up and in a direction of thought. When I presented this idea to the students they were really enthralled. They are dropping all their schedules + dates ad starting all over again with th space needs perpetuated ad cured — cured mostly inorder to breathe life into th problem too.

The process 8
1 — D> —⊙— Ⓝ⊘
2 — everything is constructed
3 — expression.

was not as clearly presented at th Princeton conference and I have suspicion of believe that I did not go across like a smash hit. Later on Sunday after th breakfast meeting I visited Elizabeth Wasser (Moch) with her brother in law William Wurster of U, of Cal. At lunch I was really lucid ad W. W. was, like I wanted him to be, impressed. He told 2 good stories.

Peret (Franz) gave a party. Wurster discussed F.L. Wright. Peret couldn't remember what he was meant (Pronunciation difficulty) then Peret finally woke up an said, "OH YES! half basement — half attic."

Eric Mendelsohn visited Eero Saarinen's. (General Motors Building) "said Mendelsohn; "But Eero I have seen these buildings before" said Eero, "But Eric don't you like Meis²?".

_____

Enough of this love making Lets — — — — I miss you very much and ⟨often⟩ wonder what you are doing at certain moments, Please tell me more of your activities ⟨and⟩ don't omit the little details I love to hear them.

Anne — I am going to deposit $400,00 in your account on Monday Dec 21 Alma is sending you a Xmas check for th usual $25.00. I don't have any cash on me now ad can't enclose a bill or two. Did you receive those 2 10's I inserted last time?

(I guess your brothers etc are gone now (are not there th office directly) mine I managed th 400,00 by my own means, so that I can get it later from th office when needed, If you do work for us please send th time card, send it any way as you judge best for your needs

I hope hope that everything will turn out well for us I love you very much very much. yours love X X Y Y, Y, / Y , , —

Merry X Mas and Happy New Year

Dearest Anne,

Last Monday I looked for your mail at Yale—Tuesday the same—it was not there. I had to leave Tuesday night for Philadelphia—Am due again during the Xmas Holiday period for the wind up meeting of the Yale Art Gallery. I hope you found time to write to me and that I have a letter greeting me. Your mother has written me several times she most warmly invites me to stay over at the new house—which I should love to do—also reminds me very coyly about the mural left undone until I make it a reality. It was really a very lovingly sweet letter—short—but good. She also reminds me that there is room enough even when Bill comes with the family.

William Tyng, Anne's brother

Last weekend 11–12–13th was the Princeton meeting on education. I believe I already wrote you who was there. Everybody appeared. I advanced my "order-design" thesis but added another area of design influence—"the nature of the space," this latter as you will see I believe helps the picture a lot. This is how the "nature of the space" came about— I am giving a problem at Yale. A Theater. We called in (to talk to us) people acquainted with the various sides of its activity

> *1. A Theater layout man—he told us about acoustical lines, sight lines, lobby requirements, the house itself the stage house etc.*

> *2. An Actor—he told us of the problems of reaching the audience but what was more important that many plays fare badly because of the limitation of the proscenium. The actor is framed the people are outside looking in etc. etc.*

> *3. An Author—the same story here as the actor*

> *4. An electrical planner: He wanted to be able to change the atmosphere of the house by electrical devices. Suddenly the place must become red or black with a pin point of light on a man (Hamlet) a blaze of light, a star like pins of overall light etc.*

> *5. The mechanical planner: The Renaissance would [have] welcomed the best and all of the machinery we can build, The Theater was then alive with creative impulses and means of illusion. This man also reminded us that Television is producing a new crop of actors with also the T.V. stage. He predicts and shows the basis that acting is back to stay and once more room to work in.*

Anny honey! I am long winded but I must write it all out. I am trying really to act as though I was talking to you and I only wish you were interrupting me with your stimulating reactions and enthusiasm and your wonderful suggestions—but here goes again.

I realized by all these unsatisfied desires ideas and pent up energies that the present theater is dead. That the students were following the construction of the first consultant and just modifying known shapes enough to save ones self respect. Enumerable architects, some of our best, are still just modifying what has long lost its life. The nature of the space of the Renaissance Theater no longer can induce the exchange between the actor and the author. Demands for illusion has changed its character. Startling exploits of man in flying thru space dims the flying carpet, Arabian Tails, the legend hardly appeals as much. We need a new kind of acting space one with a different nature one that will come to life again to give birth to much wanted expressions which the author will feed the actor and the actor the author. External shapes must wait until the 'nature of the space' unfolds, and before 'order' can be evolved or created.

Now that is the reason why I had difficulty explaining order before. The basis from which order could be derived was absent. Now that I can play with the electric like a piano on a keyboard with lights hidden in crevices of the construction—now that I must provide a room of echoes as well as a room of single words or syllables—now that I should enter the theater at first on one side and after intermission from an entirely different side of the House from the lobby (I have mechanically moved the seat backs into an entirely different looking Play Room). I have the basis from which an order can be chosen (like the Gallery really—it had to satisfy the nature of the space)

nature of the space → order < design

The genius works without separation but he must in these times of so many unsolved problems use separation. And the student and the teacher who must understand the student can profitably make the separation. And also I believe that the puzzle of who or who is not a designer can maybe be discovered and all would profit consequently.

After every page I must pause to tell you how very much I love you Anny dear. Not having heard from you is very lonely indeed. I wanted also to read the words of delight that you must have already written about the Herald Tribune *editorial. You know I sent a copy of* Perspecta *to him (Fritz Gutheim) and he wrote back that he thought that our article was really inspired and that he intends to send a copy of it to* Urbanistica. *I believe the University already sent a copy to [*Urbanistica*] and also to the American Academy in Rome. Do you need more* Perspecta *please tell me will be glad to send them along.*

now on with my 'design' explanation

Now this nature of space touches many buildings today. For instance the first Uris building of Penn Center is in the main going to be occupied by only 4 large companies. Think of it! how right we are about broader spaces—how foolish economy wise are those narrow column clustered corridor like spaces with layers of companies away from each other. I saw the Lever Building—it is dead—it looks like something made flat in

Urbanistica, an Italian publication

Hoboken in one piece and picked up, put in place in one piece vertically (the name
Whitman Chocolate rubbed off) in Manhattan. The same is true of the school with its
corridor—spine and little special shapes attached some with a laminated arch system on
a 40-foot span and a lolly column beam system for the 30-foot span. (we often spoke
about this point.) The same is true of the house and I believe a good example to bring out
the point is the

[sketch] (the process of separation to discover the nature of the space before placing
them next to each other).

  and so on—

now order

Order I believe is mostly the structure. The structural idea embodying harboring the
needs of air, light, quiet, noise etc. It is what makes the structure grow into a life of fiber
enveloping the space so that its nature can be felt. It is the seed It is integration from which
Design can work and design is the arranging adjusting (choosing?) (throwing away?)
maybe order? to meet circumstantial conditions. Though the creative mind combines
design with order and the [nature] of space, the separation happens less obviously.
It is akin to what happens in feeling and thinking.

78

[sketch]

Feeling is our great well of consciousness. Thinking is a satellite, a meteor, meant
not to be shot from feeling and never to return. It must return to the field of feeling to have
meaning in depth. But some people always separate feeling from thinking and build
their solution around thinking only.

[sketch]

(feeling will always remain the source made effective for creativity by the
adventures of thinking brought home again.)

That is only the creative mind cannot accept the separation categorically of the nature of
space-order-design and rightfully so because feeling embodies all at once intuitively,
BUT the intuitive needs help to activate and direct its field to a single objective at times
(to build a building) We must know—therefore we must separate—in order to feel
with greater creative effect.

  Now,

To satisfy the creative purists let us say nature of space → order < design = 1

then 2 in our book would be the premise that everything one conceives in a building is
constructed or built-up not (like the Lever Building) a monolith. We must then employ
every means of simulation to building,—draw from the bottom up mark our steps build on
paper as he builds in the field.

Then 3 is the aesthetic expression of this construction and the greater ever constant effort to express its spirit in the knuckles, joints. That a building is not a miracle it is a struggle and the struggle expressed will be noble thru restraint one time by exaggeration another as the artist chooses.

Dearest Anny I could go on really as you know I can when I'm wound up and in a direction of thought. When I presented this idea to the students they were really enthralled. They are dropping all their solutions to date and starting all over again with the space needs projected and lived—lived mostly in order to breathe life into the problem too.

The process of   *1—Design > Order → Nature of Space*
                         2—everything is constructed
                         3—expression.

was not as clearly presented at the Princeton conference and I have suspicion to believe that I did not go across like I should have. Later on Sunday after the breakfast meeting I visited Elizabeth Kassler (Moch) with her brother-in-law William Wurster of U. of Cal. At lunch I was really lucid and W. W. was, like I wanted him to be, impressed. He told 2 good stories.

     Peret (France) gave a party. Wurster discussed F. LL. Wright. Peret couldn't grasp who was meant (pronunciation difficulty). Then Peret finally woke up and said,"OH YES! half basement-half attic."

     Eric Mendelsohn visited Eero Saarinen's General Motors Building. Said Mendelsohn, "But Eero, I have seen these buildings before." Said Eero, "But Eric, don't you like Mies?"

Enough of this love making lets — I miss you very much and often wonder what you are doing at certain moments. Please tell me more of your activities and don't omit the little details I love to hear them. Anne—I am going to deposit $400.00 in your account on Monday Dec 21. Alma is sending you a Xmas check for the usual $25.00. I don't have any cash on me now and can't enclose a bill or two. Did you receive those 2—10's I inserted last time?

I guess your brother et al are gone now.

I managed the $400.00 by my own means (and not thru the office directly) so that I can get more later from the office when needed. If you do work for us please send the time card, send it anyway as you judge best for your needs.

I hope hope that everything will turn out well for us. I love you very much very much.

    Yours,

      Lou xxxxxxxxxxxx

       Merry Xmas and Happy New Year

Elizabeth Kassler, married architect Kenneth Kassler

William Wurster, dean of the Architecture School of the University of California at Berkeley

Peret, presumably Auguste Perret

Alma Farrow, Kahn's secretary

Dearest Anne: *Xmas Eve (after the party)*

*I just received your letter of Monday 21 when you received notice that you may expect
a call on the telephone from me. I have been planning this for a long while [gearing] it for
around Xmas even though I did realize that the connections at that time would be tough.
My plan was to call you at 5 o'clock a.m.—11 your time. I set my alarm for 5 got up—
put my overcoat over my pajamas—donned my socks for slippers opened a book and waited
for my appointed connection. Well I waited until 9:30 and no connection. I informed the
operator that I am going out for breakfast and to transfer my call to the school. As soon as
I stepped into the Gallery (after breakfast) door I was avalanched by informers that a
call was coming thru from Rome. Anny it was so wonderful to hear your melodic anxious
loving voice—I forgot all my lines—I think I told you to go see things—about the money—
I heard you call me honey!—I talked 4 minutes they charged $16.00 plus $4.00 tax—
It was the least expensive call I ever made—as far as I was concerned it could of been 1¢
it was so exciting really to hear you. Today we had our regular Xmas party. I made punch.
I drank every sip with you. I was given a recipe by some one at the last Yale Yule Party:*

*   1 Quart red wine*

*   1 pint brewed tea (to dark black)*

*   1/2 # sugar*

*   cinnamon sticks, currants, cloves, lemon peel*

*   all boiled and served*

*Your picture is very beautiful I was glad to get it I don't really have one of you taken
recently. I shall try to write more often but do you know Anny that I have never written as
much to anyone as to you. I haven't written to my parents for over a year now but there
is no excuse for that nor is there an excuse for not trying to write more often to you. About
the Xmas party. Dave W., Dave Z., Herb B., Nathan, Leonard, Marie K., Bill E., Alice E.,
Jack Lukens, I. Maintin, Barclay Jones and several other people in and out. It was a good
party my punch made a great hit no body got high not even Bill—the punch was hot
(I kept it brewing) and I made trays out of the aluminum foil for the chips and pretzels.
We all missed you very much and I believe that everyone sensed that I missed you very much
too. I hope you don't mind that I did not send you a present. I thought it would be nice but
I bungled things much these last days and am generally pretty confused and not too easy
to live with. I find the most peculiar evaluation of me cropping up from several unknown
sources let me explain—I was recommended by a man named David Marder (Director
of exhibits at the commercial Museum) to be the architect of the interior renovation there.
It is an extensive job about $1,000,000. Also Ed Stone recommended me for the job to
Mrs. Greenfield who is the chairman of the building committee (Ed is doing the Albert M.
Greenfield house over for her) I went to a reception where only a few people were invited.
Oscar was there (he was originally considered for the job and so announced in the press*

Kahn refers to a photograph
of Tyng that was later used
on the Atlas Cement
brochure that featured
their City Tower.

"commercial Museum,"
exhibition space in
the former Philadelphia
Convention Center

Edward Durrell Stone

several weeks ago—but I heard he was out because Mrs. G. does [not] like him.) Mr. G. went around to inquire of my competence and I understand that Holmes Perkins said I was a good architect, in fact a great architect for new buildings and in structure but of doubtful ability in interior design. Also that I did not have the organization to carry out a commission in a hurry (required). All of this is of course non-sense and now I understand that both Oscar and Ed Stone are being considered jointly, one the design (Ed) and one the expediter (Oscar) those unholy alliances! But I am mad over being judged so falsely.

Another thing that makes me mad at myself is that I believe I lost the job at Durham too because I told them (the committee) that I should like to produce a perfected construction similar to the Gallery (with 'newly' conceived column idea). They misunderstood—thinking I was going [to] give them a second hand job. So you see why I am mad at myself. Also the architect of the Gallery in Baltimore (very rich museum) had me show him around the Gallery at Yale—he intends to use the idea. This architect "Jenks" by name was hired by the board on which Alexander Cochran is a member. You remember he is the Architect who married one [of] the Sizer girls. I misunderstood I believe that deal over the phone too assuming that they wanted me as consultant. May[be] they still do but so far no soap. I am due to talk at their Gallery about architecture in Feb.

Anny I talked only about me but I want to tell you how much I wait for word from you— very much I wait. I imagine that [I] write often but I don't realize how quickly the weeks fly. The last letter I wrote you about the nature of space-order-design = 1 conception of the design process. I have talked to many people by now about this. I am finding the reactions to my particular lines and in general it needs some but not altogether drastic change. By now you have yourself gotten the general idea and am more than anxious to hear your reaction. I presented the thesis to Schweikher who barely got the idea. He is far from stupid but somehow I find it difficult to warm up to him. Maybe I explained it with not too much trust and held back some pertinent ties. In the end he saw enough to realize its significance. I hope you think it significant enough to write your comment. Please Anny keep working at the idea you sent me several days ago (the sketch with the letter preceding the last just mentioned). It is a beautiful sketch and I am going to stay in the office Xmas day to study it and to write soon my reaction. Incidentally that letter (the long one with sketch) was wonderful to receive with all the delicate touches. I longed so much to be near you too Anny don't forget. So far I have kept all your letters and I have reread them several times. Incidentally Monday (21) letter was received Thursday—that is the fastest yet! Please Anne have fun see places while you can. I shall try to scrape up additional money as you need it. Don't worry about money for gods sake we can always manage that within reason.

Lots and lots of love

Lou xxxxxxxxxx

Next time I shall try to insert a few extra bills. I believe it is best when sending some opaque material along with the letter otherwise it can so easily be spotted by one who needs it less.

Albert M. Greenfield, head of a prominent real estate brokerage house in Philadelphia, and his wife were major supporters of Philadelphia cultural institutions.

Oscar Stonorov

G. Holmes Perkins, dean of the Architecture School at the University of Pennsylvania

Walters Art Gallery, Baltimore

Jenks, unknown to Tyng

Alexander Cochrane, architect based in Baltimore

Paul Schweikher succeeded Howe as chair of the architecture department at Yale University in 1954.

Dearest Anne: *Xmas Day '53*

*I wrote you yesterday—mailed—forgot to include the bank deposit slip duplicate. The $25
is Xmas check. Again I feel awful not to give you something for Xmas in person. In person is
always better—fuller [. . . .] Tell me how you spent Xmas. It is very interesting in Rome
I remember we went to visit the various churches and before that bought masks and made
merry in several of the Piazzas.*

*Received a good letter from Le Ricolais which concerns you as well as me. I enclose—
I made a copy of the dates he mentions so that I may contact him when here. I heard also
that Mumford is making* Perspecta *required reading for his course. Barclay Jones wrote a
piece about me in a student publication of the college he still is attending down south.
Sidney Lerner has bought 50 copies and sold them all to Philadelphians. If you need more
please tell me. It would be well if the material could be amplified to suit the European
publications. In other words it could be rewritten to inject familiar similes. I am busy now
trying to write material for the publication of the Yale [Art Gallery] in* Progressive
Architecture. *The deadline for me is Jan 20. It is the usual torture I need you to help me you
are so very good at writing and expressing a thought. You are altogether a marvelous girl.
I am inserting a few bucks in an Xmas card (this card I received in the mail from one of the
teachers in Basic.) so you can't see thru the thin paper. I hope by next time I write (and I
mustn't keep you long) I can report that I have new work in the office. I am concerned but
not too. Dave is busy on Mill Creek as yet, and Pen is finishing (by degrees) the Mill Creek
Report. Herb Bregman just told me that they have a new boy baby whose name will be
Keith Randall (imagine a handle like that in this day and age—Moses or Sam is not good
enough). I shouldn't be catty like that but I know we would both titter over it if you
were here beside me which would be so very pleasant and wonderful.*

> *Lots and lots of love*
>
> *Lou xxxxxxxxx*

Robert Le Ricolais, French engineer, was later invited to the University of Pennsylvania where he began teaching with Kahn in 1955.

Lewis Mumford

Barclay Jones, of the Philadelphia Housing Authority

Sidney Lerner, Philadelphia bookseller

David Wisdom

Herb Bregman, mechanical engineer at Cronheim and Weger, the firm that shared office space with Kahn at 1728 Spruce Street and Twentieth and Walnut streets

Dearest Anny   *day after Xmas '53*

This is the second time I forgot to enclose the Bank slip. Now also I can point to the most unusual feat of writing 3 letters in succession to the same person. But doesn't it come at the most needed time when no amount of letters really can take the place of being together. Needed for me mostly since I do feel the gap left by your absence these days particularly. We lived them, though not fully in the conventional sense, with a great want for each other and the delight of being together from my point of feeling unequalled. Anny this letter is going to be short because this morning I have to leave on a trip to see a piece of land— maybe a new client (not bad if I don't scare her off). I've got only a half hour and I do want you to feel secure about the money business by giving you the concrete evidence—therefore my determination (foiled 2 x) to send you the slip. I am going to spend the Xmas Holidays from Yale as profitably as possible which to me means work on several details still left undone for the Gallery. Clothes racks closets (storage) pin up boards, some furniture. Also I keep dreaming about our space frames which are more and more important. Evidence of their importance is appearing in several places. I believe I mentioned that Mies van der Rohe put out an analyzed [tetrahedron] roof frame 600' x 600' with no columns on inside. To offset the 14" sag in the middle a slight camber was used in erection. This is really a good sound advanced factory or work space. My only objection is that he does not use the cantilever. I have had a chance to talk Nature of Space → Order < Design = 1 to several people and for once they seem themselves to understand. The criticism of works of art in a way other than 'I like it—I don't like it.' Of course don't mistake me I think that some people are entitled to say only ['I like it—I don't like it']. I think we are for instance don't you Anny? I am determined to make a better model of the City Hall at a large enough scale to show the floor construction too. I shall have a mold made. Now I could however make a model of a detail only. That may be more sensible for the time (immediate) to sell the idea. George H. of course (who could help a lot) still thinks the world is going to pot and the 'Decline of the West' is upon us. He trusts so much the brains of others. Creative people do not refer to the work of others but to the spirit of others. They can allow them that but never are they satisfied with the end products of their fellow artists.

Lots of Love—(my time is running out) Lots of Love—Lots of love

> *Lou*

Dearest Anny:

You said to me one time that even if you write but a word or two—still write. This is one of those times when I don't write much because I feel that all the interesting experiences are on your side now. I haven't received mail from you for several days and I know how it feels not getting word. Your letters are always so loving and warm. I received a letter from your father telling me of the arrival of Bill et al. He tells of some of the faults of the house you built but he is really very understanding—saying—"too bad Anne did not have more competent men to work for her. They should have done a great deal more justice to her plan." The furnace seems not big enough for the really rough weather. (But I believe it has a lot to do with what he mentions again—"fifty places to insulate in one way or another") ("The furnace fan set in reverse") He continues

"At any rate we are settled in our own house, have rugs down and pictures up, my books on study shelves and the very pleasant aspects of a home. Though our furnace is not adequate for these piercing gales from the N.W. the whole house is pleasantly warm in milder weather which is usual here."

Of course he wants me to visit which I shall do. He himself suggests after the winter.

I am designing several pieces of furniture and the sundry items for the Yale Art Gallery. I would rather I had you to talk them over with than Dave or Spohn who are alternately either negative or unresourceful. But I am trying to be as self reliant as is required under the circumstances. I hope Anny dear that you are busying yourself with ideas on construction and are singing at your work. Don't fail to see Venice, Verona, Florence, Pisa, Siena. Even if you have to take a conducted tour Don't worry about the dough that is to be ever our least worry. I think the tour idea is good please inquire about the possibilities and let me know if you have time otherwise take it and then tell me about it en route. I am sitting here having avoided about 15 minutes ago an invitation to dinner offered by no other than that wit of wits Herb Bregman. I turned it down for self protection giving the old chestnut of "I'm somehow not hungry." Actually I am starved having forgotten lunch (I lost track because I went down for a cup of tea just before lunch time) But now I must wait until he comes back before I go out. It's hard to write on an empty stomach if you are not officially a writer. For one working on a plan as an architect that should, according to old tradition, produce the best results. Maybe therefore I should quit eating lunches at least. Don't worry Anne all this small talk doesn't mean I am getting heavier in fact I have lost about 5 pounds I feel much better around the middle. Xmas day Sue came down to

Tyng had given Sue
Ann Kahn a parakeet the
previous Christmas.

*breakfast with the bird and insisted that everyone sing "Happy Birthday to You" for the
bird. She, the bird, is now just 1 year old as far as she Sue is concerned. It was really cute
and I thought and I am sure she (Sue) did too think of you. I hope I receive a letter from you
by tomorrow as I want to hear about your reaction to some of my rantings about space etc.
and most of all how you felt getting the telephone call. I was really thrilled to hear your
sweet voice though the hearing was jerky and indistinct. Bregman the duct man just came
in, in that sure step of a man of action. The piping of air would never have occurred to
me in my youth as a thing I wanted to live for. He speaks of it with the same love as I have
for it, so I guess there is nothing but air in it. How breezy. Think of it ¡¡¡ Keith Randall
Bregman. Keith yet!*

Dorothy Zuckerkandel,
wife of David Zuckerkandel
in Kahn's office

*I want to leave this short writing on this note of mirth but I must tell you that Dorothy
Zuckerkandel called me suggesting that she call to the attention of the press the work at
Yale and the press notices I received outside of Philadelphia. I see no harm in that. In fact it
might do me a lot of good considering the bad luck I have had with the jobs that barely
nibbled. Anyway she is due tomorrow to read Herald Tri. and other notices and will outline
a story for the Sunday papers. Dearest Anny so long for the time being. I shall try to write
often because it really is delightful being near you even in this most frustrating way.*

With lots and lots of love

Lou xxxxxxxx

Dearest Sweetheart: *Happy New Year!*

I love you I love you I love you too I received your beautiful letter of the 23rd. The
Children of St. Pauls at Xmas Eve—I felt my arms go around them and you and—No doubt
must ever cross your mind about loving you. I am glad I am your bambino and am proud
to be your inspiration teacher and mischievous imp. You are those things to me, except
the mischievous imp. You're too lovely—you with those 'occhi celesti'. I wrote you about
the telephone call. I had it all planned to shower you with all the words and feeling of love
I could think of. By the time the call came thru (since I could be glued to Dean Sawyer's
room) I was in the office surrounded by people coming in and out and I became tongue tied.
Excuse me honey, I shall call you reasonably soon again and I hope that the connection will
be better. Carlo and Lucianna seem good for you. I am glad they love you and feel with
you in moments of apprehension. You must remember what I look like and you must
imagine that my arms are around you holding you as tightly as I dare now rubbing my nose
against your cheek and whispering devilish suggestions in your ear kissing you in many
places. This is New Year's day Jan 1. I am in the office alone. It's 10 P.M. I went nowhere
New Year's Eve I was here. My habits have not changed. I am very lonely but I try very hard
to occupy myself more than I have before. I am showered by invitations to socialize but
I have not succumbed and what's more I feel that I am losing less than I ever did before
by not going out. But I want you to continue to question me about my habits. You are not
invading my privacy. I will keep nothing from you. Sometimes I fail to realize that the
everyday little things reimagine us together again in the particular way understood by us.
Anny dear you mustn't worry about your weight except as it might endanger you later.
So do keep your weight down for that reason but not for any reasons of vanity. I am return-
ing to school on Jan 4th and I don't look with great excitement toward the continuation this
next semester. Schweikher takes over after January. If he is afraid of me (intellectually or
because I am not one to follow a system as laid down) that makes me uncomfortable.
I gave him all reason to believe my cooperation but I did hint that I can do my best work
only if left to my own devices as a teacher. But as soon as I feel the least indication of
neglect (by not being in on important design decisions which affect me) I promise myself
to quit. I am such a baby really about this particular matter.

(Mill Creek is going up the contractor is lousy I am trying to do a good concrete job but
it is practically impossible with such deliberately grasping people)

I am working on some 'joints' too and I hope you don't wait too long before sending in a
time card. I would if I were you send one in for a few weeks pay so I could deposit more in
your account. It will ease your precious little (means wonderful) mind. You must have
freedom of action and you must need personal things. Don't worry about the dough. I don't

Kahn refers to Tyng's
description of a children's
candlelight procession in
Rome.

Charles Sawyer, dean of
architecture, Yale
University

Carlo and Lucianna, the
couple who worked as
housekeepers for the
William Tyngs on Via
Cassia, became close
friends with Anne Tyng
during her stay.

86

have much It'll go soon enough but while I still have a couple of thousand ($2,500) it is better in your hands than in mine. I'll tell you when to stop, in the meantime don't neglect essentials and a little more. I am delighted about your Italian, you will teach me? You are bound to learn to speak under the circumstances. My courageous wonderful she woman how I long to see you. Your picture is lovely your curly cue hair-do is just the way I left you. I waved to you much after you were out of sight completely. Your friends must have thought me a little nuts although in returning the check for the amount I loaned you Mr. Fassett made some nice remarks about me.

With All My Love

Lou xxxxx

7 January 1954

Dearest Anny:

Time goes so fast. It seems just yesterday that I wrote you last but actually it was last Saturday. Your two letters—a day apart—came the 4th and 5th Just as you had calculated. It was an exalting delight to read them and to feel the warm way you received my order-design ideas. How clear you thought those ideas were. It was so wonderful to know for sure that some one is rooting for you—believes in you unflinchingly. I often think that it can't be true and that if it is so now that it can't last for ever. But then again I know that my own people have—to this very day still—never lost faith in me. Only true love can see no failure no blemishes no wrinkles nor change in form because they read thru such transient trivialities into the spirit which they never mistake for the temporal. It must have been the plane of love that evolved man even though the marks of the primeval are still very evident. Because love is the great motivator it has shaped our laws built our cathedrals created the teacher.

New Years I was also with you. I remember well our last New Year together—in our own special way. I don't believe that we ever took each other for granted. That is rare and living—Happy New Year Honey.

The Graduate Student Council at Harvard has invited me to talk to them about Architecture (my subject). They write very cutely in doing so throwing the praise (and paying homage) to those whom as they say they like and admire. Well it ought to be fun since they remind me that they have very large turn outs from Harvard MIT and schools around. That is to be in the middle of February. I will write you of course how it all turns out.

I believe I told you that I am to talk in Baltimore the middle of March at the Gallery there. I am hoping to make a big enough hit to at least make them feel that they have lost a great deal not considering me as their architect. They are building a considerably large addition. (You notice how poorly I write it is my oak table and the thin paper)

This short note is hardly enough and shall write you tomorrow or the next day. It is very late (it is tomorrow) and I want to get this off to you. Lots of love,

Lou xxxxxxxx

8 January 1954

Dearest Anny

Dean Perkins called to have me conduct a problem (as visiting critic) on some of the days I am not teaching at Yale. I don't know why I didn't say no right away—knowing about the Harvard trip the lecture in Baltimore and how many days can a man do his best in. Over-confidence could make me accept but I really should not and I think will not. So far I have no new work—quite a few nibbles—but no new work and I simply must get some. I was thinking of writing to the City Authorities asking them to consider me for a study of the New City Building, citing the Gallery as an example of the kind of economic integration I hope to be able to establish for this particular space. Perspecta should indicate my and our sincere interest in the problem. Another idea would be to inquire into the possibility of a school job from the Board of Education. I understand from a friend that 2 new high schools are soon going to come up for planning. I am only mildly worried this minute but soon I shall not be able to carry on on the same level. What keeps my head always high however is that you think like I in these matters the bank balance is not the measure of success and that we are on the brink of a profound understanding of our art thru fragments of work accomplished and the better work it implies. This morbid note is not meant to 'blue' just to tell you without disguise what is on my mind at the moment. I have been reading The Book of Tea *and here are some gems out of it:*

> *"Those who cannot feel the littleness of great things in themselves are apt to overlook the greatness of little things in others".*

Wangyucheng eulogized tea as "Flooding his soul like a direct appeal, that its delicate bitterness reminded him of the after-taste of good counsel."

Yale University Art Gallery

"Translation is always treason, and as a Ming author observes, can at its best be only the reverse side of a brocade, all the threads are there, but not the subtlety of color and design. But, after all, what great doctrine is there which is easy to expound? The ancient never put their teachings in systematic form. They spoke in paradoxes, for they were afraid of uttering half-truths. They began by talking like fools and ended by making their hearers wise."

"Relativity seeks adjustment; Adjustment is Art. The art of life lies in a constant readjustment to our surroundings."

Laotse illustrates by his favorite metaphor of the Vacuum. (Vacuum = space)

"He claimed that only in vacuum lay the truly essential. The reality of a room, for instance, was to be found in the vacant space enclosed by the roof and walls, not in the roof and walls themselves. The usefulness of a water pitcher dwelt in the emptiness where water might be put, not in the pitcher or the material of which it was made. Vacuum is all potent because all containing. In Vacuum alone motion becomes possible. . . . In Art the importance of the same principle is illustrated by the value of suggestion. In leaving something unsaid the beholder is given a chance to complete the idea and thus a great masterpiece irresistibly rivets your attention until you seem to become actually a part of it. A vacuum is there for you to enter and fill up to the full measure of your aesthetic emotion."

89

Actually written by Kakuzo Okakura in 1916

Anny I was very taken by the little Book of Tea *which really deals with the art of contemplation and living. It is written by Kakuzo Okakura —1931. Some day we will read it— I mean you will read it to me aloud. It puts into words the feelings of beginnings. Speaking of flowers what is referred to as the Poetry of Love—"The primeval man in offering the first garland to his maiden thereby transcended the brute. He became human in thus rising above the crude necessities of nature. He entered the realm of art when he perceived the subtle use of the useless."*

(I don't like these last words but the thought is beautiful)

(Anyway it's delightful)

Jean Labatut, chief design critic and director of graduate studies at Princeton University

Mac Phaidgen, unknown to Tyng

Bob Venturi visited me today. He informed me that he is going after the Fellowship at the Academy again this year. I am to write a letter of recommendation in his behalf. At the Princeton Conference I met Labatut at the last day's dinner of visitors and faculty. He told me that the recipient of the Fellowship whom Bob was in direct competition with did absolutely nothing during his stay at the academy. What happened was that as soon as he was made a Fellow (Mac Phaidgen) he married the governor of ————-'s daughter and honeymooned in Rome for 2 years. Of course you remember I fought for Bob while Labatut fought for Mac Phaidgen. Bob met Labatut while submitting his application in New York and it seems he will be very well considered and is—likely (unless the other entries are again superior) to make it this time. I hear of several people who intend going to Rome.

If I know more definitely I shall let you know.

So much of this letter is not of me—I just realized—except for the worrisome first part of my letter about work. I believe really that it will as usual all come at once. Anny sweetheart I keep your wonderful words of love very close. They encourage me in difficult thoughts. I love you—simply I love you

> *Lou*

16 January 1954

Dearest Anny   *Friday Night to Saturday Morning 1 a.m.*

I believe from what you have indicated that I have gotten all your letters. It is sure wonderful that I have. The last two were dated Jan 4 which I got in Phila and the other in New Haven dated Jan 8. The first one I must have read over four times on the train and some more before going to bed. It meant so much to get your encouraging comments on your reaction to Perkins' recommendations—your most delightful reference to our "casual" meetings in Norfolk—harking back to the Xmas party with the punch and aluminum foil—your working hard on the 'joint'—and your outstanding figure,—not to mention the pleasure of getting a long long letter which is always a cozy delight dotted with precious amazing fabulous terrific and wonderful Luigi! Of course I read reflectively Darling Beautiful Sweetheart Wonderful Lovely Anny! I wish I could write as freely as you and express myself with such ease. You write beautifully my sweet Anny. Sue Ann got her post card and plans to write to you. She probably will not get around to it as easily as she says. She has so many projects—scrap books and all there is to learn in the world in addition to her piano and flute. I got a rather discouraging letter from Los Angeles. My mother wrote in answer to the Herald Tribune *article I sent her only recently. Her handwriting changed drastically—big scrawls very unlike her. Her eyesight is failing. My father writes that the doctor says she will not lose her sight altogether. I meant to include her letter to me (in this one) which was beautifully expressed in her love for me. I left it forgetting to bring it in the office and I don't want to wait longer to mail this note. She is going to miss her independence in reading—I feel for her very much. I don't know what to write her. If it is still around I will send the (her) letter to you. Things here are the same no additional work. I am trying to write a piece for* Progressive Architecture *about the Gallery. I just can't get up the steam and it is due in a few days. I saw the proofs of the photographers. I don't like the pictures he took. They are dramatic in the wrong sense. The quite restful atmosphere is absent. I am to see the editor on Tuesday. I will try to get him to retake some of the pictures. Not to run myself into financial difficulties again which is always around the corner with me I accepted the short teaching job at U of P (6 weeks) Turn to page 2 for my tentative schedule for Feb and March. I will tell you of any change to it. I have a copy.*

[sketch of schedule for January, February and March]

This is roughly my schedule of Teaching Days and where I will be. In addition one day in March I expect to be in Baltimore. The day is not yet set. I am preparing slides of the Gallery for this affair of which I spoke to you before.

I received a copy of Robert McLaughlin's (dean of Princeton's Arch. School) comment on the Gallery which the Progressive Architecture *has requested from several people around. The comment is fair to good (I have in mind it is really good) I say that in spite of the good praise he gave it. He saw the building at the Opening, and as he says himself saw it in a snow storm. I believe it is a mistake to suggest there ideas of "honest comment" (this is my doing) because no one really takes the time to really look at what is being criticized. Here are some excerpts (Now that I read it again its not so bad) (I underline the bad?)*

"The decision to treat the new Yale Fine Arts Building as a block of space to be divided and redivided as needs require, is a splendid piece of architectural statesmanship. Granted the validity of the major decision and it strikes me as unquestionable, any comment about detail in executing the concept becomes of very minor importance."

"——I liked the way you get <u>into the</u> building and of course I am immediately intrigued with the space frame construction. <u>How intrigued I would say, were I Yale student or faculty, I am not sure.</u>"

"The discipline that Kahn enforces by minimizing interior color is a noble one, and based, I assume, on the honesty of materials in natural state, but I find it a little hard <u>to be noble for so long, throughout the entire building</u>. The relationship of museum and school of architecture is beautifully worked out and should be a healthy one for both."

"To come back to the space frame which is exposed throughout, I was pleased with its acoustical properties, and <u>question its light absorption and visual insistence. Incidentally a high price seems to have been paid space wise for the romanticism of a triangular stair plan within a round stair tower within a rectangular building</u>. The interior classrooms seem excellent, and it is good to see common sense aspects of progressive education at last reaching the levels of high learning, by osmosis I suppose. The open office planning, <u>where faculty sit behind filing cabinets, I would have none of. Both student and teacher are entitled to some privacy, I think, both from and with each other</u>."

"Yale now has a building worthy of its school of architecture. As usual she has appeared on the field with a remarkable triple threat in Lou Kahn—who practices in Philadelphia, teaches at Yale, and now has so successfully done this excellent building."

*(note the triple threat) He introduced me that way at the Princeton conference only then
I was a triple threat from a different point of view*

*I underlined the parts which seem to me not so good but now that I write it out (in part)
it really is very good comment (I mean favorable). I believe he was impressed but did not
want to seem carried away.*

*Again most of this letter is quoting others—hope you don't really mind. What do you think
about my decision to teach this problem at U. of P.? When Alma figured out my income
tax payment for the year I was obliged to write a check for $2,500.00 which is just about
what I have left in the bank, so this $1,500.00 which I got from the U. of P. will come
in handy. There I go writing about money when I just got thru several letters back telling
you not to worry. I still insist that this is completely temporary and in a short time
I hope to be on my feet again. So don't give it a bit of thought. I am excited to hear that
you will try to manage the trip to Venice, Verona etc. It will be wonderful for you. I know
you have not seen these wonderful places, San Marco boy! oh boy! Sweet Anny don't
fail to write when you travel but don't feel you have to those times especially wear yourself out with long ones. travel is not restful, its exhausting, try to rest very often and
laugh all you can and be merry.*

92   *I am looking forward to your next letter and now that it is so late I will close with much
much love and hope that this letter will reach you in good health.*

Lou xxxxxxx

24 January 1954

Dearest Anny   *Sunday Night*

This time I waited too long to write. I am in the Dining car going to New Haven and that is not going to improve the legibility of my writing. I received 2 letters in New Haven on Monday and Tuesday. Again as always they were most wonderful to read and I rather suspect that you may be up North on the trip we were talking about. Many people inquire about you. They want to know what you are doing in Rome. They expect you to give them a picture of modern architecture in Rome and be prepared to take over where Nervi leaves off. I am responsible to a degree for the Nervi stuff. Actually I know (you told me) you saw him but once and I know that it is not very "convenient" that you see him now. Anny honey sweetheart I wish I could see you now. I would hug you really close. I would be careful not to squeeze too tightly but you would feel me feel all the love I have for you. As yet I have not received your time card for the several weeks of work you put in. You will of course give a detailed account like joint type A or type B—etc. I had a rather hectic week interrupting my Yale stay with a trip to New York to talk over the Gallery publication with the Progressive Architecture. *They have a pretty corny approach and Papadaki who is their layout man doesn't really care any more. I am over critical but I must guard against those who want to get particularly truthful at my expense. They have asked for a critical statement on the Gallery from several architects Sert, Saarinen, McLaughlin etc. Gutheim wrote in again to justify his own attitude and this time I was given a blink at a piece of it. It was very good saying in effect "That the Gallery appears like the beginning of an entirely new approach to architecture" and other nice things short but constructive. The others I am afraid of. They have no reason to be over generous and I feel I need a positive boost not one which can be taken one way or another. The train is awful. Maybe if this letter gets less distinct to read you would have to read it many times. This is the early train and the dining room is not crowded yet but I must finish this letter before reaching New York the table is convenient. The last letter I sent you contained my schedule. I thought Easter came in March but no—it begins in April. So I must be at Penn U. all thru March. I believe the best problem to give will be the Reyburn Plaza building (City Hall building). Suddenly everybody is getting interested in the building. and already I hear that the architect has been chosen. But I don't believe it! But I know also that I cannot allow the grass to grow under my feet. But how? Who? I shall write the Mayor. Dave Wallace believes it is committed—he heard that Kurtz (Penna Co.) is serving it up (That would mean M. Brown, G. Howe or Shay) Some tell me—"Lou you shouldn't be caught dead doing a building on Reyburn Plaza." How long must I wait. If a building must go there who could do better. People have suddenly begun to talk about me. They say that I am an architect with my head in the clouds. Those of course have their heads between their legs. I need a publicity agent. I need your faith in*

93

Dave Wallace, Philadelphia architect and planner

Kurtz, unknown to Tyng

Robert Montgomery Brown, partner with George Howe on the design of the *Evening Bulletin* building in Philadelphia

Howell Lewis Shay, Philadelphia architect

me. I am too impatient maybe. Many rumors start to take you off guard. Our Committee meets Mayor Clark on Wednesday—this is known as going into executive session about Penn Center. It is exactly as you left it [sketch] They have hired a California architectural firm to design the parterre. God help us with the framework as it is. I expressed myself again quite openly against Dowling at the last meeting on Friday. I am not popular with the design board of G. H., E. B. and D. But I know I am right. Darling Anny we are about to get into New York and if I wait until New Haven it will take ages before you get this. It's a terrible lousy letter full of gripes but who else can I complain to. If I did to others they would avoid me. So please Anny dear wait for my next letter in no more than a few days. I hope I shall be myself again and maybe things will be better. So long Sweetheart with lots and lots of love.

George Howe and Edmund Bacon

Lou xxxxxxxx

Penn Center

30 January 1954

94   Dearest Anny:

I was in the midst of composing a letter to the Redevelopment Authority setting up my qualifications to do the city office building. I don't think I have a ghost of a chance—I can't think of what to say so I thought maybe the thing to do is to write to you instead and gather that way some good ideas. I read your last letters about your travels. Isn't it amazing how much one can see in one day! I believe you are right about taking equally good pictures in the absence of sunlight, since the local color is so good and rich. However don't rely solely on that fact. The massing of buildings and forms and also distance needs the perspective accent which sunlight provides. Your impressions of Florence and your preference for Piazza di Santa Maria Novella I share. At times, though, when the square of the Signoria is a great stage of pagentry (historic recollection) as I saw it one day it is quite unbeatable. Do you think you'll have a chance to see Siena you were so close when in Pisa. Maybe later but don't miss this most exciting experience. This time I would, if I were you, I would go inside the buildings. The paintings in Siena are particularly wonderful. Sue's blouse sounds like a very beautiful thing. You must have wasted much time getting it but I am sure she will like it very much. And those things for Doris (though they sound a bit cheap for so many articles) must also be what she will appreciate. I met the Clauss's at the last AIA meeting which was held together with the Society of Architectural Historians at the Academy of Fine Arts. I met people I had not seen for a very long time including Talbot Hamlin and his wife Leslie Cheek, Fritz Gutheim and many people from Yale Harvard etc. Kidder-Smith was delightful to see again frank outspoken sparkling man with a good

Doris Johnson, of the Philadelphia Housing Authority

Talbot Hamlin, architectural historian

G. E. Kidder-Smith, prominent author and architectural historian

Mary Williams, executive secretary at the New York office of the American Academy in Rome

Joe Lacey formerly worked for Stonorov and Kahn.

Willo von Moltke, head planner at the Philadelphia City Planning Commission

Uris Building #3, one of the buildings at Penn Center

enough dose of modesty. I had lunch with Venturi—(as I said before he is trying the Rome Fellowship deal again). He wanted to know if he could work for me when I get work to do. Of course he may but I have nothing to offer now. I called the Academy office a few days ago and talked to Mary Williams she seemed to indicate that Bob again was side-tracked by the Jury on the first preliminary judgement. This was all revealed in confidence and [I] did not tell Venturi about it. But—I got busy and called Saarinen in Bloomfield Hills Michigan to urge him to strengthen his recommendation which I was told was rather luke warm. I asked Eero if Venturi is really good and he said "He is a very good designer one of the best." Then I said why not help his case by writing a letter in his behalf (playing dumb about the lukewarm letter he already wrote). He said "I did write but I could not think of glowing words." I did not press further but I hope he takes the hint and writes again. There is still time to reopen his application during the final Judgement on Wednesay. I do so hope he gets it. Then while on the phone he said he would like to talk to me or rather tell me other things. 1. that Joe Lacey sends his best. 2. That he needs another man— a designer without a philosophy of his own—I promised to help. 3. That he is going to remarry—to Aline Locheim the art editor who wrote that rather uncomplimentary (of Yale Gallery) article in the New York Times.*—he wanted to tell me that she is really a very swell girl and that I would like her in spite of her arbitrary (as he put it) criticism. He told me that she will never write about architecture again and that he disagrees with what she wrote about the building (He did not say however that he liked or disliked the building) and I did not ask him for an opinion. Well, Honey, you see I am very sensitive about that building I simply must be.*

Willo [von Moltke] was in earlier this morning to chat. We talked about the age old subject of Penn Center. I showed him a sketch of my latest thinking based on the foregone con-clusion of Uris Building #3 as reality. What do you think of it? I know it is not my brand of design it has no order and greatness. But it is the kind of thing which they always threaten to bring Saarinen in as consultant about. He would come up with something like it. Anyway Willo likes it very much.

[sketches and notes]

I might decide to include such sketch in my letter to the Redevelopment Authority but on second thought maybe I should say to them something about my design objectives in buildings. I was advised by the city Architect George Lovatt that they are going to decide on the architect in just a few days in next week.

Incidently George Lovatt introduced me to Councilman Blanc who is in charge of traffic and parking. I showed him the traffic scheme of mine. He was completely sold on it and told me to prepare to show it to city council which he will arrange to be in session for. I hope to get a city job one way or another.

3

Will was in earlier this morning to chat. We talked about the age-
old subject of Penn Center. I showed him a sketch of my latest thinking based
on the foregone conclusion of Uris Building #3 as reality. What do you
think of it? I know it is not my brand of design as it has no order and
greatness. But it is the kind of thing which they always threaten to bring
Saarinen in as consultant about. He would come up with
something like it. Anyway Will likes it very much.

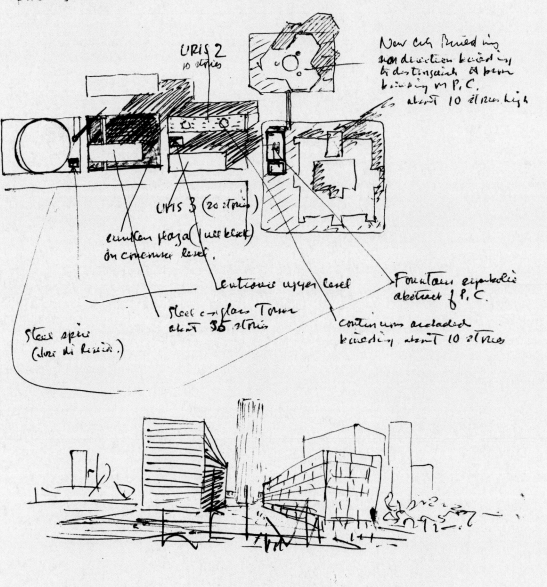

URIS 2
10 stories

URIS 3 (20 stories)

sunken plaza (use black)
on concourse level.

continuous upper level

Steel & glass Tower
about 35 stories

Steel spire
(does it remain?)

New City Building
non directional building
to distinguish it from
buildings in P.C.
is about 10 stories high

Fountain symbolic
abstract of P.C.

continuous arcaded
building about 10 stories

96

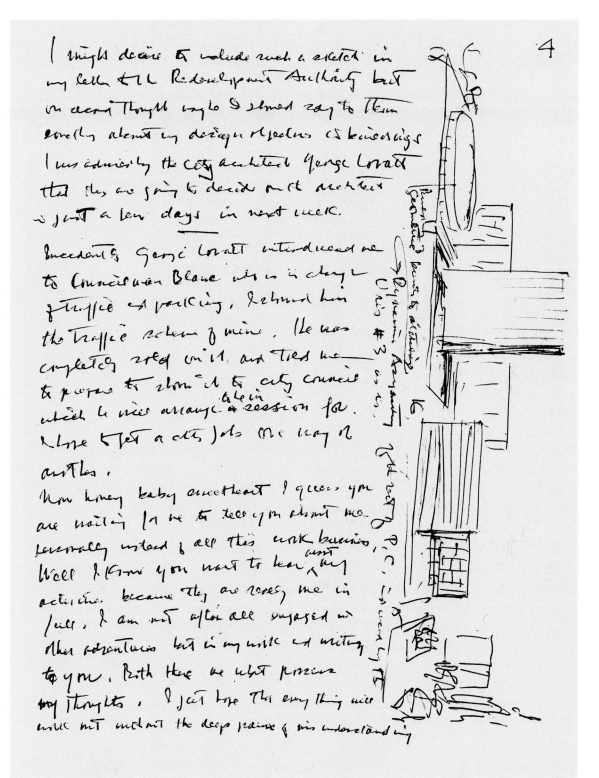

I might decide to include such a sketch in my letter to the Redevelopment Authority but on second thought why do I almost say to them everthing about my design ? problems of buildings I was admiring the city architect George Lovatt that they are going to decide on the matter is just a few days in next week.

Incedently George Lovatt introduced me to Councilman Blanc who is in charge of traffic and parking, I showed him the traffic scheme of mine. He was completely sold on it, and told me to prepare to show it to city council which he will arrange a late in session for. I hope to get a citys Job one way of another.

Now honey baby sweetheart I guess you are waiting for me to tell you about me personally instead of all this work business, Well I know you want to hear my own activities because they are rocking me in full. I am not after all engaged in other adventures but in my work and writing to you. Both these are what possess my thoughts. I just hope that everything will not end in the deep pained of misunderstanding

97

Now honey baby sweetheart I guess you are waiting for me to tell you about me person-
ally instead of all this work business. Well I know you want to hear about my activities
because they are really me in full. I am not after all engaged in other adventures but in my
work and writing to you. Both these are what possess my thoughts. I just hope that
everything will work out without the deep pain of misunderstanding. All I know is that
I think you are wonderful and that I love you.

Again I arranged my cash badly this week and am not including the bills I promised
to include in my last letter. I will write you soon again and without fail send you some
money. I keep reading your letters and constantly wonder how easily you write. You are so
gifted you have such a wonderful head on your shoulders I keep praising you to all who
inquire about you. Incidentally again, going back to Willo in my office this morning.
I asked him what may be the reason for Bacon's coldness to me. Willo said that Bacon

Edmund Bacon

considers me a prima donna! and that I am dedicated to the idea of fighting him on
planning and aesthetic ideas. (And I am not sure if Willo himself does not think that very
thing about me. It could (I mean the answer) be a reflection of Willo and not Bacon.)
I know of nothing more remote from my makeup as being a prima donna. What in hell
do they mean!! If he circulates that idea about me he could damage me (workwise) beyond
repair at least in Phila. I really don't know what to do except ignore it which I am
decided to do. Sorry honey to again blow off steam about me. I should really write you
one long letter of nothing but endearing words which you so much need and deserve.
But rest assured—I am not licked—but I do need a little foot tickling with variations and
variations. I need to feel my ego with greater honest strength. My ego is not good in that
light. Maybe it will come back It has every reason not to betray me. Prima donna!
what rot!

I love you honey and in the next letter I shall tell you about a party the school gave
George Howe at which I made a short speech calling George the Toscanini of Architecture.
Everybody said it was terrific. I just forgot to include it in this letter but now I have
material to write you soon about which I shall do!

With lots and lots of love

Lou xxxxxxxx

98

Earl Carlin worked in
Kahn's office on the Yale
University Art Gallery.

Zeckendorf, prominent
New York developer

Robert Moses, New York
City director of planning

Friends Select, private
school in Philadelphia.

99

Dearest Anny:

*Your last letter was a wow of a tome with 5 pages of text and 1 illustration full page
and explanations plus sweetnotes at the end. Your words of encouragement were welcome
and good to take but I felt so far away. Those words I know to be closer and more inti-
mately felt stretched on the bench thinking of how to make effective a thought with you
near. "You near" meaning that my courage was being extracted from the depths of
reticence and anticipated misunderstanding and thoughts of futility. In my last letter
(now some while ago bad interruptions in evenings in office by Willo, Pen, others on the
Mill Creek finishing job) I hinted at a party for George. It was most spontaneous—Carlin
being the alumni Vince Scully the faculty (———) the student body and I an old friend.
Many of all these turned out I should say about 150 people. When he entered the Baronial
Hall on a pretense he was truly surprised. We all made good speeches. I was complimented
much for mine. I told 3 stories about George. To begin with 1. About how we started
to work together. I said "George, let's associate" and he said "OK" and then we agreed to
split even, only he must get $2,000.00 more because he had everything in the way of an
office supplies girl overhead etc. and then how it all turned out that he owed me $2,000.00.
2. About the time we drove back from Middletown (our project) and he was stopped
by the cop and he got out of the Ford and said "you god damned son of a bitch bastard
of a fuckin (I left this out) Irish cop what's the idea of stopping us when we have the right
of way?" and the cop said "Hold it Fellow—take it easy—you'll be on your way soon"—
how George mad as hell finally was beckoned to drive on—how we didn't speak to each
other for a while driving and then he turns to me and says "He was a nice guy wasn't he?"
3. About the "Don't plan small disappointments story." Then sketched as a practitioner
(P.S.F.S.) some office buildings now prettier but none have the guts of the P.S.F.S. as a
cultural leader—stressed that Saarinen could not have created his arch wihout the inspira-
tional guidance of the [Jefferson Memorial] program—as a conductor of the symphony
of Architecture—I said he could swallow 10 Dowlings, 10 Zeckendorfs, maybe only 5
Moses's and still have stomach for more. George, I said, was the Toscanini of Architecture—
the performers are ready but the stage is too small and the board of directors or trustees
too narrow as a man whose stories told and his nobility etc. etc.*

*The candy came—very very delicious ate it all while composing some letters. Never
knew it done—very easy to eat. Sue's blouse came. It's a honey. I shoved it under Sue's door
the night I received it. She woke and exclaimed her delight with it. She is going to write
you, she says, soon. She talked and talked about what skirts it would go with and discovered that it suits all of them. She was really delighted and it fits beautifully on her. The
color is very unusual (I am always afraid of the unusual because her reaction to abnormal
wear is measured by stock Friends Select taste—but this went over big.) I got those (candy
and blouse) in the mail about 6 days ago. Now since I have not written as I should I find*

tonight (as I come from New Haven) that the pastel package arrived, full as I opened it with the colors I like. The red only is somehow not as intense as I expected. You honey honey darling, you bought so many wonderful colors for me to make my little pictures with. Maybe for being so good and depriving yourself of ready cash I will paint you a special private picture. It was wonderful to receive the nice box (I looked for a note inside—greedy as I am) but found none but then I have still to reread that Tome you sent and find things I missed. I always do) I read your letters quickly at first, more slowly over some tea and again before going to bed at Timothy Dwight. The train is another favorite again and now I shall wait a few days and read it again before putting it away. So it is with people who mean something to each other, and with those one loves there is no end and the beginning is far before the beginning of life altogether.

Yesterday in New Haven they (the faculty) gave another testimonial dinner to George. All the professors were there but [it] didn't have the spontaneity of the first one I mentioned. I have made some warm remarks about George these recent days—I notice that he shuns them—Does he distrust their sincerity? I think if you actually knew my words and the reactions to them that he resents my rise to a little recognition. Believe me Anny if anything I have become more humble more anxious and worried about the future. (The future is so unknown to me in many ways) I don't believe George wants to respect me. He wants to I think find fault with me. But my sense of not being wanted is too great to make the mistake of 'going where angels fear to tread.' I will stay away from him. I must I think.

I am going to change that pen.

I got a call in New Haven from a Mrs. Jaffe who happened on the Genel house. She is a Philadelphian who wants to build in the same neighborhood. She happened to drive on the Pike—spotted something brown in the trees—looked—liked—called Genel—Genel invited her to come look around—and she came home entranced (as she put it) with the "Fugue" of the house, that it was a masterpiece beyond words and that she was delighted to know that there actually was an architect (she doesn't know that there are actually [two]) in these parts (Phila) of such a caliber. I am to see her about arrangements to build her house tomorrow (Wednesday afternoon).

I am starting the Penna U. problem tomorrow at 9 a.m. I am taking the City Hall office building, getting the city program for the building from Bacon. Do you think it was stupid of me to choose that one knowing my own ambition in the matter? I shall get Venturi to take my place on days when I cannot make it. Incidentally Venturi is scheduled to be interviewed (Amer. Acad. in Rome) next Monday. He may? make it. I hope he does. Also Alpers' son Paul is staying at the Academy apparently he is getting very interested in architecture he talks of nothing else. He is on a premedicine scholarship. From Med to Arch! I suppose you are avoiding the Academy. Venturi told me he wrote to you about his friends there. Many of course ask for you. Anny honey sweetheart I long for you and hope so much that you are well and in good spirits. I must have left out many things

Timothy Dwight College, Yale University

Paul Alpers, son of Dr. Bernard Alpers for whom Esther Kahn, Louis's wife, worked as a research assistant at the University of Pennsylvania

I wanted to tell you—well if I have or even if not I will follow this late letter with another in a few days to make up for being a very bad boy So here is goodnight from a bad boy who loves you very very much.

Lots of love—of love

> *Lou xxxxx*

12 February 1954

Dearest Anny

I was mad as hops when the last letter came back from the post lacking 7¢ postage which delayed the letter to you for at least 2 days. The day is done (being almost 11 and being on the phone up to this time) and I want to write to you feeling far away. Again Anny I want to tell you that the tome was good to get and I'm a very bad boy for delaying an answer so much. Now my schedule being what it is 1/2 Yale 1/2 Penna and 0 for me there is very little time to keep my house in order even at a time like this when I am making some effort (sort of under cover) to call attention to myself about Penn C[enter] and the City Hall Office Building. Dorothy Schell Montgomery called me. She is on the Redevelopment Board. She asked me what I was doing about City Hall Building. I told her that I had written to Lammer asking to be considered. Well she thinks I should get it and that I should make a better effort. She suggested that I talk to Mitchell because the whole thing she feared (knowing the inside) was going to be decided this coming Wednesday. She thought that a competition was the way to settle the issue but if a good guy got it she would be happy (All the time she talked to me I thought of her husband and (his) partner "what does she want them to do?") But she came out with the answer. She disqualifies her husband and partner because her board decides and apparently they had talked it over about me. She warned me that Lammer favors Balinger and Co. and B. and Co says they will take in Kling if necessary. To go back—Sawyer (Exec Director to Mayor) dumped the thing in the lap of the R. Authority. Dorothy thinks the R.A. should not do the building and choose architect. Well I talked to Mitchell at Penna and he got busy with Mayor, Stevens etc. and is trying to stave off the decision of an architect. Tonight I have also composed a letter to the mayor, to Ed Bacon and to Sawyer. I stressed my previous work and knowledge of the problem and other points you suggested in your lovely letters. Maybe you can come in tonight and type them for me. Alice doesn't work Friday night Saturday Sunday. I am away on Monday and Tuesday and Wed typing means a Thursday letter. Now you see a little how my inexcusable conduct of waiting a few extra days (in my jerky schedule)

Dorothy Schell Montgomery was also director of Philadelphia Housing Association.

Francis J. Lammer, director of Philadelphia Redevelopment Authority

Robert B. Mitchell, first director of Philadelphia City Planning Commission

Balinger and Co., architectural and engineering firm

Vincent Kling, who ultimately got the commission

Lewis Stevens, Philadelphia city council member

101

can upset our talks to each other irreparably. *Marti Adler wrote to Robert Yarnall chairman of the Redevelopment Authority in my behalf including the H. Trib. article. He (in a letter to her which she mailed me) thanks her and sent the Trib. article off to Bacon (a little complicated what!) Marti also sent a copy of the H. Trib. to Stevens who (in a letter again mailed to me for record) forwarded the H. Trib. to the Mayor (a little complicated what!) Anyway it is completely cross referenced each party has now 2 copies of the N.Y. H.Trib. article about "Modern Architecture and Yale." Marti Adler sent for extra copies from N.Y.H.T. She has done more than I deserve and I am deeply appreciative. She asked for you she wanted to work with you on the idea of forwarding me. Just think! You are identified with me—who was it who said "How do you manage now?"— Oh yes Mrs Donovan—I frankly admitted it was impossible. She (D.) is a very nice person and I think Mr. D. is also. I met them at Bains where I have [been] eating Dinner to escape the Art Alliance martini crowd and save $\frac{1}{2}$ the usual cost of the same slop served in clean or dirty atmosphere. Nothing like our steak and salad served by the prettiest girl in the world. If you don't mind the Yakidy Yak about myself another thing of some interest happened.* Progressive Architecture *had the jump on the* Forum *but* P/A *cannot fit in article until May issue. Doug Haskell called to make arrangements to publish building (apparently he was worked on). I asked him what the ethics was in the case (1st comes 1st) he said it is the architect's decision which the magazine abides by. Well to make it short he wanted me to sabotage* P/A *after the trouble they went to. I could not say NO because he (D. Haskell) reminded me that he was now in a spot with Prentice and Luce regarding the building. Could I not insist that it be published by* P/A *a month earlier because* Forum *could do it in April. (all the time however I was thinking that they probably have committed the cover which to the layman and the undiscerning Architect (is) considered the "last judgment" which would relegate the work to the usual reporting status. I would under such circumstances rather not have it in now. The idea about April was as you gathered simultaneous reporting. So now I have to see what happens Monday. I must call and make arrangements when at Yale. There is little rest especially for the undecided. What can I do to keep them both friends of mine. The reason for my indecision is that* P/A *did lousy over dramatic photos—the ones a few students took at Yale are much better. I will have to insist they use them. Their drawings of the plans are also academic. So—I think* P/A *hasn't the talent. I will try to see them in New York to try to improve the article. Struggle! struggle! struggle! but if it comes too easy it has no life. Norman Rice got a small housing project on his own. I am very glad for him. He called me and expressed his happiness. All the architect wants is to work and make the thoughts of the mind live. Anny Honey Dear I am anxious to get your letter which I hope is waiting for me at Yale Sunday night. Good night darling girl with lots and lots of love*

Lou xxxxxxx

Marti Adler, wife of Dr. Francis Adler who commissioned Kahn to design a house (1954–55, unbuilt) and later had Kahn remodel their kitchen (1955)

P. I. Prentice, managing editor of *Architectural Forum*

Henry Luce, editor in chief of Time, Inc., which published *Architectural Forum*

Norman Rice, Kahn's high-school and college classmate and longtime friend, worked for Le Corbusier in the 1920s and later taught a class with Kahn and Robert Le Ricolais at the University of Pennsylvania.

Dearest Anny:

Received your great big Billet Doux and now feel quite sheepish for not thinking of Valentines at all—either you or Sue. She had a party that night—hearts all over the place for her boys and girls and it never occurred to me that I had to do anything about it staring at them. One going thru town is constantly reminded by [Valentines] but my mind is single tracked viz.—(you-work, work-you, you-work) I am so sorry Anny dear that I forgot to send you any heart on the proper day—but is it not already with you now? No wonder that I make such blunders, that I lack buoyancy which brings on humor—so could laugh off the set back which I today especially think is all around me. Your letters also remind me of things coming close, your mention of 'will' cuts me down—though said in courage and calm please think of nothing but complete happiness and love—of you and me seeing each other soon.—Anny dear I had another one of those awful Penn Center meetings where I conducted myself in good behavior up to the time when Bacon presented a little model of P.C. which incorporated the idea I sent you. He did not mention my name mentioning Willo as having suggested it. Can I trust nobody? The same idea I went over with Willo— Willo did say he would make a rough model since I had so much trouble presenting an idea to my committee on account of Zantzinger and others, but not certainly as His idea. Gee Winigers! Along with the model was a document which had many sly (sly in the light of the choice now resting with the Redevelopment Authority) conditions including the asking of our sanction of P.C.P.C. acquiring the services of an architect to design the new office building. I'm afraid he sold himself. I had myself to admit that the concept was good (since I was greatly responsible for its idea)—I just got a call from Zantzinger—that is why you feel the time lapse (laugh). I gave him my idea of the way to choose an architect. I really think it is a lousy way but here goes. Along with credentials to perform business wise present an idea of how to proceed with design or the design approach to the particular problem. The review board would be men like Saarinen, Sert, Gropius. I must not forget that the same confidence to perform is in others as in me. Nobody I found will admit in the slightest that the other is entitled to the job. All I can do is wait—so far the architect has not been chosen. This being Wednesday the Redevelopment Authority was supposed to decide this afternoon but from what I hear that is not very likely.

Giving the problem at the U. of P. I went today with the students thru one of the most complex of them—the Police Department. It is one of the most difficult to grasp. The functions overlap, the records overlap and the space now is on whatever floor or space is unfilled. City Hall when you know it like we got a taste of it today is bedlam. I pierced a beam of light thru the obscurity, at least thru the realization that the department of police is decidedly different from the requirements of other departments and cannot be treated vertically without inefficiency. So if a tower is conceived, the police may be a big broad building though simple probably in function like the spokes of a wheel with

Clarence Zantzinger, for whose firm, Zantzinger, Borie, and Medary, Kahn once worked in Philadelphia

P.C.P.C., Philadelphia City Planning Commission

the spokes extendible. How can you possibly listen to all this dribble (except that our 3 D building needs but another lower one along side it or another location)

The fight goes on between the Forum and P/A I meet the Forum (Haskell) Monday in New Haven. I have to go to Washington Sunday to talk to the people of the Greenbelt Co'op (you remember) They are building another one and need again a consultant. I don't know but I'll go and find out. From there I must take a night train to New Haven so I can see Haskell on Monday. My letters must be getting more and more boring, but that is the news with me. I am to give a talk in New Haven to the alumni (alumni day). Incidentally the alumni bulletin had an article on the reaction to the building which was very humorous. This particular jerk wrote that he "started in the basement went up every floor to the fourth and was still in the basement." I suggested after everyone had had a laugh about this wit that next time let him start on the 4th and when he reaches the basement he will still be on the 4th. Maybe that is the theme of my speech to the alumni. Lewis Stevens (councilman) made quite a point of having received the clipping from the N.Y. Her. Trib. at the last P.C. meeting. It was deliberately done to help me. I blushed naturally as though I had not seen it or bought 20 extra copies for secret distribution. The problem of eating alone is not comparable to your confining state—result I eat less—less careful with the little—hungry later— eat late can't sleep well —not hungry morning—eat soon after getting hungry in town etc etc. in a highly silly irrational system of living. Of course in other respects as a hermit I am amazed at my own restraint. I thought to stop smoking was heroic but this is hard— hard as can be but nevertheless I found possible of control too. A few days ago I went to the Hendler Gallery to listen to the latest. Frank Weiss seems to be the philosopher holding the chair. I believe he seems to be trying to discuss himself. Barbara and Sam dropped in last night when I wanted to start this letter. They stayed late. They are admiring of you and inquired very much of you. I told them of your many adventures. They asked if I received mail often—yes and I write often. Their new address is 2008 Chancellor. Anny honey I know you need dough and I will send it to you in the usual letter way—it seems to work. I do wish though that you would send in your time card for several weeks of work. To my most sweet and wonderful Valentine to whom I freely give lots and lots and lots of love more than I am able to give any other.

Yours

Lou xxxxxxxx

Greenbelt Co'op, cooperative market for Greenbelt Housing

Hendler Gallery, venue where Philadelphia artists and architects met

Frank Weiss, architect who graduated from Harvard while Tyng studied there

Barbara Crawford and Sam Feinstein, artists and teachers married to one another

104

On board train from Washington to New York—New Haven

Dearest Anny:

Am just returning from Washington where I consulted on a shopping building of 30,000 sq. ft. for which I recommended the use of a 3D Truss a natural for the problem. The Truss would be built of 'tooth pick' members with reflecting panels for acoustical absorption and light. Harbored of course would be the airconditioning ducts and electrical source. The whole area would have no more than 4 columns.

[sketch]

The architects Graham, unknown to Tyng

Sweet and Schwartz, unknown to Tyng

The architects Graham are the ones who built the Flamingo apartments in Philadelphia. Sweet and Schwartz were the local architects who I believe (judging from the other work shown in the office of Graham) that S. & S. were the real designers. Again I believe I am dealing with a small—mediocre architect but one who was completely taken with the idea and is no dope as to grasping the idea very fully. His 'man' a rather easy going southerner you could see learned all his architecture in one day this day. The sketches he showed of his idea "Adee" were soon withdrawn. You may think the tower corny but actually very necessary since the entire neighborhood of this shopping area of a newly developed section of Washington is a bedlam of neon arms jutting out into the highway each negating the other and it is impossible to read any of them driving along the speeding highway the stores face. The sign is required to be visible from 3 distinct points which "ye olde" triangular tower is able to do. I whetted their appetites and so twisted their minds away from the usual solution of assembly by catalogue that the very complacent architect had to take notes, ask me the spelling of some of my words and became despondent over the prospect of increased costs. My clients the coop boys of course jumped on this point as important. The architect hoped they would express hope that my idea (obviously good for them) would be insisted on. Since they did not express hope, he began to defend my idea (because he saw 'fame' around the corner). Well I was holding all the answers. I suggested Macomber as the builder and engineer. I am to get him on the phone tomorrow.

I had to rush for the train—I was driven down to the Union Station on the way I was asked (by the coop boys) what my fee would be. I said $15.00/hr. They asked from portal to portal? ans: yes—silence. This was near the stop—I got off—missed the damned train and had to wait an hour. I shall probably get in N. Haven about 12:00 o'clock midnight. Undoubtedly they were shocked by the fee. But Kelley (lighting consultant on Gallery) charges $20.00 per hour. Was it not worth something with which to pay for the many nights you and I spent on dreaming about these ideas.

105

A few nights ago I was given a call from Sam Feinstein asked me to come over for supper. They were having some friends from New York amongst them one of the writers with Sam on the Art News. *He then, at supper, revealed to me his intention to do a profile of me for the* News *and I believe he wanted a check on his ideas (from the co writer) and he also wanted a reaction from her about me. They have fixed up their place most ingeniously with the broad approach to space Sam has a real feeling for. The Phila artist who was there was the funniest teller of stories I have yet seen or heard. His store was endless mostly Jewish tid bits of rare quality. Everybody was slain by his finesse. I had to leave early to get back to the office and left them all with many ideas and angles (angles which they saw not by me) that they thought [they] could use about yours truly. When I think of it all though it makes me self-conscious and [I] feel untrue to my deeper self. NO person can really be portrayed except thru their work and their acts. It is good that facts about a person's life are lost. There are so many circumstantial veerings that are made too much of. The deeds tell the story even if they be only transmitted thru children. The angle of the* News *in my case is the similarity of my thinking to that of the vanguard painters who believe themselves unique. Here I must say that it is wonderful for me to feel so relaxed in your presence—that I need not restrain words for fear of being taken for a didactic snob. They say I talk like they do but I can't make them out. I truly taught them what they did not know. I know also that I must learn not to take myself so seriously—that is to appear that way outwardly. I don't—don't worry. I really make it easy to take—besides I am constantly in a critique state of myself. One must find truer soundings so that even a child, thru them, can understand and work by the tenets of order discovered (not invented). Anny darling sweetheart the train is approaching Newark and I better start licking the stamps on the envelope. It's a long ride from Washington to New York (couldn't manage thru train) and must rush from the Grand Central to the Pennsy to catch the New Haven. The problem at Penn is going well. The architect has NOT been chosen for the Office Building and may not be for some while. Stone (Ed) got the Commercial Museum with Thalheimer and Weiss. Greenfield now blows from 2 ends of his anatomy front and back. Ed is renovizing their house you see. I wonder if Philadelphia architect will be commissioned by the City of New York. Zantzinger is acting generously toward me. He thinks I should get the Office Building to do. I understand from Gabriel Roth that he is going to do a building in Penn Center which one! and he told me also that Emery Roth (Uris's architect) is getting another apartment building to do on Logan Square! What the hell do we strive one might say. But we do we must!*

Lots and lots and lots of love my love xxxxxxxx

Gabriel Roth, New York architect, brother of Emery Roth

106

Dearest Anny:

*So far I haven't received any time cards from you. When did you send them? To me
or to Alma? Do so again right away Honey and try to make it come out for about slightly
under $ 300.00.*

*A few days ago I received your Feb 19th letter which sounded welcomely cheerful.
How desperately lonely you seemed by the other 2 previous letters which I also hungrily
read the 2 days at Yale. I guess we are about even on letters. No new developments except
that I have gotten Macomber and Pfisterer interested in working on the 3D truss for
the coop store. The architect in Washington is glad to allocate part of the engineering fee
to Pfisterer. I wish I didn't have to be involved in so complicated a position with owner-
builder-responsible architect. But one needs to point to accomplishments even though of
divided character. Up until now (to-day) I was working at the office with Venturi and
the other member of the program committee of the Senior class doing the problem of the
City Hall Building. Venturi got word from the Academy just an hour ago that he is
made a fellow. He is of course delighted and could hardly keep a straight face. I am indeed
glad for him. The problem is extremely complicated and part of the complication is self
inflicted because I want to make something out of the building for ourselves. Tonight
I shall continue work alone—alone I can be with you too and I can do much better work
when I dream about what you would go for. I am waiting anxiously for us to be together
again in our own wonderful way of love and work which again is nothing really but
another form of that love. I believe it can only be that way with a few. Anny sweetheart
you ask me many questions—questions which I have tried hard to answer before.
Those questions pass thru every incident of our lives together involving many people many
situations with hopeful stabs into the future—the answer is always full of love for you—
that I do know—though I am aware of unanswered things in many bundles with lots
of string and sealing wax. Some single way must be found though now I am tied in knots
hard to pull apart.*

*Now that I am full of students from the rear and from the front I can truthfully say that
I would much rather have a big practice or a good practice with only some contact with the
academic life. When I see those faint scribbles after 3 weeks of seemingly stimulating
directions I get a bit doubtful about the gain I give or take. Still you can't get me to admit
that it is wholly the student's lack. We don't know our own job well enough. I don't particularly limit the scope enough in order to make good performance possible. Now that I have
no work to do in my practice (except the little house) I must sound like a school marm.
Please forgive me Anny my dear sweetheart little girl darling. It must be terribly confining
for you tied to the house. I couldn't myself stand it! I hope it's all over with soon and that*

Henry F. Pfisterer, structural engineer who worked
on the Yale University
Art Gallery.

107

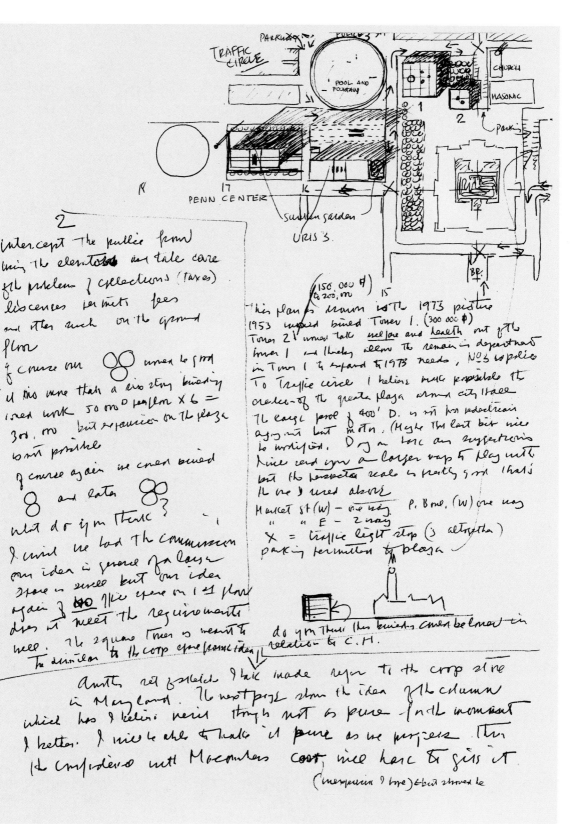

TRAFFIC CIRCLE

PARKING

POOL AND FOUNTAIN

PUBLIC

CHURCH

MASONIC

PARKING

PENN CENTER

17 · 16 · R

sunken garden

URIS 3.

2

intercept the public from using the elevators and take care of the problem of collections (taxes) licences permits fees and other such on the ground floor

of course our ⚭ would be good if this were then a six story building would work 50,000 per floor × 6 = 300,000 but expansion on the plaza won't possible

of course again we could build ⚇ and later ⚭ ?

what do you think? I could see had the commission our idea in general of a large store is sweet but our idea again of no office space on 1st floor does not meet the requirements well. The square tower is meant to be similar to the corp office from idea.

(150,000 $) (200,000)

this plan is drawn to the 1973 picture 1953 would build tower 1. (300,000 $) tower 2 would take welfare and health out of the tower 1 and thereby allow the remain in dept in tower 1 to expand to 1973 needs, No 3 is applied to traffic circle I believe most preferable the creation of the greater plaza around city hall the large pool of 400' D. is not for pedestrian against but motor. (Maybe this last bit nice to be modified. Do you have any suggestions since I sent you a larger map to play with but the perspective scale is pretty good that's the one I used above)

Market St (W) — one way   P. Bone. (W) one way
"   "   E — 2 way
X = traffic light stop (3 altogether)
parking permitted to plaza

do you think this bridge could be lower in relation to C.H.

Another set of sketches I have made refer to the corp store in Maryland. The next page shows the idea of the column which has I believe merit though not as pure. In the moment I better. I will be able to make it pure as we progress then it corresponds with Macomber's cost will have to give it (inexpensive I hope) but should be

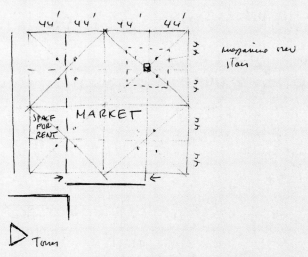

44'   44'   44'   44'

mezzanine over
stair

MARKET

SPACE
FOR
RENT

▷ Tower

forget about the walls consider the building in essentials the problem is the 176' X 176' building or 30,976 sq ft.

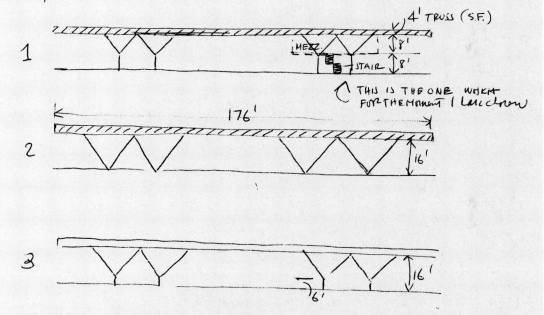

4' TRUSS (S.F.)

1

MEZZ

STAIR

8'
8'

↰ THIS IS THE ONE WHICH FOR THE MOMENT I LIKE + LOOK OVER

2

176'

16'

3

16'

6'

I believe the column cluster idea as in 1. is a good idea They submitted their idea (that is this architect Isaac graham) which has 35 columns and also depends on some exterior walls for support in this case I resigned for the walls to be independent

⤴

☞ this damned pen!!!

Now Anny dear I have just about told you everything about my work except I forgot to mention that the little house about $30,000 is I believe going through. On planning its clients Jaffe saw the Weiss house is were even more thrilled about that and said that these expenditures don't radiant heat glass etc etc is now new. If you want it can find a little time you wish to spend from your many coming duties suppose you look with the house the requirements are

a large living room (dining also)
Kitchen laundry
2 baths, and 2 bed rooms
1 study (spare room)

with the usual need for ample storage car port etc.

the lot is nearly.

View of the houses

View / air

NORTH

all trees are beech some we have to go.

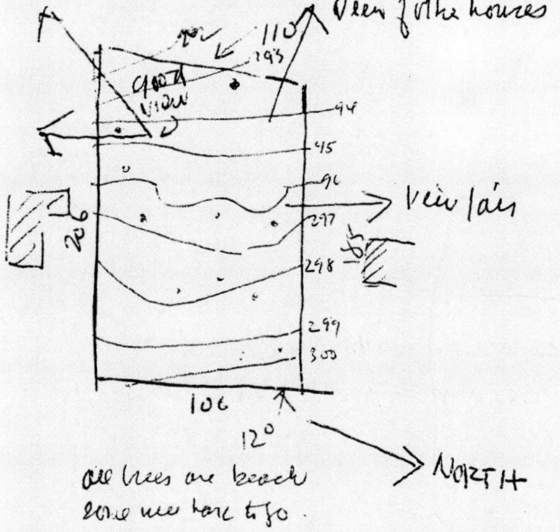

It seems like I am trying to put you on time — Another bit of business — Your time cards I submitted them to Shma for payment and you can count on money by the time this letter reaches you.

Now I have almost the you put in 48 more hours in 1953. But she cannot enter that now so she will distributes the time in 1954 and deposit 2 checks to cover the time you submitted and the time just made up. That showed square deal 300 net. For the time being this may help some.

Again Anny honey I hope I hope that all is well and will be well and close with all my love & my sweetheart

you both are healthy strong and cheerful and that you will have some freedom of
movement and write me many many love letters (even if it does take up some of your time).
Surrounded by all the papers which are to be called for the full draft of the program,
I get a bit disgusted. Of course I am not finishing the program alone since the boys are
coming in again tomorrow Sunday. George H. and Macomber came in the office yesterday.
They were very high and George and I took M. to the railroad station. Driving back
with George he showed great affection (man to man) for me. Martini I believe does it.
I have I think written you about the doubt I have had about George's affection recently
but maybe I was wrong. Sweetheart forgive for not writing a long one this time.
I feel sort of lousy (ate at the L'Aiglon) [   ] the spaghetti platter. [It] seems that
I ate the porcelain and not the pasta. So with lots and lots and lots of love to
my wonderful sweetheart Anny

Lou xxxxxxxx

7 March 1954

Dearest Anny:

I read your letters (recent) with anxiety and hope that everything will be OK.
To be lonesome and confined takes the strongest human to live thru. Only the ones you're
living for must appear to give encouragement and moral strength it seems. You are
wonderfully a woman with a spirit that many could envy. I too am waiting when we will
work together again on our projects and love each other. My wonderful wonderful
Anny we have problems but we are so good at solutions. I love you. I love you.

With 2 universities to serve I have my doubts about the 7 day week. Stop to think of it
I have always worked the 12 day week—All of which adds up to making your own calendar
which somehow recognizes that the world is round—that night is shade/shadow and day
is light that sleep is rest and love the thread that ties together divergent paths into a single
will to create.

Penn interests me most right now because it is the most difficult. I am beginning to
understand the program of required spaces and their relation to use. The Reyburn Plaza
site is small and very hacked up with underground difficulties. A new building must only
supplement the existing City Hall and City Hall Annex and at same time must satisfy
immediate and the needs of 1973 without building more space than necessary now.
On the next page I shall draw for you my solution of 1953−1973. I made an analysis

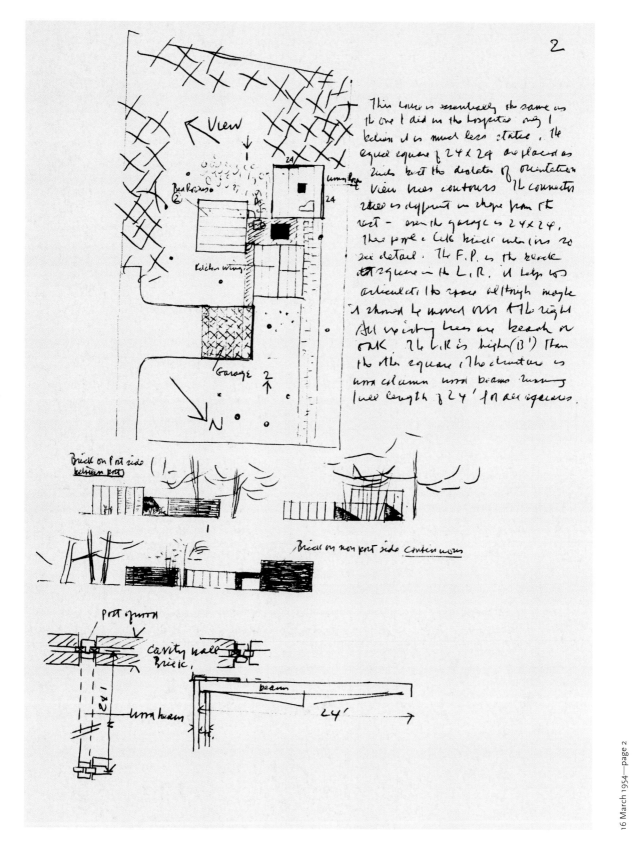

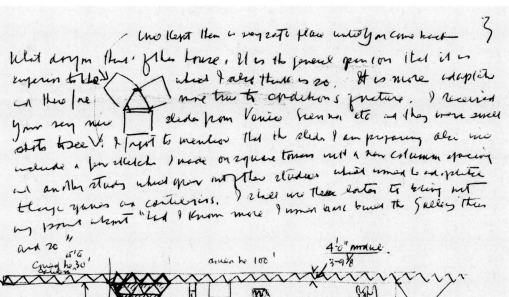

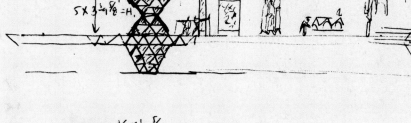

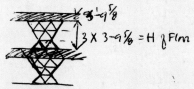

113

Thursday night (to be ready for Friday class) which led to a comprehension (for the first time) by the students of latitude possible in the allocation of new sq. ft. area in the new building. Venturi is helping me in teaching and is going to draw up the scheme I have on the next page. The reason for the square tower (about 40,000 sq. ft. per floor or about 8 stories high) is 1st that much ground floor area is desired to intercept the public from using the elevators and take care of the problem of collections (taxes) licenses permits fees and other such on the ground floor.

Of course our [sketch] would be good if no more than a six story building could work 50,000 sq. ft. x 6 = 300,000 but expansion on the plaza is not possible.

Of course again we could build [sketch] and later [sketch] What do you think?

I wish we had the commission—our idea in general of a large space is swell but our idea again of No office space on 1st floor does not meet the requirements well. The square tower is meant to be similar to the coop space frame idea.

[Annotation for Sketch:] This plan as drawn is the 1973 picture. 1953 would build Tower 1 (300,000 sq. ft.). Tower 2 (150,000 to 200,000 sq. ft.) would take welfare and health out of the Tower 1 and thereby allow the remaining departments in Tower 1 to expand to 1973 needs. No. 3 is police. To traffic circle I believe make possible the creation of the greater plaza around City Hall. The large pool of 400'D is not for pedestrian enjoyment but motor. (Maybe that last bit will be modified) Do you have any suggestions. I will send you a larger map to play with but the Perspecta *scale is pretty good—that's the one I used above.*

Market St (W)—one way, P[ennsylvania] Boul. (W) one way
Market St. E 2 way
X = traffic light stop (3 altogether)
parking permitted to Plaza.

[Annotation for sketch] do you think this building [tower 1] could be lower relative to [City Hall].

Another set of sketches I have made refer to the coop store in Maryland. The next page shows the idea of the columns which has I believe merit though not as pure for the moment better. I will be able to make it pure as we progress thru the confidence with Macomber's cost (inexpensive I hope) but should be—will have to give it.

[Annotation for sketch] mezzanine over stair—tower—forget about the walls around the building—essentially the problem is the 176' x 176' building or 30,976 sq. ft.— This is the one which for the moment I have chosen.

I believe the column cluster idea as in 1 is a good idea. They submitted their idea (that is this architect Hans Graham) which has 35 columns and also depends on some exterior walls for support. In this case I visualize the wall to be independent.

This damned pen!!!

Now Anny dear, I have just about told you everything about my work except I forgot to mention that the little house about $30,000 is I believe going thru for planning. The clients Jaffe saw the Weiss house and were even more thrilled about that and said that their apprehension about radiant heat glass and the floor etc. etc. is now over. If you want and can find a little time you wish to spend from your many coming duties suppose you fool with the house. The requirements are—a large living room (dining also) kitchen laundry 2 baths and 2 bedrooms / study (spare room) with the usual need for ample storage carport etc.

It seems like I am trying to put you to work.

Another bit of business—your time cards. I submitted them to Alma for payment and you can count on money by the time this letter reaches you.

Now I told Alma that you put in 48 more hours in 1953. But she cannot enter that now so she will distribute the time in 1954 and deposit 2 checks to cover the time you submitted and the time just made up. That should equal about $300.00 net. For the time being that may help some.

again Anny honey I hope that all is well and will be well and close with all my love to my sweetheart

Lots of lots of love Lou xxxxxxxx

Dearest Anny:

On the train again to New Haven. Want to gauge it so that I can mail this when I get to New York (I hope it can be long enough to call it a letter). How little Bill knows when he calls you a problem child. You are my adorable love, a love I believe will never change. It so happens that when I finished that last sentence I got my sandwich. I can't write and eat. The 2 gentlemen across from me started a conversation. They are sailors (in plain clothes) returning from a trip with the merchant marine. They are Assyrians—Trans Jordan to be exact. Two of the most disarming guys I have met in a long while—attractive warm friendly DAMNED PEN! and a sense of justice borne of deep experience. He insisted on paying for a drink.

I started this letter on Sunday on my way to [New Haven]. The pen skipped so I had to stop and now its Monday late in my room in TD with a new cheap pen ready to finish my letter to you.

The schedule I sent you some while ago is substantially changed and I will now try to correct first of all the schedule so that your anticipations about my activities are more accurate. This is March 15 'The Ides of March'—Income tax day.

March 15, former deadline for filing income tax return

U of P. problem ends April 2. Judgement at U of P.

Harvard Lecture—March 23 8 o'clock

Baltimore Lecture—March 18 will be back very late probably 19th at 2 or 3 in morning

Spring Vacation Yale—March 27 to April 5—but actually I shall go from Boston on the 24th back to Phila and stay there until 5th.

Incidentally there is not Easter vacation per se.

Le Ricolais comes to Yale—April 12th and 13th. He made special notice in his letters to Yale that he wanted to come when it suited me to meet him. I have received several letters from him and he is most warm and writes he is grateful for our friendship. It all stems I believe from a letter I sent him expressing my admiration for his pioneering work. He writes in one letter he wants to learn from me. I wrote him right back that he should not expect any information from me except what he has seen in Perspecta *and what I can explain to him about the Art Gallery I will send you a new calendar but in general I anticipate nothing new except to carry out the above dates. I am having slides made of the* Perspecta *pictures for Baltimore and Harvard and a few slides of those new structural patterns of the market and the house which is turning out in a direction I will sketch for you on the next sheet.*

I forgot to mention that I am going to a reception for Eero Saarinen and his new 'critic'
wife given by Johnson in the Rockefeller House on Sunday March 21. It should be fun to see
all the friends again.

[Annotations of sketches] This house is essentially the same as the one I did in the hospital
only I believe it is much less static. The equal squares of 24 x 24 are placed as suits best
the dictates of orientation view trees contours. The connector still is different in shape from
the rest—even the garage is 24 x 24. These people like brick interiors so see detail. The
[Fire Place] is the black square in the L.R. It helps to articulate the space although maybe
it should be moved over to the right. All existing trees are beech or oak. The L.R. is higher
(13') than the other squares. The structure is wood columns wood beams running full
length of 24' for all squares.

View—Bedrooms—Living Room—Kitchen Wing—Garage
Brick on post side between posts
Brick on non post side continuous
post of wood—cavity wall, Brick—wood beam—beam

What do you think of this house[?] It is the general opinion that it is superior to this
[sketch] which I also think is so. It is more adaptable and therefore more true to conditions
of nature. I received your very nice slides from Venice Siena etc. and they were swell shots
to see. I've kept them in separate place until you come back. I forgot to mention that the
slides I am preparing also will include a sketch I made on square towers with a new column
spacing and another study which grew out of these studies which would be adaptable to
large spans and cantilevers. I shall use them later to bring out my point about "had
I known more I would [have] built the Gallery thus and so."

[Annotations for sketch] could be 30' cantilever—could be 100'(span)—4'-0" module,
3'-9⁵⁄₈"—5 x 3'-9⁵⁄₈" = H[eight]—3 x 3'-9⁵⁄₈" = H of Floor

Dearest Anny I must stop now since my eyes are closing up on me. It is now about 2 A.M.
(Thursday 16th) and I must get up before Sawyer comes into my room, which on Tuesdays
happens to be particularly early. I am hoping and praying for you darling that everything
will turn out well and that you are happy and that you are not upset by Bill's remarks
about problem child. Your last letter I got at Yale was most welcome because it seemed so
cheerful with the kids [2 nieces 2 nephews] in your room and the light you shed on Bill's
philosophic attitude. I thought myself that he was a pretty tops fellow.

With lots and lots of love

    Lou xxxxxxxxx

Dearest Anny:

*I am particularly lonesome tonight so I write to be excused for writing so late last week
and to tell you that my lecture last night in Baltimore was a good success (I believe)
I got home after 3 in the morning so am pretty awful tired tonight. I was debating whether
or not to write as a matter of fact as I am exhausted. The Cochranes have a fine house there.
The cedar boards are aging to a gray lavender really the way wood should be allowed to
weather. On the way back on the train my shoes off and tickling my own feet on the rough-
ness of the floor I reviewed the evening past. Arriving at Baltimore to be met by the director
of the Museum a nice guy but young man full of humor, warmth, love of architects,
himself an Annapolis Navy man—quit for art history. He drove me thru old section of
Baltimore (never seen by me before) and ended up finally in Cochrane's house. And as I said
a good restrained modern well articulated structurally sensitive house with interplay
 of the delicate with the more delicate. (Of course the stone work is not the Anne Lou type).
We had cocktails (you should excuse the expression) and then dinner. I sat at one end
of the table and Alex Cochrane on the other (the Missus was in New Haven). We each had
to serve our section with wine which was good and I was taught a new lesson in table
manners (having delayed the pouring on my end not knowing the custom) by my next in
lineage to my right who delicately hinted it to be my duty to do the pouring. (I had sat
back for some while expecting to be waited on.) The dinner of ham and mint ice cream was
truly delicious. I am, thinking of you, reminded of the time I had dinner at Bill's house
in Rome that was also a very memorable dinner. You know I often remark about
the narrow table and the "diagonally" seating. The table [Cochrane's] was covered with
a bright red table cloth which made everyone look particularly healthy (good trick for
anemic people) the candles were like the ones Bill's table had all very festive pleasant
friendly and warm. Good conversation enthusiastic reception of me and anxious anticipa-
tion of my lecture. I left earlier than the rest to be on tap at the Museum. It's a paid
admission deal about 100 people of architects planners directors of the authorities etc.
and also of course the dear old Ladies of Baltimore and the dear young pretty ladies of
Goucher and Hopkins. I spoke about planning, the Gallery, the 3 D structures, how
I would plan the Gallery now (new slides of drawings I made) I showed your mother's
house in [Eastern] Shore and the 3 D of the Bucks County school, and slides of the house
with the 4 squares with elevation—again a new drawing. I have also by this time some
fair slides of the Gallery which new items help me to like my own material and consequently get better results speaking, in short my lecture was well received and the comments
were all good—some came over and said "Mr. Kahn you are a genius" to which I made my
well known reply "I know." This always draws a laugh, even, if you remember, from you.
One said "if you were not an architect you would have been a great sculptor." One said*

Goucher College and the
Johns Hopkins University

"Buck's County School,"
Tyng's independent
proposal (see pp. 39–41)

118

"you were going so fast we missed half but it was wonderful." One said "you articulate so well you see I am deaf and I heard everything you said." (It is my well known weakness I do not articulate well—however she was a kind relative of the Cochranes) etc. We had wine after the lecture which lasted for 2 hours—no questions. I took the train back and as I sat tickling my feet on the floor thinking what I just wrote my thoughts came back to my Anny whom I love. Today I inspected Mill Creek—it is coming very well the houses are going up 4 to 5 stories and the proportions are very good. The white brick and the gray cement is likely to look very good indeed. The bricks (poorly laid) are going up in the quads [4 attached in a square] The Formiglia joists are up (very good and clear) and the whole idea of the cement beams white brick and mortar I believe is going to blend to uniformity appropriate to the low cost materials. Oscar's job looks very good on the heights there. his houses are good in plan but I don't really like them in elevation. His towers are good to look at. I hope you don't mind my not sending you any money this time I will though in a few days. You must need it desperately for your independence and needs in general. Don't worry Anny I will not inconvenience you by my neglect or thoughtlessness. It's just that I don't have it being Friday and the Banks are closed tomorrow. But what am I saying—I know that you understand without all those unnecessary excuses. Wait a minute! I can let you have Ten so cancel the above. You got my corrected time table and the next thing of interest is the lecture at Harvard. I shall make extra drawings for that. The cost of slides is atrocious but Mr. Cusati the photographer at Yale makes them for me for 75¢ and that is quite better than $4.00 of the [Heigh] Studios. It's raining. Bob Venturi is in helping with the office work. He has been of good help especially in regard to the city hall office building. He is now making a model of several floors of construction. One solution which is ordinary by our standard but still I believe good is the square.

Lots and Lots of love Lou xxxxxx

[Annotations for sketches] stairs, toilets, elevators, stair / heating, lighting / the columns are the shafts for the supply and return air ducts NO core per se This of course is my idea and it completes the function of the 3D construction / I believe the columns used this way over each other make sense another form possible is in elevation.

Kahn refers to Oscar Stonorov's East Falls public housing.

ITALCABLE

24—3—1954

TO ANNE TYNG VIA CASSIA

488 ROMA =

      ALL MY LOVE TO BOTH OF YOU =

              LOU ++++

28 March 1954

Dearest Anny

Last night I dreamt about you. I was in our office telephoning you walked in and motioned to me that you could wait no longer. You had on a yellow dress your golden hair was dressed in pony style. Your eyes some how were black and flashing looking at me reprehensibly. You were (and are of course) beautiful—Anny Anny I think of you always. I miss so much our meetings together. I hope nothing changes about our way of life—Your telegram was read to me over the phone some day or so after it came, I sent one off to you right away— did you get it? You said you would telephone—I want to do the same—but where? I do not know. I hope so much that you and our little one are well and above all that you love me as much as you tried to express in the last love letter you sent me. I welcomed it more than the others. It felt like something new will occur soon and soon came your telegram.

I don't feel I can write a lot this time because all the things that have happened here seem unimportant. I will write you a day or so after this. Before I can write much I must first hear from you there are so many details to hear from you about I am looking at the lovely picture of yourself you sent me a while ago. You are truly beautiful and bright A true woman one can love. Your courage gives me courage. Right now I have too little courage. I feel a bit beaten by conditions and unknowns. I met the new Mrs. Saarinen (previously Elaine [Aline] Locheim) She came over to me to apologize for the lousy article which she wrote about the Yale Building (you remember I told you). I put her at ease but let her know also that she has a lot to learn and that irreparable damage can result from such thoughtless criticism. She seems like an operator to me. She tried to get me in an argumentative discussion with Eero—she did—but Eero got the worst of it. I suppose that will not help things very much but others were listening and they all saw much more in my approach. But hell! what about work to prove those wonderful theories. I was warned that I might get a Synagogue to design. I believe Sam Genel is the instigator. I will write soon and for now all my best love and lots and lots of it.

Lou xxxxx

Tyng had used a previously arranged code to insure privacy to tell Kahn of Alexandra's birth on March 22, 1954.

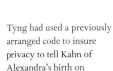

121

Dearest Anny:

I have been trying to write this letter for several days with no success. Interruptions confused mind new conditions and my damned schedule. I got the letter I was anxiously waiting for about Alexandra—its a beautiful name—your letter came several days ago. I started to write back that night Wednesday—whatever I started to say seemed not the way I felt and had to give up. I'm sure I felt every pain you felt during your delivery Anny Darling it must have been so trying with no one around you must have mustered all your strength physical and moral to live it thru. I am so relieved that it is all over and I hope that you are recovering well and will [be] active again soon. The little foot, twisted you believe during delivery, will I hope be soon corrected. She must be certainly beautiful if she looks the slightest bit like you. If she is like me she may grow to become beautiful in other ways. If she has your wonderful ability and courage she will love to live and work in the creative field of the ever fascinating universe. If I may just say a word about me even as I write I must strain to feel happy things are so indefinite work is not coming in the jobs I wrote to you about have strict limitations and there is little cash in it. I don't mean to worry you above all because I know how much you truly love me and need me. All details beside the immediate one seem so trivial that I cannot get myself to write about them. The Harvard lecture went extremely well. The professors were not there except Le Ricolais and I already wrote you about that. I now remember I got a letter from José Sert who lets me know that he is sorry to have missed my lecture but heard that it was 'very good' and represented a 'new revelation into the truth of the creative process.' The U. of P. problem came to an end yesterday finishing at 1 a.m. this morning. The solutions are good in general running the gamut from bad to mediocre. I fed them a good bit but they gained in no direct proportion. But I did not see all the final presentations so I expect for a surprise (always surprise) at the display for judgment on Monday. I had Gallob make photographs of each scheme represented by block models placed in the City Hall center Penn Center area model which I had made up for the problem. As you will gather from the post marks this will be mailed from New Haven. There is a meeting in about 15 minutes of the Advisory Committee of Architecture I must attend. I believe I already said that Osborn Eero Cheek etc. will be there to question us on the future of architectural education. I am frankly sick of education. I feel too prepared these days to do a world shaking job in architecture. Bob Bishop, who teaches at Penn, I sense has a high regard for me. [He] said he would sometimes like "the privilege to work for me" sometime and I cannot understand why I am not now making the city plans instead of Bacon. He believes he is sincere at least I should like to feel it is true I am sorry to write so little Anny but I must now get this off.

With all my love to both of you

Lou xxxxxxxxx

122

Alex's foot was not twisted; she suffered from a stretched muscle which quickly corrected itself.

Edward Gallob, former client with wife, Tana Hoban, also a photographer, for remodelling of their carriage house (unbuilt)

Cartoonist Bob Osborn; Eero Saarinen; Leslie Cheek

Bob Bishop, architect in partnership with Newcomb Montgomery

9 April 1954

Dearest Anny,

Carl Feiss, chief of
planning and engineering
at the Division of Slum
Clearance and Urban
Redevelopment

*I am on my way to Washington to talk to Carl Feiss on the possibility of work on
Planning. He has not seen* Perspecta *and other more recent publications of ideas of mine
(and yours). I shall also get in touch with a Mr. Lawrence of the State Department from
whom I got a letter requesting I send a brochure of my work to the S.D. for possible selection
as architect for foreign work. The latter interests me very much as you can imagine!
We are just leaving Perryville—I am in the dining car getting some tea—don't want to fill up
since my date is for lunch. In the office we are still finishing up Mill Creek. Pen has been
most painfully careful about unimportant things. Bob is working on City Hall area and has
found to be a sensitive aesthetic person. We have been working mostly on arrangement
of buildings—essentially it remains however as we thought it should be long ago. Dave is
making a drawing of the market in Maryland. Mill Creek Housing is up to the eighth story
and going fast. The Quads really work space wise. The row house can now be junked
because the space relationship of courts are most friendly. The space between houses could
be more but landscaping can do much.—I was asked to be the speaker at Carnegie Tech.*

Now Carnegie Mellon
University

*(Pittsburgh) on the 29th of April. I am also to speak in Hartford Conn. on the 14th as
an educator on an A.I.A. panel Haskell presiding. (sorry train jiggles so)*

123

*The problem at Penn is finished. The results were good not startlingly so. Bacon was
on the jury but came about 10 o'clock p.m. after the judges had placed the final decided
marks on the drawings. He looked around superciliously with mums and yawns. I was
asked out for a beer and he came along Venturi—Qualls—Geddes—and Bacon and I.
Bacon after a bit said that the problem showed a negative approach that they had missed
the boat, that there was no integrating of Penn Center with the City Hall Center.
He also said that I had misled them educationally. I kept my head as long as I could,
but I could sense that the others expected me to answer both completely unfounded
accusations. But I did keep my head. Amongst other things I accused him of inhibiting the
entire solution with his stubborn insistence on the Dowling plan. I showed that he
was the real negative force. He could not explain what was negative about the students
and also it came out upon questioning that what he meant about "misled educationally"
was that he was not called upon to give the students a pep talk on how the center
should be designed. Everyone there got a taste of his complete arbitrary approach and
childishness. But everybody felt that he is a powerful force to reckon with because
his word (when false) can poison many. I have decided not to let him worry me too much.
But I cannot hold grudge like he can and when I become friendly to him which will probably happen the next time I see him he will take it as a tricky maneuver on my part. What
does your wonderful little wisdom head say to that! There are many plotting against*

George Qualls,
Philadelphia architect,
principal in the firm of
Geddes Brecher Qualls
Cunningham

Robert Geddes, professor
at Princeton University and
principal in Geddes Brecher
Qualls Cunningham

Sunday March 7

Dearest Anny;

I read your letters (recent) with anxiety and hope that everything will be OK. To be lonesome and confined takes the strongest human to face them. Only the ones you're living for must appear to give encouragement and more strength it seems. You are wonderfully a woman with a spirit that many could envy. I too am waiting when the ones we're together again on our projects and love each other. My wonderful wonderful Anny no less problems but we are so good at solutions I love you I love you

—

With 2 universities to serve I have my doubts about the 7 day week. Stop to think of it I have always worked the 12 day week — All of which adds up to making your own calendar which somehow recognizes the 16 week is round — that night is shadow and day is light that sleep is rest and love the thread that tied together divergent paths into a single will to create.

Penn interests me most right now because it is the most difficult I can begin, to understand the program required space and their relation to use. The Reyburn Plaza site is small and very hacked up with underground difficulties, a new building must very supplement the existing City Hall and City Hall Annex and at same time meet rates by immediate and the needs of 1973 without building in more space than necessary now. On the next page I shall draw for you my solution of 1953 1973, I made an analysis Thursday night (to be ready for Friday class) which lead to a comprehension (for the first time) by the students of latitude possible in the allocation of new sq ft area in the new building. Venturi is helping me in teaching and is going to draw up the scheme I have on the next page. The reason for the square tower (about 40,000 sq ft per floor and about 8 stories high is that much ground floor area is desired to

Sunday
Monday
Tuesday — March 16

Dearest Anny:

On the train again to New Haven. Want to gauge it so that I can mail this when I get to New York (I hope it's long enough to call it a letter). How little Dick knows when he calls you a problem child. You are my adorable love & love I believe will never change. It so happens that when I finished the last sentence I got my sandwich. I can't write and eat. The 2 gentlemen across from me started a conversation. They are sailors (in plain clothes) returning from a trip into the merchant marine. They are Assyrians Trans Jordan to be exact. Two of the most disarming guys I have met in a long while. Attractive warm friendly, I AM NEOPEN,! and a sense of justice borne of deep experience. He insisted on paying for a drink

I started this letter on Sunday on my way to N.H. the pen skipped so I had to stop and now it is Monday late in my room in T.D. with a new cheap pen ready to finish my letter to you.

The schedule I sent you some while ago is substantially changed and I will now try to correct from all the schedule so that your anticipations about my whereabouts are more accurate. This is March 15. The Ides of March — Income tax day.

U of P. problem ends April 2. Judgement at U of P.
Harvard Lecture — March 23   8 o'clock
Baltimore Lecture — March 18   nice to look very cute probably 19th at 2 or 3 in morning.
Spring Vacation Yale — March 27 to April 5 — but actually I shall go from Boston on the 24th back to Phila & stay there until 5th.

Le Ricolais comes to Yale — April 12th and 13th. He made special note in his letters to Yale that he wanted to come when it suited me to meet him. I have received several letters from him and he is most warm and writes he is grateful for our friendship. It all seems I believe from a letter I sent him expressing my admiration for his pioneer work. He writes in one letter he wants to learn from me. I wrote him right back that he should not expect any instruction from me except what he has seen in perspecta and what I can explain to him about the art gallery.

I since could you a new calendar but in general I anticipate nothing new except to carry out the above dates. I am having slides made of the perspecta pictures for Baltimore and Harvard and a few slides for the new structural patterns of the market and the tower which is turning out in a direction I will sketch for you on the next sheet.

I forgot to mention that I am going to a reception to Eero Saarinen and his new 'critic' wife given by Johnson in the Rockefeller House on Sunday March 21. It shall be fun to see all the friends again.

Sidenote: this is not Easter Vacation for us.

him Dave Wallace being one but he also admits his powerful position. Now Anny
you have been most patient because I haven't mentioned Alexandra or you. I think about
you so much really that my every move is somewhat stopped by the tension I now feel.
Actually I don't think but only feel. I am so worried about Alexandra's foot. I have
been absent now from Yale (because of the Penn last week drive) that I have missed the
usual letter waiting for me. Soon I shall read it and I am most anxious to do so.—
(We are now stopped at Baltimore)—I confess that I have tried to get everybody out from
my mind in order to start again to see things clearly but no results. I need work and
confidence I guess and so maybe my trip here in Washington—foreign work—
people reassurance of my ability—someone to talk to and compare notes with, and
no demands on the decision wheels of the brain. I am going to go back to the man who
is coming up from New York Mr. [Rannels] architect going to start a new integrated   Rannels, unknown to Tyng
publication of the arts centering around architecture. I want to mail this when I get off
the train and I don't want to keep you waiting. So Anny honey so long for a few days
and I promise most faithfully to write in a few days and also immediately after
I read your letter (which I expect) mailed at Yale.

With all my love to both of you

Lou xxxxxx

Ended Sunday May 2, explanation on why it took so long on page 3

Dearest Anny:

*The last weeks you wrote so much and I so little. My last letter tried to make up
I still feel far behind. Whenever I start to write, except for the close feeling of you I get,
it seems I have little of interest to relate. I am for the moment just beginning to—yes—
Samuely again—I wrote you last on Sunday—/ Monday and Tuesday. [Samuely] lectured
to the students. He said about the same thing his article indicated and I believe you
and I felt that it was very important. It is. The students, many of them—maybe all,
knew nothing of his work and those drawings of simple principles went over big. They felt
it more instructing than Le Ricolais. What they missed about Le Ricolais however is
his unconcern with final shapes (though implied) and preoccupation with detail and area
principles towards enclosure. Samuely, (incidentally a small guy about 5'-1" with sparkling
black eyes and German Jewish face) though a strong thinker in principles is service
minded toward the architect. If the architect wants it and has a good reason for
it he is inclined to work it out for him. Understand now that is not worded to imply that
he is compromising. NO! but rather that he is unaware of the beauty that lies in
growth of a form from elements of combined members or surfaces which the architect
when he wants what he wants does not have in mind. The engineer might find for him such
elements or show why not he is able to—because the [architect] wants what he wants—
this all before it is decided that a direction is the one. (The last bit of sentences are about
as clear as my mother's potato soup). However Samuely is a wonderful engineer
well deserving of a place with Fuller, Nervi and Le Ricolais. I announced him in that way
(he was grateful). His criticisms of structures on the students thesis problems were
excellent and one observation emerged which is well worth keeping in mind.
One student developed this idea.*

*[sketch with notes] 1, if you take a paper tube and slice it you get
a series of rings which when placed above another forms a triangulation of rings.
When glued together it becomes very stiff—oh, la, la. / 2, This contains the
same material as 1 made of rings 2 x the depth of a single ring in 1.
Samuely felt that 1 is better than 2 BUT please turn to next page.*

*In general the circular form is doubtful because the stresses take a devious way—
go a longer distance—to get to the support. [Samuely] believes that straight members
go the shortest distance to the support and therefore must be the most economic of
material [sketch]. He also believes in breaking the structural elements to a greater number
of parts especially in large spans—in order to continue the triangular planes to practical
sub spans within the great span. He has to deliberately start with a small element to
get the whole but usually he thinks of it as whole first then solves it by breaking up the*

Felix Samuely, London
structural engineer,
published an article in
The Architect's Journal on
tetrahedral structure.

127

large span. He believes that the tetrahedron is basic in all structures but does not call a tetrahedron of Fuller's dimension the criteria. He believes that tetrahedra of any combination of angles becomes a structural basis of form.

Tomorrow I lecture at M.I.T. I keep adding slides to my collection of drawing and diagrams. I am going to talk about space order design now my standard gag. [You] kept asking me about my talk at Harvard and I thought I wrote you, I know I did, a most detailed account of it. It went over very big indeed. I showed much of your work.—next time when I have a chance to observe more accurately my reaction to Schweikher I shall tell you what I think of him. I know that I am not being told the things I should be if my position at Yale is what I believe it is. However it could very much be a matter of shyness on his part or a reading of his character into me. He may be watching me for what I am up to. Anyhow I am waiting for more interesting developments in practice. The first good jobs either the foreign one or the synagogue one which also seems a good thing. I shall ease myself out of Yale. I should hate to be told to accept instruction from Schweikher, though I don't believe it can happen. Belluschi is going to Rome as the Resident Architect. He is on the committee for the selection of the architects for foreign work (State Department) He called me up to tell me that I am on top of the list for a job. It may not come thru too fast but maybe within 3 or 4 [months]. Where? no one knows. Maybe I shall know more next time. I am preparing a brochure of my work for their review although I am assured by [Belluschi] that it is only a matter of formality to need it at all.

Pietro Belluschi, architect and dean of architecture and planning at M.I.T.

I started this letter on Wednesday and now it is Sunday. Thursday I was away to Carnegie Tech (Pittsburgh) I took the plane (over the clouds all the way forth and back) arriving there in 1 1/2 hours. The students met me and I had a few [hours] in the school with the teachers before cocktail hour the dinner and the lecture. I talked for 2 1/2 hours and the students after the talk hung around for another [hour] before we all went home. The reaction was really very good. The next morning I walked over to the Alcoa building All aluminum with the port hole like windows. I think it is a wonderful bit of detailing and bares out the validity of the principle of joint making by separation which was employed consistently thru out the building [sketch]. All the details were designed by the Aluminum Company of America (Alcoa) and not the architects Harrison and Abramowitz. The Alcoa spent $1,000,000 on research before the architect was called in. The architects of course did a lot of choosing of appropriate design elements in aluminum, but the interior design of board rooms and any other special rooms are really stinko. Enough of that. I got back Friday afternoon and had hardly taken off my coat when I received a call from a Mr. Raybill a Quaker who explained on the phone that he intends building a 20 story office building for the Friends (he being one) "Montgomery and Bishop are the architects but I would like that Frank L. Wright and Louis I. Kahn be consultants." Would I agree to such a consultancy. I said yes of course.

Wallace K. Harrison and Max Abramowitz

Johannes Hoeber,
Philadelphia Deputy
Commissioner of Welfare

He asked that we meet that very day and it seems after discussion to be a promotional job but still a possibility of good content. Saturday I was busy all day—in the morning with a confirmation service which lasted until the middle afternoon. That afternoon I met a real estate man about an alteration he wants done and in the evening I was invited by the Montgomerys to rehash the Friends proposition again. This I did at the Montgomerys in Germantown. At 8 they had to go to a party at the Smiths' who are an old Philly family. They asked me along (wanted to show me an addition that Montgomery and Bishop did for the Smiths) and I stayed for the party too—having met the mayor the Hoebers, the Bacons and other city officials there, and so having gotten back to town very late on Saturday here it is Sunday and I am finishing your letter and I feel very much ashamed first because it took so long and secondly because it was so thoroughly all about me only. But my thoughts are not for me only. I constantly am in Italy wondering really about your movements with Alexandra and trying to see and feel you smile hoping you are laughing much and that you are given the love which you so much need and deserve and should get plenty of. You must also understand I am a thorough Pick puss nowadays for many good and bad reasons. The only thing I can't say is that my life is uneventful.

With lots and lots of love and a concentrated all my love to you and Alexandra

Lou xxxxxxx

6 May 1954

Dearest Anne

The days pass like mad. It seems I just wrote to you it was Sunday and now it is Thursday night. The reason is clear—the two days at Yale bring me to Wednesday to start the week on my own work and this is what I did yesterday: I started off with 2 conflicting appointments neatly arranged by Alice. Labatut of Princeton was to be in the office at 8:45 a.m. and I was to attend a board meeting of the Union Health Center (Melamed) at 9:00 a.m. (breakfast meeting). I got out of that dilemma like a State Department diplomat. I met Labatut and arrived at the breakfast meeting on time at 10:10. It so happened that L. came to Philadelphia as one of the judges for medals of this year's crop of architecture at Philadelphia. (Noble and Martin got it for the Mercantile Library on Chestnut St. very nice job) so had to leave for judgment at 10:30, the breakfast meeting was really a lot of fun with Melamed making himself understood by his integrity etching thru a personal esperanto. Incidentally the new principle set down by President Harbeson is that no one can receive the medal of the chapter more than once. I submitted nothing (saving thereby about $100.00). I did not see the exhibit because I had to speak that very night at the Honor Society of the Architects at Penn. Le Ricolais was there and after the talk and discussion I went out for a beer with him and we talked as usual. He is a tired man not interested too much in work. He refers to himself as old and longs for his tree chair and Romanesque chapel around the corner in Brittany. I appreciate the touching scene but not the negativism of "why work when no one appreciates it anyway." But I did not explain my entire Wednesday. In the afternoon I attended the weekly meeting at Mill Creek and went over the usual building problems. I believe the job is coming very well—badly executed but the idea is very strong. I got back just in time to be wisked to the dinner at Penn. It was at 12 midnight when I got back from beer with Le Ricolais and flopped down on the bench in the office, tried to sleep and decided to go home to bed. Thursday (today) I got up early to meet the Psychiatric Hospital people for the settlement of the last payment on the Hospital. I have about $1500.00 coming to me which money at the present time I need desperately. I had to finance the end of Mill Creek Redevelopment Plan and maybe I can recapture a little of that from the last payment due us on the job. I am not too worried only I have accumulated quite a bit of debt in making photos etc. for brochures. I tell you its murder the touch and go of dough. But I still say to hell with it.

Clauss (Zepp) called me to try to get Orr (New Haven) to collaborate on possibly getting the Air Academy to do. It is a fabulous $125,000,000 job. He wants me to go into it too. Well to be honest with you I hate the idea of associating with Orr or Zepp (that is in

130

Isidor Melamed, local Philadelphia union leader, commissioned the American Federation of Labor Health Center, St. Luke's Hospital, 1950–51.

Martin and Noble, Philadelphia architects

John Harbeson, president of the Philadelphia chapter of the American Instititute of Architects and principal of Harbeson Hough Livingston & Lawson

Psychiatric Hospital, Bernard S. Pincus Building and Samuel Radbill Building, Philadelphia Psychiatric Hospital, 1948–54

Zepp Clauss was a principal in the firm of Gilboy and O'Malley.

Douglas Orr, New Haven architect associated with Kahn for the Yale University Art Gallery

the later case Gilboy and O'Malley) I believe probably Eero or Skidmore Owings and Merrill or Walker or any of the big guys will probably get it anyway. I had a good notion to submit my name unattached giving my qualifications suitable for a designer or a consultant. I called Doug Haskell for advice he said that he did not believe that the judges (all Air generals or engineers) would see the point of me. He thought Doug Orr a good bet because of his Washington connections. I think the whole thing of me in that picture is fantastic and I should drop it. (unless someone offers me a position and that is out because the Institute advised immediate application and no one has asked me except Alfred.)

I know the news so far is pretty dry but it is the best I have. So far I have not anything tangible enough. The house is kind of dead. The others Synagogue and Office Building is still not cooking, the State Department job not ripe yet. But as I recapitulate any one of the bigger ones will do me.

Whenever I pass your desk it is you all over. I went to the Colonnade with Dave and others in the office. We began to talk. When I mentioned Rome a lady who sat next to us said to me are you Mr. Kahn—she knew because I mentioned Rome—and then said what do you hear from Miss Tyng—It was Miss Pim? (is it) the sec'y below you on Rittenhouse. She wants to be remembered and hopes you write to her. Incidentally I forgot to mention that Labatut was very much taken by the model we made of the City Hall area. It is really quite nice though cheaply made. The P/A article is out. I did not as yet get a copy but I understand it to be very good. Haskell, when I spoke to him today remarked about how fine it was. He wants to run an article on the Gallery which brings out the principle of flexibility and the theory of space order design and in that way be unimitative and superior. Well he is going to think about it. Your letters are wonderful—full of milk and pink. I am glad you are being treated so lovingly because I am not there to do the same. Alexandra must be delightful though she would have been much more beautiful if she resembled you. She sounds terrific really and if she has a little of what I was as a kid maybe she will be OK at that.

All my love to you and Alex

Love Lou xxxxxxx

Air Force Academy in Colorado Springs, ultimately designed by Skidmore, Owings & Merrill

Ralph Walker, New York architect

Alfred "Zepp" Clauss

The Colonnade, a Philadelphia restaurant

131

Dearest Anny:

*I copy for you the poem by E. E. Cummings which awakens the creative instincts
from feeling—the nerves of our psychic order.*

*So many selves (so many fiends and gods
each greedier than every) is a man
(So easily one in another hides;
yet man can, being all, escape from none)*

*so huge a tumult is the simplest wish:
so pitiless a massacre the hope
most innocent (so deep's the mind of flesh
and so awake what waking calls sleep)*

*so never is most lonely man alone
(his briefest breathing lives some planet's year,
his least unmotion roams the youngest star)
how should a fool that calls him "I" presume
to comprehend not numerable whom?*

*I came across this in a catalogue prepared by Yale Art Gallery for the show—
"Object and Image in Modern Art and Poetry" which is now on the first floor of the
Gallery. It places side by side the painting or sculpture a poem in sympathy. The show is
particularly good because it is uncluttered and one sees hardly more than 1 painting
or object at a time.*

*I just (an hour ago) mailed a letter to you—could not resist sharing this wonderfully
expressed concept of the universality of "I"—the numerable whom. How can man assume
the artist isolated when he is the gifted one who senses infinity from o to 1.*

*I just heard that Mr. and Mrs. Robert Montgomery Brown have gone off to Europe
for a 6 week stay. I suppose they'll drink up Europe (most people drink it in) I am told they
will buy an automobile, I suppose mostly for the trunk compartment. I saw George
and he looks pretty bad. I believe his retirement from Yale did him no particular good.
He seems to want to avoid me somehow. Last time I was at [Yale] I saw him in the morning
of Monday. He promised to have lunch with me on Tuesday, he also explained he was
staying over at the Schweikhers (newly acquired friend). He must have had a 'full' night—
he forgot my date (very unusual for G.). I had Louise Britton call up and the message
came back—he is out to lunch with the boys (Schweikher's workers in the office*

Mr. and Mrs. Robert
Montgomery Brown owned
1728 Spruce Street where
Kahn had his first inde-
pendent office.

Louise Britton, executive
secretary to the dean of
the architecture school at
Yale University

132

Harrower, unknown to
Tyng

Earl Carlin worked for
Kahn on the Yale
University Art Gallery.

Harrower and Earl) and intends to stroll over to the Gallery later. I went out alone (poor me) and when I got back George was full of apologies and of course I let on that it made no difference. But for a guy that admires him for what is good in him and forgives him without question for his other idiosyncrasies it did hurt. I will send you several copies of P/A as soon as they arrive. I believe your name appears too. I hurt two fingers in a taxi door that slammed on them. This was about 3 weeks ago and it hurts even more now. I must have broken the 2 fingers right of the thumb on the right hand. I should and will get them x rayed to make sure. It does not bother drawing or writing somehow, but I cannot clench my fingers in a fist without pain.

I do so hope that little Alexandra's foot is normal and that the x rays also reveal nothing abnormal about the hip. The cast must bother her. You describe her so vaguely but she must be as beautiful as you.

Roy Carroll, of the firm
Carroll, Grisdale, and Van
Allen, was president of the
Philadelphia chapter of
the American Institute of
Architects 1952–53 and later
became national president.

Friday—Earlier today I got your letter with the drawing of the cast. I hope you are not minimizing what is wrong. Don't ask me to decide anything you must know the feeling of so many unknowns and so many conflicting answers. Only thing I know is that I love you. I went to see the A.I.A. exhibit. Kling had about 8 jobs shown, Carroll, Grisdale and Van Allen almost as many. The new ruling (only one gold medal) throws out Kling for the gold medal though he was eligible for and got an honorable mention for a house. He got nothing on his Lankenau Hospital (near Genel) which proves the good judgment of the jury. Eligible for the G.M., [Carroll, Grisdale and Van Allen] got nothing for their Youth Center (parkway) but got Honorable Mention for a house. They did not show the airport. The winner was really the best (Mercantile Library). All exhibits were attractively shown, even Beryl Price but Oshiver had his usual Toledo (El Greco effects) sky in tempera the background for a building extravaganza, the only really corny part of the show. Big and Gaudy. It was wonderful to read your words of good spirit and a will to have fun. How confining it must have been before Alexandra came. Your trip around Rome, the fabulous, I could just feel it in even the few words you wrote. Today I attend another meeting of Melamed's board (health center) and they approved my going ahead with a few sketches for the new building in town. I am still waiting for some photos to complete my brochure to send to Washington (State Department). I will write soon again. I could see your wonderful face in front of me on your little body moving about.

Beryl Price and Oshiver
(first name unknown to
Tyng), Philadelphia
architects

My best best love to both of you.

Lou xxxxx

Dearest Anny   *Postmarked 19 May 1954*

*Today I opened your box of chalks you sent from Rome. You know that quite a few
came broken and none of the reds are the right color. Luckily I ordered enough and I still
have a bit of red which will do me very well. Incidentally I found a shop that sells
La Franc in New York. They are sets and that is a disadvantage. Well getting down to the
point I started to do a few sketches just to amuse myself and relax from the extra curricular
activities of mine—travel, talks, meetings, all of which though stimulating and are adventures to look forward to—are time consuming and in the long run expensive. I am badly
behind my work and still can't get down to it, so I try to relax first by working on
something easy on the mind and that is drawing and color for me. Oh! I know other ways
of relaxing but that must wait. Yesterday I took a stab at the Mill Creek sketch. I worked
all day and almost finished the overall perspective which is the most difficult of the
sketches. Pen laid out the Mill Creek initial Housing perspective, looking thru an opening
between 2 of the quatrefoil houses to the towers. I was out last Wednesday to see them
coming along. I believe if we can manage somehow to get the electric service lines
underground those houses will look exceptionally well.*

[sketch]

*Now I have still the drawing above to draw (from Pen's perspective line drawing).
Also a perspective of a promenade and a few sketches showing the progressive steps taken
to develop the greenways. You being a collaborator I go into such detail to impress you
of course with my value in the organization. The overlay drawings of the various colors for
the big plan are very good and should make a handsome map. I suppose they will start
printing as soon as I finish those perspectives. The text, though finished to our satisfaction,
is not somehow to theirs. Willo tried his hand at it and he promptly dried the whole
thing up. I suppose that will also fall on our shoulders. Though it seemed that Pen was
ungodly slow on the drawings, he produced a very good job. But as a result of this much
time consumed we can barely hope to break even if at all. Well that is the usual fate
of jobs under my wing. They just don't make money. I was told, and you remember this
too that we undercharged for our services compared to the outside consultants.
They got about double what we bargained for.*

*Zepple came in—he saw my light burning—we chatted for a while. I showed him
the model of the City Hall Plaza and the new slides I developed on the hollow columns.
He told me he received his copy of* P/A *and was surprised to find that I hadn't as yet.
When he left it occurred to me to run over to his place and see it. He was gone—I asked the
Swiss young man to look in his room I walked in too. He didn't find the magazine but
looking around the walls I was surprised to find an attempt to imitate the squared*

Zepple, Alfred "Zepp"
Clauss

134

off painting idea and it was marked to be followed as a wall decoration for a job of his. Also he is imitating the tetrahedral ceiling in one large room of a building. He is doing it in plaster to resemble a structural ceiling. A complete fake!

Everybody is desperately trying to become outstanding even if they have to stand on some-one to reach such a position. Zepple left himself only 3 weeks to complete the working drawings for Riverview. The design group of his were working on the details of the design but they changed very little from the preliminary scheme that won the prize. I think it is a miserably unlivable plan. They have to cheapen the construction because they were forced to spend $1,000,000 more for foundations. The administration is rushing them also because they have to finish the construction to be ready for the next election. I believe I did already tell you that Dr. Hoeber of the Department of Welfare thought that had I finished my plan I would have won that competition. But I believe you should have won. Well we both didn't and I have and I know you have by now completely forgotten about it. I have a slide of your and my schemes and it looks pretty damned good (as a pattern). I believe Zepp did have a good central control area. I don't know what has come over me. This is the 3rd letter I have written in a week. Of course I am saying hardly anything that really should interest you. I forgot to mention in the last letter how glad I was to receive the photos of your parents' house. They are very good and I agree that you could do so much to develop the details. You have not written how they like the house now that they are living in it for some time. I remember your writing about their complaints at the beginning but you must tell me how they like it now. It is indeed a fine achievement and I hope that soon you will be active again at your work. I feel kind of lousy today I think I am getting a cold. I sat near Bolton of the Art Alliance for dinner—he had a terrible cold and I must have gotten it from him. Sue also came down with the flu yesterday (maybe I got it from her). So far it isn't too bad. The letter from Sue and my parents were very delightful and I am returning them to you as you wanted me to. I am getting the chills and so will go home now and maybe continue this tomorrow. Tomorrow I have a Penn Center meeting (Monday) so had to take a day off from school. I expect to take the 6:23 (you remember?) that day. So long until tomorrow —

This is tomorrow I feel lousy but got to the P.C. meeting anyway. They had this California architect Welton and Beckett who were hired by the Pennsylvania Railroad at the suggestion of A. Kaufman to make a survey of the marketing possibilities of P.C. they came back with a display on cardboard a smooth sssmmoooooooooththth tongue. They took the buildings as is

[sketch]

and proved that it is good for commercial use on the level of the concourse. Then they showed perspectives of what this meant. Pure corn the most nauseating crap I've seen yet. Everybody was enthusiastic Bacon was ecstatic and of course disgusting. Zantzinger proposed a resolution that Welton Beckett be commended for their fine work and Bacon

Riverview competition for housing for senior citizens; Kahn and Tyng each submitted an entry.

Welton and Beckett, California architects

Arthur C. Kaufman, chairman of Citizen's Advisory Committee on the Penn Center

135

immediately added that why not add to the resolution that W. & B. be retained as the architects. Of course I realize that a good political move is meant by this. No Philadelphian could convince the Pennsylvania R.R. of the concourse scheme. It would take an outside expert to make them take notice. I am not blind to the politics but architects of their caliber! God help us. In the light of such an atmosphere of mediocrity I could not ask that they all adjourn to see my model of the area. I did manage however to make arrangement that G. Howe see it with Le Ricolais on Wednesday. I just got back from the meeting and so I feel rather poor inside and out. I am about to take the train to New Haven where I expect to have a very busy day since I lost a day because of the meeting. I shall try to finish this letter on the train.

Looks like I did not get around to this until today Thursday. I got back very late from Yale on Tuesday and Wednesday morning went over to the Leise Metal Works to inspect the table legs I had made for some furniture [for] New Haven Art Gallery. Incidentally I just saw for the first time the P/A copy of the Art Gallery. It is a fair job, though poor in picture layout, does not minimize its importance in my opinion. I will send you a copy post haste as soon as I get my mitts on the extra copies I am to receive. Sert does say good things about it. Of course Gutheim still believes it is the beginning of the renaissance. I just got back in time to see Le R. and George at the Art Alliance and from there we went to my office.

136

G. H. was very impressed with the triangular building on the Plaza and said he would talk to Mayor Clark about it. Le Ricolais thinks anything I do is wonderful (he doesn't know the half of it). From the office we visited the Bulletin job which I believe is a jungle structurally (There are many good but not excellent features) Le Ricolais was respectful. From there a quick tour of the Mill Creek project and G. H. was very much impressed, so [was] Le R. It looks its best now I'm afraid because as it gets finished in spots it reflects the poor workmanship. It was exhausting being host to these two rather exhausted architects, though the one Le Ricolais is refreshing for his honesty and thoroughly disarming sweetness of nature. We have become fast friends. Wednesday evening I simply had to go to bed starting on my bench and ending in bed. Today I feel somewhat better and am finishing up the little models I must make for Melamed's committee on the new Health Center. Z. Clauss is after me to collaborate on a [. . .ateum] for Annapolis. I am to see the man of his office to see how we may present our credentials to obtain the job. I hate this whole business of collaboration with these grasping half baked architects full of excuses based on the circumstances of our time for their mediocre performances. However I shall not keep you from this letter any longer and not wait for tomorrow to ship it off.

To keep the record straight on the Monday P.C. meeting, A. Kaufman sensed Bacon's proposal out of order and was quite piqued of Zantzinger's resolution to commend the Calif. architects. I heard from George on Wednesday that Kling is no doubt in for the job but I believe the people are going to be Martin and Noble because of the Mercantile Library you mark my words. Your charming letters are all read and reread and I am

The new *Evening Bulletin* Building by George Howe and Robert Montgomery Brown

particularly pleased by your last letter because you seemed happy and your encouraging
enthusiasm for my nibbles was also nice to read about. So far of course there is nothing
coming in in the way of dough which I by now need desperately but mind you I am
not worried nearly so much as I should be. I have a goodly check due me from the Hospital.
The city Planning commission will not pay me the rest until I finish those sketches of
[Mill Creek] which I am finishing. When I do I will be repaid what I advanced for Pen's
time. So! if that comes in I will send you some cash. Please wait just a little longer until
then, Anny because I really can't now. Right now I live by the regard people have for my
work. The regard they may have of me I personally discount because I know what a better
man I could be in many respects. It is now very late and I enclose the letters from Sue
and my parents. I have not written to them now for almost a year. You see what I mean
about being a better man. I read a letter my father wrote to Sue in answer to a letter she
owed my parents for about 2 or 3 months also. My father said to Sue that letter-writing was
a distinct antipathy of the Kahns and that he was glad that she inherited the good qualities
of that particular clan. He explained to her what pain he goes thru to write and mention
my laxity as an uncontrollable instinct. He's really a sweet guy. So now on the 4th page at
1 a.m. having written all about myself. But though I mentioned you only once or twice,
I am after all writing to you and always see you and Alexandra before me and it is
with the deepest love that I close and kiss you both many times.

Lou xxxxxxx

Dearest Anne   *Thursday, Fri., Sat, last day of May '54*

She is a perfect darling! I believe too that she will be a beauty and will have much much to offer this world—and You! You look so wonderful to me so beautiful—so loving. I believe I also recognized the blanket you made—Alex is peeping over it. You can well understand why I have looked at you two now tens of times wondering about it all—looking back how it all came about. I can really say no more except to add again how moved I was in seeing you again as though actually.

I haven't gotten extra copies (they are so slow) of the Progressive Architecture *article on the Yale building. I get many compliments and the more I get the more I feel like doing another building which is really good. So far nothing tangible has arrived although I have not lost hope. My bank account is still lousy and will be so for several weeks more when I expect some money from the P.C.P.C. to close our account with them. We spent in finishing up Mill Creek Redev. on the last lap $1,400 which I advanced and need now to carry on for a few months. I could I believe manage O.K. and I will send you next time about $50.00 so I can make up for the long lapse and my utter neglect of your penny needs. Gee Anny I do feel so lousy about my inadequacy even in so unrespected a thing as money. But it is all temporary and believe me I am not living in a sea of hopelessness but I see nothing that I am not ready to penetrate to the truth ultimately.*

What I expected in the way of reaction to Schweikher's real intentions showed itself I believe. I received my usual notice from the Yale Corporation announcing my re-employ- ment for the year 1954–55 but it did not indicate the usual raise in salary and dropped the "Chief" in front of Critic in giving my title. I called G. H. (knowing he was in on the arrangements for next year) and seemed "not to remember" discussing that particular point with Schweikher. He advised me to talk to [Schweikher] directly and not to do anything rash. I got him and asked for an explanation. He explained that it was his thought to drop the title of critic altogether explaining it as a misnomer as applied especially to assistants in design. But the Dean did not like dropping "critic" at least yet. Schweikher went on to say that he thought I wouldn't mind his dropping "chief" from my title since he understood I didn't give a damn one way or another and that if critic had to be used in the catalogue as a title, mine would be the only one used in that way and the others would be known as assistant critics or associate critics or research assistants etc., etc.— Then I said "why did you drop chief without my permission" he said he should [not] have done so but thought it made no difference to me. I agreed that it did not but to the outside world it would be taken as a demotion and that I was tired of explaining my worth to people who want to see you trodden under actually. He was very sorry said he was rather misled by George—he did not caution him about my possible reaction. He tried to get me to drop my objection—but I did not permit that. He said most likely the catalogues

were being printed. I said they would have to correct the printing. He said he would try
to do so. He was so so sorry. Of course it is obviously an attempt on his part to minimize
my importance. Everyone knows that a director is a desk man and I as "chief critic"
would appear more important. He concocted all this business for purely selfish reasons
and I will definitely quit if the catalogue cannot be altered. I am sorry that George seemed
"not to remember" I believe he knew it would happen although I am sure he did not
suggest that it happen.

The thesis problems are particularly good this year though the students are not the best.
It all came about by my growing understanding of architecture and my recent discoveries of
order. The Nature of space—order—design theme really dovetails with history and art
in the psychic order. I showed you the diagrams on those ideas and keep them constantly
in mind as the guide to teaching.

Dearest Anny your picture of you and Alex is so loving and as I start this page with wonder
at what you are doing now in Rome. Many people inquire about you. They believe you're
studying with Nervi. I tell them, since they come to [me] naturally for any news of you, that
you mention little about work.

Everybody seems to be studying for the State Board of Registration. Bob, Pen and Bill were
over to review questions by Bregman (the great wit and social philosopher) on plumbing,
conditioning and controls. In a slow drolly way he is a good teacher. I listen in with
one ear while working on the perspective drawing for the Mill Creek Booklet. I finished all
the sketches yesterday (Friday) and took them over to the city Planning Commission.
Now as I mentioned earlier we can be paid our remaining sum in the contract. We have
still $700.00 in the Redevelopment contract which I am going to try to loosen to make up
the deficit of about $400.00 I laid out and stand to lose. Because I am sure my partners
will certainly not dig down in their pockets to cover my loss (really their loss or rather they
gained so much). The booklet should be tolerably good. The sketches are a bit dry but
better that way for public purpose. Pretty soon I will send you copies (I have the negatives)
along with P/A on the Yale A.G. I have had more offers to lecture. What is going to come of

me? I must build one of the great buildings of the time. My new theorem fascinates every-
one. You must help me build this particular building I doubt if I can do it without you.

Rome may be hot in the summer. I so wish you could go away to Switzerland with Alex.
Maybe I can get hold of some money if I do will you go? Is it a good idea? I want you so to be
happy in spite of having so confused and befuddled a sweetheart like me. Anny I must busy
myself to get off many obligations I have much much neglected. I still haven't written the
correction to the Princeton conference which is long overdue and I should hate to have
them print my words as I spoke them. I want to do this chore immediately after this letter
to you. I must also prepare an outline of my next article in Perspecta (3) *which will be on*
the Gallery and I could develop my more recent theories, even explain how I would build
that building today. Le Ricolais gave a wonderful problem of a stadium at Penna.
It turned out to be 4 teams producing 4 magnificent structural ideas.

All of my love and kisses to Alex and you until next time soon

Lou xxxxxxx

140

13 June 1954

Dearest Anne

I have been lax in my writing and feel ashamed because of the long ones you sent me.
The Reasons are manifold but still not justified because I could have found time and I had
so much to tell you several times this week. I am glad you got my late letter and I hope you
will excuse my late writing this time too. I went to a Mayor's Citizens Committee meeting
last week at which several vice-presidents of the Pennsylvania R.R. told us about their
plans for the service level of the Penn Center Plan, also that McClosky was hiring Vincent   McClosky, developer and
Kling to design an apartment building and the Annenberg plot for the Center.   contractor

[sketch with notes]

I knew of this development but surprisingly I am/was unconcerned now that I have
developed a stronger idea around the center City Hall Plaza and the East Market Street
area. I therefore was much more relaxed at the meeting than I am usually with the result
that I made more sense to the other members of the Committee and it induced constructive
questions on my part easily recognizable as such by the other members of our committee.
Fortunately Bacon and Zantzinger were not present. At the end of the meeting Stevens
proposed that I show my model 50' = 1 inch at a meeting scheduled in the Mayor's office
next week. This should be the break I am looking for.

Dearest Anne.

I have been lax in my writing and feel ashamed because of the long ones you sent me. The reasons are manifold but still not justified because I could have found time and I had so much to tell you several times this week. I am glad you got my late letter and I began several of my late writing this time too. I went to a Mayors Citizens Committee meeting last week at which several vice presidents of the Pennsylvania R.R. told us about their plans for the service level of the Penn Center Plan. also that Mc Cleary was willing to design an apartment building at the Annenberg plot of the center.

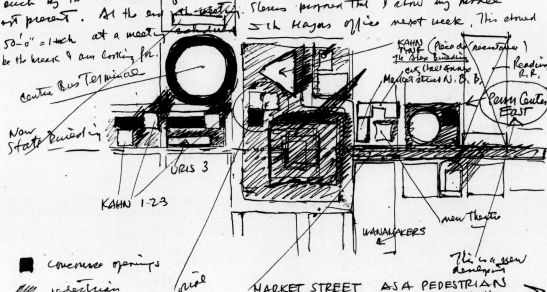

Apartment building
P. Barlo.
Market.
18   17
Annenberg plot turned over to Mc Cleary.
entrance to Transportation Building on Bus terminal on Commerce street

I knew of this development but surprisingly I am unconcerned now that I had developed a stronger idea around the center city Hall Plaza and the East Market Street area. I therefore was much more relaxed at the meeting than I am usually with the result that I made more sense to the other members of the Committee and it reduced constructive questions on my part as easily recognizable as such by the other members from committee. Fortunately Bacon a Zantziger were not present. At the end of the meeting Slesers proposed that I show my model 50'-0" = 1 inch at a meeting scheduled 5th Mayors office next week. This should be the break I am looking for.

Kahn Tract (Place de recentofice)
The Slater Building
City Hall Annex
Market street N. E. B.
Reading R.R.
Penn Center East

Centre Bus Terminal

New State Building

URIS 3

KAHN 1·23

memorial spot.

WANAMAKERS

new Theatre

This is a new development

concourse openings
pedestrian

MARKET STREET AS A PEDESTRIAN SHOPPING STREET (from city Hall to the Independence Hall. This ties up the financial and real estate interest on east Market and Penn Center

141

This is essentially my new plan.

1. The extended Plaza (in the style of Plaza) containing the city Hall Building overview plaza

Sculptus group 1-2-3
paved (space 100 × 100)
proc. 100 × 100
covered opening 100 × 100

2. Turn around terminus of Broome garage from Vine to P.C. (no in Parking's plan in P.C. from (7th & 18th enlarged) but bad entrance conditions.

3 New Market St.

with all poles wires plugs litter out no Trolleys but buses

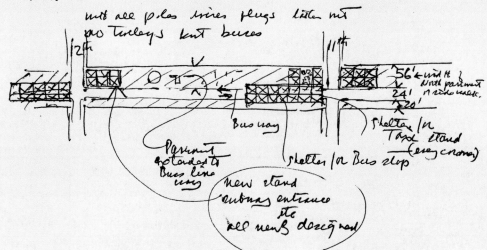

12th   11th

56' curb ht
North pavement
14 sidewalk.
24'
20'

Bus way

Shelter for Taxi stand (every corner)

Shelter for Bus stop

Pavement extended to Buss line way

New stand subway entrance etc all newly designed

and new Penn Center east which should bring about an outlet for the merchants protection on East market.

please Kaufmann at Greenfield.

A cooperative arrangement of jewelers hats skin wigs & Clothes → warm modern & needlecrafts stores to provide for their own self protection.

Marti Adler wants a house built for her family. I am to do it. small about $40 000. Another client recommended by Marti also wants one about that big. The health center is definitely going ahead Melamed called me about it yesterday. So far no word from the State Department. I received some wonderful letter about the gallery. one or more gallery involved or rather identified with 3 D constructions and the new order

142

I am sending you a copy of P/A May and P/A June. May is
the gallery addition (your name appears) and in the June issue again
and this time prominently in connection with the City Hall Building.
I am so proud to be identified with you on that. Your letter about
Sloss is so understanding a friend but to remove any discomfort you so
this about us just cuts the hell out gone. Just yesterday I
deposited $50.00 in your account and will do it again for the same
amount in about a week. Please send me a time card for about $150,
so I can deposit that as soon as possible. I don't take any retainers
fee from the houses as Helman's job is still not in a position for
payment. I am careful about funds but I can manage the
amount I just mentioned. It's hell to think that you are stripped
or uncomfortable and not thoroughly independent. Please try
to understand and I know that you are so patient. Next week
I shall go to New York — in intent to see the new Japanese house built
by the Reeeeeen. (Invitation from the Japanese Ambassador no less)
Now that school is over I feel much more free. but mentally I know
I shall feel less so — Two trips to Yale take my mind off
things. Now I need work and plenty of it to do the same. I
am of course very encouraged by the possibility of making a good
showing at the Mayors Meeting this Thursday. The model does work
very well. On Monday (that is tomorrow) I show the model at the
Citizens Council on City Planning. Aaron Levin is nuts about its
triangular building on the corner of Market Street East.
I will write you immediately after these meetings and promise
never to hold you off without writing so long any more —
So love enough for the moment. But all my love to
you and stay love

I included the page I wrote June 6 but never finished
My intention was good but I got very lazy.

The snap was taken by this class mate of mine (lady) we met in
Rotterdam 39. You remember?

143

It would be a good idea—one that will be infinitely useful to your later work—to be in frequent touch with the work of Norris. The University of Rome I understand is N.G. and the work of N. does not filter thru. Having had very friendly contact with La Ricolais and Samuely now I feel they are very much the equal of Norris in their way, I find La R. of particular consistency and by far the purer engineer and philosopher. His study of Topology is the reason for his advanced positions and his preoccupation with geometry per se is another. He has a whole note book of diagrams and formulae (of his own) which are based on Topological formulae in forms and plan. It is precisely the scientific knowledge which an architect needs if he is at all interested and intends to work in the 3D field. Samuely is a practical engineer with, as I noted to you before, an immediate decorative sense. His emphasis on intersecting planes lets right in line

with La Ricolais' Topology. If you get a chance get a hold of information and construction if possible on Topy. It is not so much the intense study now as the acquaintance with its worth in the construction of the envelope of spaces. I believe in small doses then enough to seep thru for me. The little touch I got from La Ricolais here at Yale at least puts me up to date on source material. When I write this I wonder at U save Time the deep value of all. When you recall my little diagrams of the psychic order you realize that intellectual mind is not to be set aside if we desire great works of art. Philosophy and science guides works of art to [scope] and expression techniques in the of the era.

[sketch with notes]

This is essentially my new plan.

1. The extended Plaza (in the style of Pisa) containing the City Hall building, Memorial Plaza [sketch with notes]

2. Turn around terminus of Bacon's garage from Vine to P.C. (now in Dowling's plan in P.C. from 17th to 18th underground) but bad entrance conditions.

3. New Market St. with all poles, wires, plugs taken out no trolleys but buses [sketch with notes] and new Penn Center east which should bring about an outlet for the investments protection on East Market, pleasing Kaufmann and Greenfield. A cooperative arrangement of Gimbels, Lits, Strawbridge and Clothier, Wanamakers, Snellenbergs should be possible for their own self protection.

Marti Adler wants a house built for her family. I am to do it. Small about $40,000. Another client recommended by Marti also wants one about that big. The Health Center is definitely going ahead Melamed called me about it yesterday. So far no word from the State Department. I received some wonderful letters about the Gallery and more and more getting involved or rather identified with 3 D construction and the new order.

145

I am sending you a copy of P/A May and P/A June. May is the Gallery edition (your name appears) and in the June issue again and this time prominently in connection with the City Hall Building. I am so proud to be identified with you on that. Your letter about Alex is so wonderful to read but to sense any discomfort you go thru about us just cuts the hell out of me. Just yesterday I deposited $50.00 in your account and will do it again for the same amount in about a week. Please send me a time card for about $150.00 so I can deposit that as soon as possible. I don't have any retainer yet from the houses and Melamed's job is still not in a position for payment. I am careful about funds but I can manage the amount I just mentioned. It is hell to think that you are strapped or uncomfortable and not thoroughly independent. Please try to understand and I know that you will be patient. Next week I shall go to New York to see the Japanese house built by the Museum (invitation from the Japanese Ambassador no less).

Japanese house, built in the garden of the Museum of Modern Art, later dismantled

Now that school is over I feel much more free but mentally I know I shall [be] less so— those trips to Yale kind of take my mind off things. Now I need work and plenty of it to do the same. I am of course very encouraged by the possibility of making a good showing at the Mayor's Meeting this Thursday. The model does look very well. On Monday (that is tomorrow) I show the model at the Citizens Council on City Planning. Aaron Levine is nuts about the triangular building and the idea of Market Street East. I will write you immediately after the meetings and promise never to hold you off without writing so long any more—so long sweetheart for the moment.

Aaron Levine, designer at the Philadelphia City Planning Commission

With all my love to you and Alex

Lou xxxxxxx

I included the page I wrote June 6 but never finished. My intentions were good but I got very lazy.

The snap was taken by this classmate of mine (lady) we met in Rittenhouse Sq. you remember?

[Sunday 6 June 1954. Mailed with 13 June letter]

146   *It would be a good idea—one that will be infinitely useful to your later work—to be in frequent touch with the work of Nervi. The University of Rome I understand is [no good] and the work of Nervi does not filter thru. Having had very friendly contact with Le Ricolais and Samuely now I feel they are very much the equal of Nervi in his way. I find Le R. of particular sensitivity and by far the purer engineer and philosopher. His study of Topology is the reason for his advanced position and his preoccupation with geometry per se is another. He has a thick notebook of diagrams and formulas (of his own) which are based on Topological formulae. It is precisely the scientific knowledge which an architect needs if he is at all interested in forms and plan and intends to work in the 3D field. Samuely is a practical engineer with, as I noted to you before, an immediate diagnostic sense. His emphasis on intersecting planes fits right in line with Le Ricolais' Topology. If you get a chance get ahold of information and instruction if possible on Top'y it isn't so much the intense study now as the acquaintance with its worth in the construction of the envelope of spaces. I believe in small doses thin enough to seep thru for me. The little touch I got from Le Ricolais' talk at Yale at least puts me up to date on source material. When I write this I wonder at the same time the deep value of it all. When you recall my little diagram of the psychic order you realize that intellective mind is not to set aside if we desire great works of art. Philosophy and science guide works of art to order and techniques in the expression of the era. The last bracketed sentence should read "just think if each doctor practiced his own way without regard for scientific understanding as the departure point. We should also regard this understanding not as a hindrance but as the means of releasing the creative level possible in our time."*

Dearest Anne

I just came from the meeting in the Mayor's office where I showed my model of the Center City area. I set the model up yesterday at 6 p.m. had a long drink of ice tea and flopped on the bench in the office. Apparently Bacon and his commission had their model delivered after mine yesterday because when I got in for the meeting at 9 a.m. this morning Bacon greeted me by saying my model was swell pointing to several features. I had a very good opportunity to explain the idea to the Mayor, Sawyer the Mayor's special sec'y, our committee of the 2 councilmen, Mitchell Kaufmann a V.P. of the railroad, a number of newsmen and a member of the General State Authority. The upshot was that Lew Stevens came out with the remark that he would like me to be the architect of the plaza and the city building. The side remark was if we can keep this fellow (me) down some we would undoubtedly have the most beautiful building in the world. (Ta Tara Ta!) Kaufmann admitted that the Market St. idea was good. (he wished he had suggested it I read in his face because who is more obviously in touch with the problem of Market than he). They took movies and photos of the event (I don't still know who took them I mean for what purpose). I hope that Stevens word carries weight and if we ever get this job it would truly be a good building. So far so good. The Monday meeting at the Citizens Council was very successful. They had a large turn out and [. . .] Stonorov was also amongst those counted he made no remark openly but I asked Bob Bishop who sat next to him. "Who helped Lou?" Bob of course knowing the situation was never more definite as to who (he told me about it). I tried at the meeting to give credit to the various people I asked to collaborate in the event it was necessary. But Bob Bishop and Sidney Martin both felt they had absolutely no claim to it— which really is right. Bob Venturi just called me to inquire about the outcome of today's meeting. He has tried right along to think of ways to overcome resistances to me. He was most kind about helping and charging me the minimum for his time. Here lately my colleagues have been unduly solicitous but I am positive that that is the warning to be most on guard except from my most trusted friends. An instance of what I mean is this. I have been hearing rumors that "I am too busy to take on city work" that—"the fees are too small for Kahn" etc. Where in the hell that started I can't imagine and at first I discounted these rumors. But—when Bob Bishop said to me "what is this I hear—that you don't want city work because the fees are too small" I thought it best to investigate the source. (Bob referred to Bureau of Recreation Playgrounds etc.) I called Bassett. he was most surprised about the rumor and advised me to see Mann about work. I happen to know he made much effort to get a playground for Geddes which he did get for him. I knew by his unwillingness to do the same for me that he must harbor some definite resentment. Then again some of our "friends" in the profession can always make a little "harmless" remark about my "superiority". Believe me Anne I don't care, now, so much because

Mitchell Kaufmann, vice president of Pennsylvania Railroad

Lewis Stevens, Philadelphia City Councilman

Bob Bishop, architect in partnership with Newcomb Montgomery

Sidney Martin, Philadelphia architect

Bassett, worked at the Bureau of Recreation

Frederick Mann, head of the Bureau of Recreation

147

it can't harm me in the long run as long as I have the backing of men high up in the
Administration. But I do need work. All my projects are still to be gotten as jobs.

I am starting the house for the Adlers and the De Vores. I will send you my plans for your
suggestions soon as I have something. Both houses are small on present terms (about $40,000
each) Still some waiting on the State Department work. Melamed will come thru soon—
also another Union alteration. I have a feeling that all things will break loose soon but now
I am living on hope and expectation. Today I sent off the two copies of P/A I wrote in my
last letter about. Incidentally I enclosed $20.00 in the last letter and I hope you got it.
* I am most disturbed in your last letter about your social apprehensions and please note my*
funny words not like me. If you still feel insecure you might suggest another site to send
our missiles to. This short letter is deplorable I know but I do want to tell you about latest
developments on the god damned Center of Philadelphia. Pretty soon I will be completely
cured and I won't care one way or another. that may come with foreign work which
I really more than ever hope for. All my love to Alex and you and give my regards to Bill
Anna and the kids. You must excuse this drab letter and consider it as just a memorandum.
I want to get into the swing again of writing more often. I am terribly impatient to send
this off to you and Alex.

House for Mr. and Mrs.
Weber DeVore, Springfield
Township, Pa., 1954–55
(unbuilt)

All my love, Lou xxxxxxx

148

18 June 1954

Dearest Anne

Yesterday I wrote you—Today I received your letter of June 12–13 which made me sad,
helpless and feel stupid and guilty. We are both so apart from things we so normally
did together that your present state of unhappiness and insecurity stem from it. You need
me I know and I need you. I also want to hug you and kiss you like mad. This depressing
state of things for you in Rome expressed really for the first time with such glaring certainty
just tears the heart out of me. Things around here are lousy so far but I am constantly—
hopeful. Nothing is going to let me down. I must get work—big work—otherwise my whole
sense of courage—pride—will to work—will fold up also whatever I hold deep in my
desire to live a life good for both of us will also suffer. Courage! I know it's easier to say
than realize—Courage! and hope we both must have lots of. I am going today to put a
substantial sum in your account. I must think hard and work some kind of shenanigans
to accomplish it. But I promise you that I will try very very hard, so that you will have
as much freedom of movement as possible and be proud as one like you deserves so much
to be of both yourself and me.

I believe that the Jewish Community Building owes me $500.00. If that is so and I will check soon I will try to have them give it to me in cash. In so doing I can deposit that amount in your name. That is one idea. I hope I can do this soon.

Alex sounds wonderful. How I should like to see her and hold her. I am not really a bad sort though I am a picklepuss and an apprehensive-bound nit wit. It's easy for me to joke a bit only because I have the advantage of working away at my job which you cannot do. That I think is most terrible and also your lack of independence from the home that can never be your home[. . . .] This one page must suffice. Your long letter was not too easy to read believe me. I am going to try to read it again tonight but right now I will close and I will try to write you in a few days.

All my love Lou xxxxxxx

21 June 1954

Dearest Anne

No word as yet from the State Department and I understand from another source that it may take 3 or 4 months yet before anything is decided there. Your intuitions about Turkey are interesting because I was thinking that some such remote place would be my lot which of course is "OK by me." Something must happen to release the tremendous tension I feel the sudden emergence of many problems has caused. Money damned damned money!— Your income portability problems—your taunting hints of how to be released from them—no immediate work in sight which means so far no new source of income—very discouraging news from California—(my mother, in addition to failing eyes, has developed an infection from her diabetes which could mean anything)—my continuing deliberate habit of staying away from home (really Sue) and continued hounding about—why? I feel terrible about Sue. She is growing up fine who needs, like every girl, the love of a man and who expressed that to me with her question of why don't I come home once in a while. I am trying continually to make them feel no need for me—Well I'm trying!—What keeps me up is confidence in the final outcome—hope—and a dogged patience and Sanity. Until recently I felt encouraged knowing your faith in me—your understanding of my frame of mind—I feel your unhappiness and I am in turn depressed no end.

Where the first page is blue this page may have more light. Bacon called to tell me that Willo saw the model of P.C. and environs and likes it very much. I had yesterday worked very late to develop a building for the State. I chose as a possible site the circle between 15th and 16th Penna. Boul. and North Arch St. The building itself followed the circle in this way.

[sketch]

I like an open space very much more in that particular space but I felt that the auto-mobile is causing the characteristics of consolidation and dispersion at the same time. The State Authorities want to move to Broad and Spring Garden. I say and so do others that it would be best if they were in the center of town. My argument is that the State building, 350,000 sq. ft. (as big as one of the Uris buildings) would place another strong energetic life into the center thereby actuating new movement there and may turn the trick of com-plete development up to expectations,—where now it could die half done. Consolidation means economic stability. Consolidation means of course depleting other areas and forcing abandonment of other areas but it is the present method by which new open spaces will be established by neglect of one area and by the movement toward consolidation of such areas as Penn Center. Dispersion or decentralization as the opposite is the other obvious result of the automobile. So you get

[sketch with notes]

Well more about the building. Willo liked the building very much. It looks like the design of a crown with the 6 major facets and six minor truncated ones forming an interior hexagon. Each six major contains about 8,000 sq. ft. the minor elements are the elevator and circulation area. The center is an open court connecting with the concourse and is about 150' across (about 40' wider than Broad St.) When Bacon called he made particular mention about how beautiful he thought the building was but felt (like I do too) that the open space was much more to be desired. I won a point though in proving my ability as an architect and that even if I had to be forced against my will to produce a work it could still be significant. (I am glad you know me for what I am otherwise my last sentence would certainly be taken as pure conceit.) (Actually I am delighted to be of service and all I really demand is recognition).

Willo and Ed B. both believe that my Penn Center East Idea is terrific which accompanies the idea of a new Market Street. I told you in my last letter that Stevens said I should design one of the buildings. Well I called him again on Saturday and he repeated that he is anxious to have me do one of the buildings. I might I figure win out on the central city deal by more work. But I am also aware of snakes in the grass. I still don't trust Willo.

A Jaruta (Mexican name I forgot) came with praise on seeing the Gallery. Bob Geddes came back to say it's great. George still sings my praises. I should be happy but I am not really. My head swims with conflicts a will to lead a life of love around me with you the vortex— no strings and it's stronger than the heaviest cord no knots and it's stronger than heaviest

Where the first page is blue the page may have more light. Bacon
called to tell me that Wilso saw the model of P.C. and environs and likes
it very much. I had yesterday worked very late to develop a building
for the state, I chose as a ~~possible~~ the circle between 15th and 16th Penna.
Boul. and North Broad st. ~~possible site~~ The building itself followed the

circle in this way ↓   I like an open space very much more in that

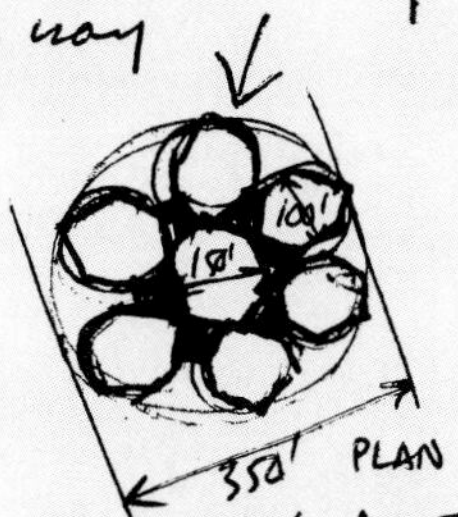

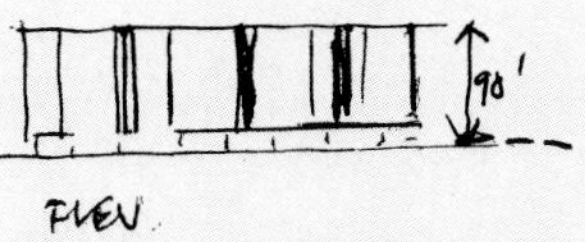

PLAN

350'   PLAN

particular space but I feel that the automobile is causing the
characteristics of consolidation and dispersion at the same time.
The State authorities want to move to Broad and Spring Garden. I say and so
do other that it would be best if they were in the center of town. My argument
is that the State building of 350,000 sq ft. (as big as one of the Uris buildings) would
place another strong energetic life into the center thereby actuating new
movement there and away when the traffic of complete development up to
speculations, — who now it cannot die half done. Consolidation means
economic stability. Consolidation means of course depleting other areas,
and forcing abandonment of other areas but it is the present method by
which new open spaces will be established by neglect (and by
the movement toward consolidation of small area as Penn Center.
Dispersion by or decentralization is the opposite so is the obvious
uses of the automobile. so you see.

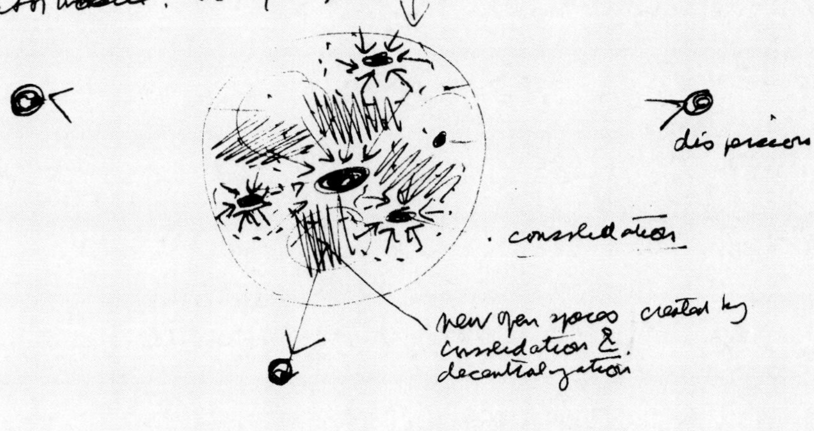

dispersion

consolidation

new open spaces created by
consolidation &
decentralization

*chains. I sent you another $20.00 the other day. I hope you received same. I did not
deposit additional yet don't have will try to go thru with the $500.00 deal I don't know
I never tried such a thing. Please write me a time card it's the only way right now.
I will call New Haven soon.*

Lots and lots of love to Alex and You,

Lou xxxxxxx

22 June 1954

Dearest Anne

I sent you the 2 editions of [Progressive Architecture] *by earlier mail. Those will get to you
rather later now that I received the tear sheets I sent them to you in the meantime.
In the books you will read the comments in full, referred to on p. 101. I think the coverage
is fair—you will notice that the captions under the photos have some quotes but don't refer
to who said them. They used my words as though they were theirs. It's appalling how
barren most people are. This magazine missed the big idea except in the opening statement
on page 89. But the comments of architects from whom I received letters are really good
and of course the excerpts from comments on p. 101 are also very complimentary. I saw Ted
White at the Art Alliance. He said to me, in his usual manner, that any time he mentions
my name in an off-hand manner to* [George Howe]—*G.H. reminds him that I am a great
man—fancy that! He sure doesn't show it but G.H. does think a great deal of me,
and I understand you do too!*

Ted White, Philadelphia
architect

Note the new stationery—too much?

Sent you a letter last night

Exhausted writing

L   O   V   E

Lou

Dearest Anny

It was wonderful to receive your recent mail all about Alexandra. The pictures
you sent are so awakening of reality. I kept thinking of the night with you also in July
and the month after when you told me about the possibility of Alex. I remember
as though it was yesterday the night I left you on the boat—that night especially I felt
a great love for you. I also felt a hope that all would turn out for the best—how?
I did not know—how? I still don't know except that I have not lost hope and at times
I am quite confident. I am I know a terrible pickle puss fungingi puss and a lot of
other pusses. Alex is wonderful looking and I agree has a distinct personality.
I believe she does look like me somewhat although in her more serious poses looks
very much like you.

Now may I be permitted to talk about other things for a moment. This money
business comes as you I am sure know by now at a lousy time when I have practically
nothing and can expect only little for several months. In addition to my ordinary
expenses I have obligated myself to have some extensive dental work done. My teeth
which were missing for many years have caused the others to be displaced so badly
that I was in danger of losing quite a number. In saving them I have to have a number
of them (in the molar section) capped and bridged (whatever the hell it is) and it is
very expensive—the work is half done and the bill is coming up any moment.
This is a bit of most romantic news but can't be helped. I deposited $50.00 in your
account and if you will please send me post haste a time card amounting to $150.00
I believe I can manage to deposit that amount in your account. It must be terrible to
have to put up with what you do knowing your proud temperament it must be hell
for you. I agree with all your intentions about going away but I hope you don't isolate
yourself too much from the centers of activities. After all you are a doer and I am
glad you mentioned going to the library of the [American] Academy and that you will
see a couple of new faces and maybe hear a few chit chats about our ilk.

Mr. Meyer, unknown to
Tyng

I heard from [————] that Mr. Meyer is in New York. You remember we went to visit him
(with the Chinese art collection). His sec'y called informing me that the ground is now
negotiated and he asked me about how I wanted the survey made of the ground.
Mr. Meyer is in Europe and will be back in 5 weeks to sign a contract with me. That
should be a good job to work on for you now. You know his requirements. We were
talking about space rather formal well related to the piney exterior. It might be

153

possible to make the house of light materials though I have some recollection of his
liking for stone. Well what's the difference—try it one way or another. Have some fun
and maybe something really swell will result. Just remember this—that whatever
you do think first about the nature of the problem from which the order is derived and
that means to do it can be a circumstantial condition. It should not deter if the
nature and order are satisfied.

I was visited by a congregation who want a synagogue built. (This is not the group
who I mentioned before). They decided on me and I am being asked to develop
a preliminary idea of my thoughts on Synagogue. This is a good size job. I will get no
money now and I don't care. I am confident that the conditions they set are sincerely
made and am also confident that I can produce a synagogue they will like. I am
working on this now. I have until September 10 to do the imagining. I believe it will
cost about from 3/4 to 1 million dollars.

Adath Jeshurun Synagogue
and School, Philadelphia,
Pa., 1954–55 (unbuilt)

[sketches with notes]

Must go to New York tomorrow to make arrangement for article in PERSPECTIVES USA.
Must get this off to you before midnight—nearly so now.

With lots and lots of love to you and Alex

Lou xxxxxxx

I heard from that Mr. Myers in New York (you remember we went to visit him with the Chinese art collection) His secy called informing me that the ground is now negotiated on he asked me about how I wanted to survey made 3th ground, Mr, Myers is in Europe and will be back in 5 weeks to sign a contract with me, That should be a good job to work on for you now. You know his requirements. We are talking about space rather formal well related to the exterior (privacy). It might be possible to make the house of light materials though I have some recollection of his liking for stone. Well what its difference. Try it one way or another, I have some [new and may be something really excellence nice result. Just remember this— That whatever you do think first about the nature of the problem from which the order is derived and That means to do it can be a circumstantial condition. Materns not deter if the natures in order are established.

I was written by a congregation who want a synagogue built (This is not the group who I mentioned before) They decided on me and I am being asked to develop a preliminary idea from my thoughts on Synagogue. This is a good size Job I will get no money now and I don't care. I am confident that the conditions they set are sincerely made and am also confident that I can produce a synagogue they will like. I am working on this now. I have until September 10 to do the imagining. The whole it will cost about from 3/4 to 1 million dollars.

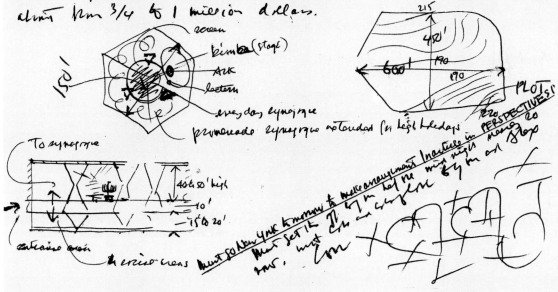

5 July 1954

Dearest Anny:

Your last pencil letter made me feel so well to think that you have revived your will to work. Your will is contagious because I needed stimulation too. To work on 3-D construction with you would be delightful and probably would be the only way to amount to anything from my part. Get acquainted with the material in Rome—who is doing what and write your opinion from that angle first. Doug Haskell could then be reached by me and on that basis and maybe I could arrange a tangible means of supplying the resource for work abroad. Certainly I look with favor at your idea and I would be most stimulated to work with you. I went out for a beer with Pen just about an hour ago. Beer loosens the tongue. I complained that I was bogged down in the last week or so—could not persevere and that I need someone to kick me in the pants and say "get to work and no nonsense out of you." Pen then ventured that the only one who could do this is you (he said "Anny") she has the tenacity, the indestructible will to carry out what she starts to do. I believe he misses you too. There are I believe very few people who really understand the importance to architecture of the space frame. As you say, no one has tackled the multi-story space idea. When I show my slides on the multi-story building (not necessarily using the diagonal column system or vertical space frame.) The one which goes like this

[sketch]

with the growing column, they are really taken with it. The transitional aspects of this tower is what they are willing to accept and I don't see why it is not OK on a small square building of type. Thus not clearly a space frame but has infinitely more reasons to exist than the Lever Building considering the base for 1. wind 2. for the meat (space) in proportion to the elevator concentration. The stories above are narrower for the precisely opposite reasons.

I wrote you last time about the synagogue job and the limited funds I have to work with there. I am not worried if I can produce a good building and I appeared enthusiastic a few days ago but I worked on the cubages and there my intuitive sense did me dirt. I had 2 x the required cubage and you know what that does to a scheme—there just ain't one. Now I am beginning over again, maybe can incorporate the school rooms with the form of the synagogue. I believe the nature of the 2 functions are not incompatible both being sectarian. Maybe the building must be made square to simplify the shape of the classrooms under.

Dearest Anny;

Your last pencil letter made me feel so well to think that you have turned your mind to work. Your will is contagious because I needed stimulation too. To work on 3 D construction with you would be delightful and personable would be the only way it would amount to anything from my part. Get acquainted with the material in Rome, who is doing what and write your position from this angle first. Any [...] could then be reached by me and that basis it may be I could arrange a tangible means of supplying the resources for work abroad. Certainly I work with form at your side and I would be most stimulated to work with you. I went out for a beer with Pen just about an hour ago. Beer loosens the tongue, I complained that I was bogged down, in the last week or so cannot persevere and that I need some me to kick me in the pants or say "get to work, and no nonsense out of you." Pen then ventured that the only me who could do this is you (leave in "Anny") else has the tenacity the understanding will to carry out what one starts to do, I believe he means you too. There are I believe very few people who really understand the importance to architecture of the space frame. As you say no one has tackled the multi-story space idea. When I show my ideas on the multi-story building (not necessarily using the diagonal column system or vertical space frame) the one which gives like this [...] with a growing column they are really taken with it. The transitional aspect of this [...] tower is what they are willing to accept. I admit see only it is not [...] OK on a small square building type. This not clearly a space [...] but has infinitely more reasons to point than the lower building considering the base for 1. Wind 2 for the meat (space) in proportion to the common concentration. The clues alone are narrow for the precisely opposite reasons.

I write you last time about the synagogue jobs and the theater (which I shall work with them). I am not worried if I can produce a good building and I appeared enthusiastic a few days ago but I worked out an acoustics and then my intuitive sense did me dirt. I had 2X the required cubage and you know what that does to a screen — there just aint one. Now I am beginning me again maybe I can incorporate the active rooms with the [] form of the synagogue. Notice the nature of the 2 functions are not incompatible seeing of the recticion. Maybe the building must be made square to supress the shape of the class rooms under.

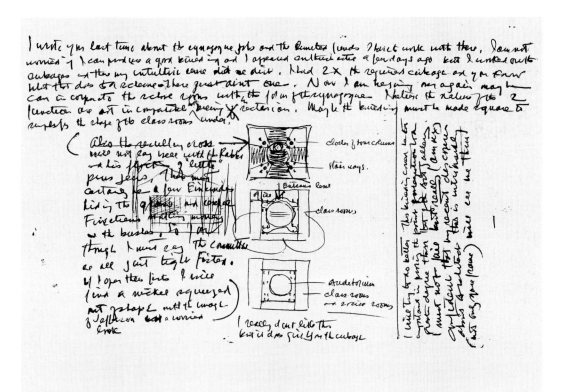

(Also the recital [] cross will not say well with the Rabbi and his flock of little pews Jews. There must certainly be a few Einsteins living in the [] and where Franklins matters money — the busses. So I am though I must say the committee are all just tight fisted. If I open their [] I will find a nickel squeezed out perhaps with the image of Jefferson and a worried look

I really don't like this but it does give you the cubage

Clocks of tower clums

Stair ways.

Balcons here

class room

Auditorium class room and active rooms

[sketches with notes] cluster of four columns / stairways / entrance level / office / classrooms / Auditorium / classrooms and social rooms / I really don't like this but it does give you the cubage.

(also the resulting cross will not lay well with the Rabbi and his flock of "little" pious Jews. There must certainly be a few Einbinders hiding [in] the grasses and several Finesteins making money in the bushes, so far though I must say the committee are all just tight fisted. If I open their fists I will find a nickel squeezed out of shape with the image of Jefferson with a worried look.)

I will try to do better. This building could be too important in proving the point of integration to a greater degree than that of the Art Gallery. I must not fail but really I am very confident that my recent discoveries about Architecture that is intrinsic (not only space frame) will see thru.

I must [now] more than ever put my shoulder to the wheel. Constantly events cross and recross my mind—things that I should have done and things I should not have done. I confess that here lately I am somewhat worse about myself than usual. There are explanations, some of which you know about, others which will iron themselves out I hope. But here I am crying in my beer when I should be exploring things and feeling well because your outlook is again enthusiastic for accomplishment. Your charm depends on your courage and your convictions and your tenacious will, your beautiful work—and the more truthful evolvement of even better work thru practice and experience. Sure I will encourage you. In that field I am an expert who feels confident to guide others with a sure hand. (Experts of course can do little for themselves—they need experts to help them). Anyway wisdom points to no worry. time proves wisdom right. Obligations are destructive of freedom. Freedom without order is impossible. Order releases freedom. How many incongruent things can the mind think of. What I am trying to say is that the greatest hope can be derived out of the fruits of labors. The accomplishments are the stones of a great fortress against the poisonous points of view of our present social system. I can't say social order because order can produce only good designs. You should be thoroughly hot in Rome this time of year (never experienced Rome or Italy in summer). Keep cool and give my love to everyone

All my love to you and Alex

Lou xxxxxxx

Dearest Anne

I am reminded this being Saturday that I have not bathed today. There is every reason that I should have since it is very hot and sultry. I am greatly in need of a vacation being touchy as blazes one reason—I called Ralph Walker chairman of this foreign work business—asked him about what to expect since I heard Wurster got a job in Hong Kong— I very jokingly mentioned what Belluschi told me about being on top of the list— Mr. Walker the almighty "800 men office Mr. Walker" said "well I don't know if you're on top of the list I know only you are on the list." One must of course never assume his position as better. I am always conscious of that but it seems that no one will assume your position for you. You've got to assume something. I am also not so sure that I am unemotional enough to look at things objectively enough. I am going to Washington on Monday to look around a bit. Being in a lousy frame of mind it might do me some good. I had a little bright moment today—Melamed called to tell me they acquired a property to build on and that I am going to be called on soon to prepare the plans. I shall ask them for a fair retainer so I can keep going. Even with all the things I have to work on— synagogue—2 houses (another coming soon) and some odd things I don't have any resources to go on. Well let's not cry in our soup. Flash! Kling got an honor award from the A.I.A. (National Convention) for the Lankenau Hospital (that awful hulk on a hill near Genel) Stubbins was on the jury this time and he was on it the last show of the Chapter where Kling got nothing for it. Honest to goodness. What price Architecture! I adored your last letter because it was cheerful and hopeful and had a breath of you of old—enthusiastic, a desire to do great things, to pitch in and cut the red tape + not so much caution so much security so much strings and all the rest of the apprehensions which I can gather more of in a short time than anyone and hate myself for. Well am I touchy!—Went to see the Clausses last Sunday. Jane called me thinking that Esther was on vacation. We had a pleasant time together they are very nice. They asked about you of course. I told them great things about you when you were in the office before you left and about how wonderful you are. I am sure that my reaction to any questions about you must show on my face or speech because I do miss you.

Today I am most barren having had a most uneventful week. Dave is away and the lot of supervision (with Pen) came on me. Ken Day of course is always there to add the ZIP/ which makes things rip along. Things can go wrong under their noses things which could ruin the job, but they thumb thru the specs for the answer where change or horse sense is necessary. An example of this—we are using screw ties throughout—they (the screw ties) leave a hole about 1″ deep after the forms are removed. This gives a strong construction rhythm to the concrete and tends to erase some of the pour disfigurings. Now they come to the penthouse and the contractor decides to form up without those

Kahn was attempting to secure a commission from the State Department, where Ralph Walker was chairman of a committee for U.S. State Department buildings abroad.

Hugh Stubbins, Boston architect

Kenneth Day, a principal associate with Kahn and Louis E. McAllister

159

ties (they use snap ties which have to be snapped off resulting in a nasty surface scar).
Nothing is done! The field tells me when it's already formed. Kenneth Day looks thru the
specs (where it is not mentioned to do as we like) and says we can do nothing. I recall
the verbal agreement and insist that the pouring be delayed until properly done. Well I will
know how I made out on Monday. Very very interesting to you I am sure! but I did raise
bloody hell on the phone and when I hung up K. D. said he agreed with me. but now
the whole staff on the job will say I am an arbitrary bitch to get along with where Mr. Day
was calm and is always a gentleman. Calm = lousy work—a most unworthy reward in our
field. The Mill Creek drawings (redevelopment) I believe I told you have been finished
a long while ago. We just got in one plan which was printed. It looks good, I will send you
what I feel you will enjoy seeing. I am tickled that you are tickled about the City Hall
mention. Poor reporting but deserving credit. I am anxious to hear about your exploits
with the outside world. I am most glad that you are planning to see people and do
things. I can well understand your desire to do so. I suppose that P/A has arrived in Rome.
That should make you feel somewhat better about getting back into the circle of archi-
tects. Isn't it the truth though that very few indeed understand the modern
potentialities in the same way we do.

Nature of space	*Order*	*Design*
desire	*seed*	*composition*
what do you want?	*What are the principles which lead to its being.*	*What are the circumstances (environment) which are at play?*

From an Order of common usage emerges style.
Design does not evolve style. Imagery is gotten from order.
etc., etc.
This meets the approval of George Howe

All my love to Alex and you Anne. xxxxxxx

I hope I get that foreign job soon but from indications NOT TOO SOON. They tell me
that no appropriations are yet made. It might be another 6 mos.

Dearest Anny

I just received your letter of the 7th and glad you just made my $20.00 letter of July 1. Just had that bill sort of hanging around the drawer / not used to a bill of that denomination. You got a check in the mail from the Treasurer of the United States (a refund on taxes) for $265.95. I opened the letter because I know you would have had me do it. I was just about to place the stamps on the original to forward when I realized that it might be intercepted (though I did not know the amount) Oh hell no matter what crossed my mind I opened it (excuse) and will deposit it in your account. I wrote you but a few days ago and as I remember I also had very little to say except hope about everything. I just came from Washington (as I wrote) and deposited the brochure they requested. There were many folders probably too many (including Perspecta *and my European sketches). A letter of transmittal indicated my willingness to serve anywhere. My one concern was that I hoped that Belluschi could be one of the judges as to where and what for me because I could not expect the best from Shepley nor Walker who are the other members of the committee. But I found out that Belluschi is coming back shortly probably in a few weeks for the next meeting. So I hope I am put on the active list soon. What I should like to do is a new embassy for Rome! If you see Belluschi you might mention jokingly that I wrote you hoping that that were my problem. I can feel a problem like that thru every fibre of me. With my classical training and my modern ideas. This is going to be a real short one Anne because I really wanted only to tell you that you received this nice check (I hope it isn't a mistake) and that after a week of doldrums I intend to today go to work again and try to forget or take a different attitude toward things that bother me very much. If I work a good solution to the synagogue problem may result and that would please me very much and get my confidence back. Your [tetrahedral] animals are nice but I really hoped you would think about the little sketches I drew. Maybe they were too indefinite as to size so I will try to send you a drawing next time to scale which you might work on—if you cared to of course. Please excuse my breezy emptiness of content in this letter it's really awful to send nothing and take so long saying it.*

With love to Alex and my dear dear Anny

    Lou xxxxxxx

Henry Richardson Shepley, Boston architect

Ralph Walker, New York architect

161

Dearest Anny

Just received your 4 pages of July 13–14 with the F. LL. W insert. You took just one look and knew we could do better. The only thing that is different is that the one which I am doing must cost no more than $750,000 which must include the school as well as 20 classrooms offices and a social hall. I don't need the height he shows and I believe I can economize in other respects but the difficulty is really very great. I have decided however to show by Sept 10 what I believe in and not worry about the budget. Today in writing to you I want to send you the receipts of the bank deposits I made so you can be up to date. I write as though I have been depositing more frequently. Anny dear I don't have it this moment yet but I will in a few weeks I believe, though even then not too much if I am to use the money for necessary resources to accomplish the work. I must hire a few people. Dave—Mill Creek Housing, Spohn, De Vore House—I need people for the Synagogue and for the Health Center (Melamed) which job I just got today in the mail. That last is going to be nice as far as money goes—They pay on the nose—the commission is not big, possibly $400,000 but the commission on a 7% basis would be about $30,000. I am going to make better arrangements regarding the engineering than I have made before. This letter is for the birds—Oh I forgot to tell you that the De Vores were in (nice people) They like my scheme for the house.

[sketch with notes] garage / 6 posts to each 24 x 24 section / columns doubled when 2 sections meet / outside room

If you can read that little plan you're good. Will send you a print of the plan when it's made—(Monday or Tuesday). I have only a model now. Excuse the short short letter. I had a few minutes of uninterrupted time before another meeting I have tonight.

All my love to Alex and you.

Lou xxxxxxx

21 July 1954

Dearest Anny

I forgot to mention how much I liked your suggestions for the synagogue shapes. I think you will agree that the deliberate use of the Star of David may boomerang— be thought of as a tired or obvious shape—I think though that it answers the problems of the greater auditorium on the high holidays very well. Right now it still stands the way it was several weeks ago.

[sketches with notes] focal area / supports / main seating / added seating / circulation / column / stair / one arrives from the bottom (that is from below) by the stairway at the 3 points of support.

I am struggling with the budget to make it not exceed $1,000,000. the one you sent of Wright's to seat 1200 is to cost $750,000 (I don't believe he can make it). But I am to seat 1500 and must include 20 classrooms offices and a social hall for not much more money. I have employed a young man from the U. of P. (one of my students) to help me on it. He is making only seating diagrams for me now. He is sensitive very good. Name Jouco Illvonen (Finn) fine looking and is supposed to be a concert violinist (gave it up doesn't like to talk about it) (That part is for the birds) So far also I don't have much to go on but do expect soon to give you prints for your most valued critique. I am going to start that Health Center for Melamed soon (He hasn't arranged for contract yet) The 2 houses are going slowly with Pen working on them. I told you we had a good session with the clients in which Bob V. also participated. Bob is a very good architect. He looks for the right things and is very well backgrounded historically which helps his judgement. The unfamil- iar however still scares him—though he is likely to accept things new which I know will not look well. But give him just a short time and he I believe is going to be one of our best if and when he gets the work. Cornelia Hahn is here this evening working with Dave on the Mill Creek Landscape drawings, which part of the contract is going to be rebid. She seems more relaxed less confused less likely to jump to change her mind to suit the political situation of the moment. I guess her Peter is doing her good.

163

Cornelia Hahn, landscape architect, and her husband, Peter Oberlander, both attended the Harvard Graduate School of Design with Tyng.

Wanda Nostrum of the Container Corporation

No word yet about foreign work. I was also asked to do a Jewish Community Building in Trenton, N.J. Will meet the committee next week. Wanda called me to offer that I do a supermarket. Those jobs in the hand and in the bush in addition to the New York house for Meyer should keep me busy. But, out of all I have but a retainer of $1,000 from the Synagogue which amount must do until Sept 10 day of presentation. Soon I shall have a little money—when I collect for preliminaries on the houses, from Melamed on the Health Center. To start the Health Center I need another person I believe (unless Dave runs out of work which I expect) but must wait for money. Soon? I must wait.

I have a feeling I shall hear soon from the State Department one way or another.
This job interests me mainly because of the unknown surprise awaiting its arrival. I will
of course write you as soon as I hear any interesting news.

I am being introduced all around as the ———architect! Too embarrassing to say.
Seems that all have known this for years. You and I know how much we must accomplish
to be ———. and how far we have still to go. and that it will always be far to go for
those who have chosen long distances to travel and decided that they must be extended
more time to complete to some degree this mission. With a late start as I believe is
true in my case (especially in regards to architecture). I must not forget however that the
training I had in other related fields made it possible to emerge from a thoroughly
misguided start to one of a relatively realistic direction respected by quite a few but
those few still waiting to be shown more, to make sure.

This note is one of those dashy ones but should not be considered lightly because
I wanted to write to you and Alex as I sat down, I said "I must now write to Anny—I can
see her as though she sits beside me." I received a telephone call from California. My father
is in the hospital about to be operated on. They were quite upset—he was on oxygen—
looked like I had to fly there. I said I would call back that midnight (9 o'clock their time).
I called to find to my relief that he was better and resting and somewhat more articulate
and joking about life. He has a terrific spirit and will to live and I gave them the
Kahn brand of encouragement which tolerates nothing but life. I hope secretly for
the best and I know you do too.

Love and love and love

  Lou xxxxxxx

Dearest Anny

Your 6 page letter came late Friday and I was happy to feel that your will to work has come back. As ever your suggestions of structures are stimulating and as I mentioned in previous letters I should like you to contribute more concretely—this when I send you more data to work from. The Meyer House is not signed up yet but am sure it will be soon. Your suggestion of a combination wood and steel is wonderful and I think we ought to do it. I am constantly reviewing possibilities in the light of the problems and such an area spanning idea supported by (on as you say stone coming up from the ground) could be a beautiful expression of order. I always thought that the house should be thus

[sketch with notes] ceiling / stone rooms supports

and if the points of support of the roof structure could fall in an orderly fashion on the walls it matters little what the wall's shape is. This being Saturday I can't get you a print of the De Vore House but I will attempt to sketch it for you at a larger scale (enclosed). The synagogue is coming slowly and not still to my satisfaction. Again I believe that the symbolism should not dominate the shape of the building, as [Star of David], though I believe it functions very well. Besides indulging in the pleasure of writing to you I had another purpose to write and that to enclose a copy (tentative 1/2 scale) run off of the Mill Creek plot plan. I believe it is about the way you remembered it when you sailed. Now it makes me think how long ago since you sailed and how you looked when I waved you so long! Still got my beret. Your little vignettes on Alex are delightful—It seems that I have written quite often lately. I can't believe myself and don't get too used to it because it just ain't natural.

A thought comes to me that in suggesting construction it's got to be within reason for the time we have to conceive it and build, but it must answer the new problems in the new way, otherwise it is completely "for the birds". This [sketch] triangular beam idea (Samuely) is immediately applicable (very good in concrete) (fair in wood) (good in steel) is therefore within the killing time demands of the client. On the Adler House I believe we could benefit from time a little more. Please excuse this short one because I have somehow little to report though I know I left many things unanswered which I must reserve for later. I don't feel particularly chatty.

With lots and lots of love to you and Alex

Lou xxxxxxx

Dearest Anny

Saturday July 24' 54

Your 6 page letter came late Tuesday and I was happy to feel that your nice to work has come back. As ever your suggestions of stimulus are stimulating and as I mentioned in previous letters, I should tell you to contribute more constantly — Then when I need you more data to work from. The Meyer House is not signed up yet but am now it will be soon. Your suggestion of incorporating wood and steel is workable and I think we ought do it. I am constantly bringing permutation with respect of the problems and such an area spanning idea [supported by (or as you say stone coming up from the ground)] echoed here a beautiful expression, matter of order — I always thought that the house should be thus and if the points of support could fall in an easy fashion on — the walls it matters little what the walls shape is. This being Saturday I can't get you a print of the De Vore House but I will attempt to sketch it for you at a larger scale (enclosed) The zynograph is coming along and not steel to my satisfaction. Again I believe that the zynograph should not dominate the shape of the building, so — though I believe it function very well. Besides in dashing in of pleasure of writing to you I had another purpose to write, and that is enclose a copy (tentative ½ scale) run off of the Mac Creek PLOT PLAN. I believe it is about the way you remembered it when you called, — Now it makes me think how long ago since you called and how you looked when I called you so long! I got my kernel? Your little vignettes on Alex are delightful — It seems that I have written quite often lately I can't believe myself and don't get too speed to it because it just aint natural —

A thought comes to me. That a supporting construction has got to be well in reason for the time we have to conceive it as timed, but it must answer the new problems in a new way our time is completely "In the birds". They very △△ meaning a beam idea (Samuels) is immediately applicable (good in concrete) (fair in wood) (good in steel) — is not those with in the killing time demands of the client. The Adler house I believe we could benefit from too. A little more. Please excuse the short one because I have some too little to report though I know I left many things unanswered which I must reserve for later. I don't feel particularly chatty

with love and — to you and Alex

166

ceiling

stone coming up supports.

24 July 1954—page 1

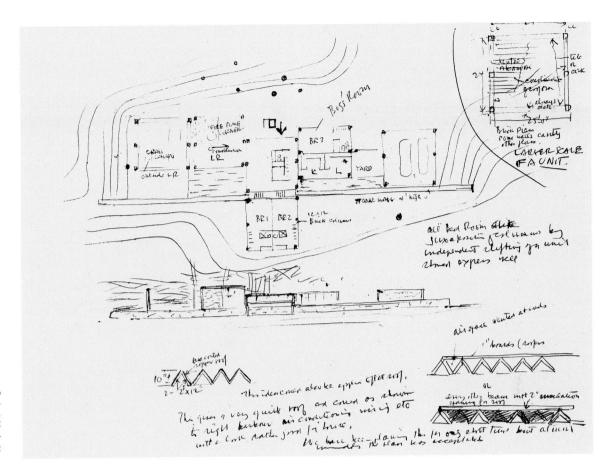

[sketch with notes, plan and elevation] grass lawn outside L.R. / fire place
corner / construction / L.R. / B.R. 1 / B.R.2 / B.R. 3 boy's room / K, L, yard /
stone wall 4' high / 12 x 12 brick columns / all bed rooms alike,
juxtaposition of columns by independent shifting of a unit should
express well

[sketch with notes, "larger scale of a Unit"] 24' x 24' /
lintel or beam over / construction of roof over / tile or cork / always slate /
brick piers, some walls cavity others glass.

[sketch with notes, bottom of page] lead coated copper roof /
this idea could also be applied to flat roof / air space vented at ends /
1" boards (roofers) or every other beam with 2" of insulation,
spanning for roof / this gives a very quiet roof and could as shown to right
harbor airconditioning, wiring etc. with a look rather good for
the house. We have been planning this for only short time, but almost
immediately the plan was acceptable.

Dearest Anny

I am very ashamed Anny dear for not writing for some time. My excuses could be tolerated but there really is no excuse. I several times had a few moments of leisure and will to write, but it has been one charette after another trying to evolve the structure for the synagogue which (though still not right) is now coming along. I had to go to New Haven too in order to save their doing some badly conceived additions to the courts and the interior. What they did in my absence is unbelievably bad. They just don't know how to keep the spirit of the place up and around them are many who do know how. but the ones in charge are really "for the birds." Your last most fabulous letter with equally fabulous sketches of space frame ideas was wonderfully received not only by me but by those I showed it to. The overlapping criss crossing of wood joists with connectors is a good idea but I have modified it thus for the more direct expression of structural need.

[sketch with notes] [. . .] / more on edges / less material in center / support

I am going to show it to Nick [Gianopolous's] outfit. I have an arrangement with them to help on all 3-D work. Etter, the PhD on 3-D from M.I.T. is now in their firm.

Nick Gianopolous, engineer
based in Philadelphia

Charles Etter

Your beautiful drawings took time so please as I wrote you several times send me your time cards. I have not heard as yet from the State Department about foreign work. I sure hope that doesn't fizzle. I was warned however that it may take more time than I would have it. You're the one who supplied me with the info about Central Africa or South America. I did not receive any notice as to place as yet. I may call Belluschi this week to get the latest dope. I shall write you as soon as I get it.

I have just finished a letter to Sue who is in Camp Deerwood surrounded by music and to my surprise liking it [better] than her hockey. She has suddenly taken a bee line in that direction inspired by a few young people she likes and being told she is good by people she respects in the field. Her flute is very good and her sense of humor is maturing rapidly. This latter development I am most interested in since she'll need it to understand her dad. Now I know we can expect wonderful things from Alex. Willo was over to take a drawing away for publication. I explained to him the latest development of the synagogue which he liked very much. He is still under suspicion as a friend of mine though I know he respects my work. He just came back from seeing the Yale Art Gallery and he had all praise for that. This is also a surprise since his design mindedness should interfere with good reaction. The usual design faults were overlooked because as he himself put it, "It's so damn good that design doesn't matter." I had a visit from the school editors of Perspecta 3. *They showed me some new photos of the Gallery done by one of my students. They are very good. I am told to write a 5 page editorial of my latest theories with sketches. I shall*

Dearest Anny,

Wednesday Aug 18

I am very ashamed Anny dear for not writing for some time. My excuses could be tolerated but there really is no excuse. I several times had a few moments of leisure and need to write but it has been one cigarette after another trying to evolve the structure for the synagogue which (though still not right) is now coming along. I had to go to New Haven too in order to save their doing some badly conceived additions to the courts on the exterior. What they did in my absence is unbelievably bad. They just don't know how to keep the spirit of the place up and around them so many who do know how, but the ones in charge are really "for the birds." Your last most fabulous letter with equally fabulous sketches of space frame idea was wonderfully received not only by me but by those I showed it too. The overlapping criss crossing of wood joints with connectors is a good idea but I have modified it these [drawing] more direct expression of structure need.

4

Truss
more on edges

less material in center

support

2

I am going to show it to Nick's outfit. I have an arrangement with them to keep on all 3 D work. Even the PHD in 3 D from M.I.T. is now in their firm.

your beautiful drawings that time so please as I write you several times send me the time cards. I have not heard as yet from the State department about Foreign work. I still hope that doesn't fizzle. I was warned however that it may take more time than I would take it. You the one who supplied me with the info about Central Africa & South America. I did not receive any notice as to place as yet. I may call Bellanchi this week to get it worked done. I shall write you as soon as I get it.

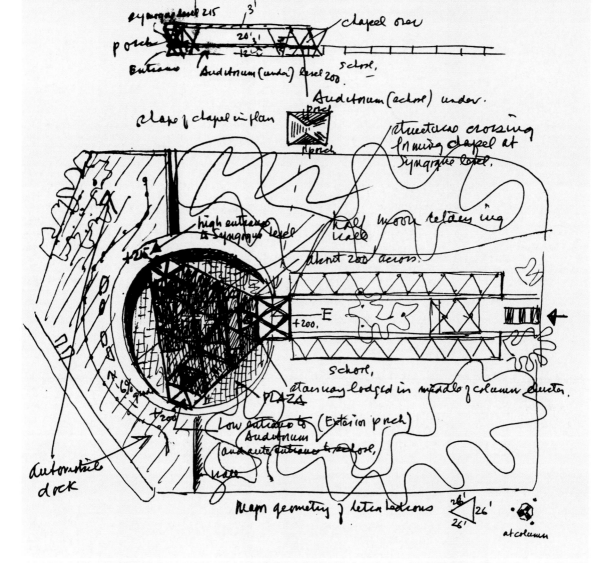

I haven't gotten the drawings back from the clients. They are seeing Macomber factors to get them to bid or take over the construction. One of the committee members was assigned a visit to the gallery and to Macomber. That guy may of course take the restored concrete and may also thank Mac.order to lovely for them. I have my fingers crossed. This lousy sketch will have to serve until I get the plans back or until then send you photostats. I almost like so I'll say much of you but leave just as some ideas on the structure expressing the columns.

synagogue level 215   3'

porch   20'   chapel over

12'

Entrance   Auditorium (under) level 200   school

Auditorium (above) under.

shape of chapel in plan   roof   structure crossing forming chapel at synagogue level.

porch

high entrance to synagogue level   half moon relieving

about 200 across.

+215

+200   E

School.

stairway lodged in middle of column cluster.

PLAZA

+6' grade

+200   Low entrance to (Exterior porch)   Auditorium and auto entrance to school.

Automobile dock

Major geometry of interlocations   26' 26' 26'

at column

be able now to include the synagogue as a good example of order. In the original design
I had the school embodied in the single building. This presented many difficulties—one—
expansion, two—conflicting noise problems. So I decided to separate the two. Basic shape
the same for the synagogue (reduced—better that way) but the appendage is much a relaxed
and familiar affair (construction somewhat same as synagogue) Next page for bad sketch.
I haven't gotten the drawings back from the clients. They are seeing Macomber of Boston
to get them to bid or take over the construction. One of the committee members was
assigned a visit to the Gallery and to Macomber. That guy may of course hate the exposed
concrete and may also think Macomber too fancy for them. I have my fingers crossed.
This lousy sketch will have to serve until I get the plans back and will then send you photo-
stats. I should like it very much if you could give us some ideas on the structure especially
the columns.

[sketch with notes]

The idea basically is a 3-D structure expressing itself as posts for 2 entrances on different
levels and the other entrance is more elaborate and gives room for a chapel (seating
200 or 215 on the synagogue level). The synagogue seats 1500. The stair is in the center
of the 3-D column supports (hollow to take the services) and the effect of going up
the stair from the coat room and lounges below should be good with light from above
lighting the cluster of column supports. I am trying to lay out the seating in a way which
does not follow the angles of the walls. I consider the space not the confining angles.
The interior I hope to perform in our gossamer not sure network very good for synagogue.
Please send me ideas soon after I send you the more accurate sketch when I print them.

Again your last letter was so wonderful to receive and I feel such a terrible skunk for
not writing right away. I am due again soon to spend a few days at Norfolk—remember?
It was so wonderful to sneak into your room I shall never forget the wonder of it.
This time I shall confine myself to sneaking in the bathroom when I have to. It will be
my only vacation but I am quite content because I have work and if everything goes well
especially with the [synagogue] I shall be satisfied. I have my fingers crossed on many
things that concern me and I need not mention one in particular. It is very late Anny and
I am going to close this most selfishly centered letter but though it reads this way
you know me well enough to take it right. I spoke so little about you two so next time
I shall write about that.

With lots and lots and lots of love to you and Alex.

Yours Lou xxxxxxx

Dearest Anny:

So far I have not heard from the State Department. I wish they wouldn't pick you up and throw you down in so short a time. The summer is a draggy time to expect much action so I still have hope to hear soon after the summer vacation period. I received your last 2 page letter and glad to have found your impatience simmered down. When I read the letter before this one I was in the middle of the damnedest set of disappointments (later somewhat straightened out) and the tone of it so difficult for me at that moment that I could gladly have buried myself in the nearest hole. I don't get that way often but that day was unbearable to begin with and then I opened your letter an avalanche of responsibilities poured down on me. Now that I read it again it was good to hear every word of it—it was just the combination—like oysters and ice cream. Today the synagogue people were in. I believe they want the impossible. My figures show that they need $1,000,000.00 They want to build more school space and then pay only $800,000 for the buildings—even more space for less money. I have no contract just a token retainer. I want to build that building like mad. My figures I believe are below what it would take to build it and they want the bakers dozen of bananas for the cost of 6. It already cost me more (much more) than the token retainer and now I really have to get to work. You know in me a dope a real dope who because of anxiety to build a building will finally be left holding the bag. But I am still (I realize as I sit here) determined to show them! They do like the sketches I prepared for them and that is my only hold—since they are as they say unusual and realize that they cannot be copied. The only really solid job in the office is the health center. There I am dealing with civilized people who respect your opinion and don't question costs as they are. I have of course been using the retainer I received from the Health Center for the other job.

So what so something else'll pop up. I don't sound so good nor funny. Don't feel it really.

Your stories of Alex are delightful and I could just see her growing up in such loving arms as yours. I wish things were different too anyway I hope that they will be different. But just the same I feel lost and uncertain and thoroughly, as a result, unbearably unsettled and disturbed. But hope still and all dominates in me and with the new day there is more and more of it. (I didn't intend this to be a cheerful letter and I see I have accomplished just such a tone and I hate myself for it too—mainly because I know how wonderful you are and what you are going thru and how much I would want it to be otherwise, and how unreal my waiting for the circumstantial is.)

The lack of wisdom I showed on the synagogue is what is responsible for my present attitude in the main. I just sent out for Photostats of the damned thing and before I mail

172

this will include. By next letter will include the other work. Should I send a copy to Le Ricolais? You will note that the space frame is not complete (columns straight but could not get around doing it because the idea of the stairway in the center keeps the frame from being as easy thing to do. I haven't found yet the answer but will find it because it is right. I am getting Wambold to make a breakdown of costs to present to the committee which may put an air of rest into the situation. There's hope!

Edgar Wambold, contractor
on Weiss house

[sketch]

I just received mail from 3 of the students working on Perspecta 3. *They had seen the Mill Creek Housing Apartment Buildings. This is what they wrote I quote ". . . It is real great the best of its kind. Your principles will be known far and wide. . ." I am blushing and I keep thinking how much you contributed to the high standard of that job. Now Day is going around proud as a peacock boasting about the apartments which if you remember he was dead against. He defends apartment living now—how ludicrous but how wonderful to be like you in spirit in courage in conviction and how fortunate to be gifted to the point of action. Work and sanity are synonymous interactions. Sanity is impossible without the satisfying products of work. Why my impatience? Because I know how more than ever. How could one keep his patience under such a will to create and make born of how. (I am still waiting for the Photostats so can include them in my letter.) Maybe you could think of what I could write for* Perspecta 3 *on the subject of Nature of Space—Order— Design. Should I look up precedents to prove my point or just begin as though nothing ever happened except what always was there? Give me some hints. It will help to get me started. Its like what the Indian said to the Mermaid—How?*

173

Lancelot Sims, director of
the Philadelphia Housing
Authority

A call just now from Lance Sims reminds me of my delinquency in producing the 3 perspectives of Mill Creek Housing. We did one but the others are not started and must be finished by Sept 1. What a racket. I told him they're started which is a big lie with a little tail of truth. I have a thumbnail sketch.

The photostats came and am anxious to send this off to you.

All my love to Alex and you

Lou xxxxxxx

Dearest Anny:

Now the "situation is the same" only reversed—I haven't heard from you now for some time since I sent you two letters and an insert of the synagogue plans. Your brilliant suggestions on structure are a constant reminder of constructive collaboration with nuances far beyond. I am only now getting around the more possible type of construction for the synagogue with the employment of the angled columns. I found difficulty every time I rely on the engineers. When I think independently I really come up with things. When I lean on them or assume more than they know I get nothing in return. After all the talk about intent I got a measly bitten off match stick construction of unequal members glued with Le Pages glue that fell apart when produced from the vest pocket with a story of how it could be adapted to the problem and fireproofed by blowing asbestos on the members. Those guys can't think outside the book or the last lecture. I am now talking about Charlie Etter. But still I think he will emerge of benefit. I learned that I must talk to them with less enthusiasm and more probing in their minds and training. I found that a star frame means literally a frame of members—the members having direction held

together where three of the members come together. No membrane is involved. I did not reach them because I used the term "space frame" when I should have used "space slab" (a word I invented for the concrete construction at Yale) As soon as I did use space slab he said "oh that's different!" Space frame—space slab there is really a difference. How to form such a slab is still a problem in spite of Yale because it is by experience and one should stop until the answer is humanly complete. I began to think (this all happened in the presence of Etter who just asked me repeatedly how do you do this instead of venturing how himself) and came up with the general attitude. Concrete is masonry with reinforcing for tension built in. This molten masonry is marvelous but it is heavy but should do wonders with the tension ability added and much lighter than

(The sudden large writing is caused by the road bed from New York to New Haven. Am going to Norfolk tonight) [sketch with notes]

Now as masonry it may/can be formed by making each [tetrahedron] = a stone (hollow stone) and brought together with the others with metal and grouted in (we discussed that before)—or we could assume with the absolute purity of form for a likely way equally valid from my point of view.

[sketch with notes] The waste may be justified to answer shear problems / if you can understand.

175

— [The sudden large writing is caused —— and bad reform
New York to New Haven — I'm going to New York tonight;]
an in ←——— ——→ now before ↑↑ —— —
Navas masonry it can be formed by making each
tet = a stone (limestone) and brought together with the others
with metal as pointer in (he discovers that before) — or we cover
against with the absolute purity of form for a likely way equally
valid from my rising price

The most easy
justified —
lower those
problems

if you can
understand

The entire and discovers the doms of tet reg tedious
are thought of as free of concrete with the reinforcing
freeing tet ledded and opening provides thin not
for the recessing slab. Actually that picture is
wrong & inaccurate because you would probably get
forms hollow slabs (I a series of hollow
containers dipped in place by a self spacing design.
honest, licks the cost problem but the tetra can't be
least, from looks. I intend to make each element 4'
On the side the rare concrete the sides can be than as
4" (like now at Yale). The only reason I don't want to see
get by something new for the Synagogue is my present frowsy
of the tet — as because I get no stimulus from its
engineers. But your suggestions are a constant
stimulus and inspiration and I know that
circumstances will lead our minds together, Verlim
has been here and gave us his most welcome reaction
to my work, he is an excellent critic with a completely

National group of Architecture. [...] love me by [...] one

are based on the square space idea — one in brick and one in stone.
The brick one is graceful with its square 1-4" piers [...] square.

piers
beam
joists

joists

2-2X12 nailed with flat nail on top
to 9½" vertical dimension
space for heat and air conditioning
beam

The other is

the beam
joist system modified

square 3'-6' stone piers

space where pier meet the
space for stairs, closets, toilets,
clearing the space of the light of
encumbrances.

[...] plans which I am taking
[...] order and design and
[...] Thursday. I will give you a copy. I belong to you [...] and
[...] I have received letters from Phil Johnson [...]
[...] faith in my work of the [...] gives fits
[...] in the truth of the faith [...]
[...] because I was deeply upset by the judgment
[...] delight I felt was the [...] shown you [...] your parents
[...] It was a good judgment in fact I feel it should have
[...] the big prize even if the hospital was properly considered
[...] I was most gratified as the letter enclosed will
[...] Now! your undying letters as so good
[...] Alex and you I wait for with much anxiety
[...] kept all your letters an have hid them away but I am
[...] a certain obvious place I am going to read them all
[...] again. The room is so terrible I must stop and shall
write soon soon again . Now! now! all my love to
Alex and you Lou +++ +++ +++ ++

The continuous direction of the rows of tetrahedrons are thought of as joists of concrete with the reinforcing following the [tetrahedron]. Pattern and opening provided thru out for the servicing of the slab. Actually that picture is wrong or inaccurate because you would probably get forms like the Yale forms (of a series of hollow containers dropped in place of a self spacing design). I must lick the cost problem but the [tetrahedron] cant be beat! for looks. I intend to make each about 4' (like now at Yale). The only reason I dont want to as yet try something new for the synagogue is my present knowledge of the [tetrahedron]. And because I get no stimulus from the engineers. But your suggestions are a constant stimulus and inspiration and I know that circumstances will lead our minds together. Venturi has been here and gave us his most welcome reaction to my work. He is an excellent critic with a completely Natural grasp of Architecture. The two houses we are working on are based on the square space idea—one in brick and one in stone. The brick one is graceful with its square 1'—4" piers six to a square.

[sketch with notes] pier / beam / joists / joists, beam / 2–2 x 12 worked with flat nailing top to 9 1/2" vertical dimension / space for heat and air conditioning etc.

The other is

[sketch with notes] The top / your system modified / square 3'–6" stone piers / space where piers meet offer space for stairs, entrance, closets, toilets, clearing the space to the light of encumbrances.

I just finished the preliminary plans which I am taking to show at Norfolk as another example of order and design and I will on my return Tuesday mail you a copy. I believe you will find them interesting. Now! The enclosed letter from Phil Johnson gave me a wonderful feeling of faith in my work of the worthyness of its characteristic of unfamiliar— in the truth of the faith that those who love me showed me—because I was deeply upset by the judgment. The only delight I got was the favor shown you for your parents' house. That was a good judgment in fact I feel it should have gotten the big prize even if the hospital was properly considered. Anyhow I was most gratified as the letter enclosed will convey to you. Now! Your wonderful letters are so good to me. News of Alex and you I wait for with warm anxiety. I have kept all your letters and have hid them away but I am sure in a quite obvious place. I am going to read them all over again. The train is so terrible I must stop and shall write soon soon again. Now!

With all my love to Alex and you.

Lou xxxxxxx

Dearest Anne

I received all your mail—was in bad state money wise. Now everything O.K. again.
Am going to deposit $300.00 in your account tomorrow Tuesday 26th. Continue sending
time cards. Want to get this off special have not much to write I imagine but I know
when I sit down to will have much. Been on charette constantly. Just charette constantly
yet not much work done. Need rest too much drive—reason for my dull design of the
Health Center so far—tired—Will write day after tomorrow. for the moment
so long sweetheart.

All my love to the two of you.

> *Lou xxxxxxx*

Dearest Anny:

I did receive your monumental letter of 10 pages and also today the one on Alberobello.
Your sketches are so wonderfully full of your genius for geometric form and topology. Those
that don't have intermingled your words of love I show with great pride. I feel so dumb
not able to show them all with pride and praise. What gets me about the Alberobello
picture is the incongruent facades. Were they redone or are the ones I mention those which
are copies of the old? I am referring to [sketch of house with notes] What this [arrow] got to
do with [arrow] I have a hunch that they may have been renovated for more practical use.
ce cas! Your trip to Amalfi and places near gave me a twitch alright knowing what a
fabulous place (romantically and picturesquely) it is. It is truly Italy of the song. There
can be no place like it. Your seeing those places thru the eyes of Alex is also delightful to
read. With all my insecurity and apprehensions I assure you I love her and I am delighted
with your bits about her as her mother. I am swamped with duties and the problems of
feeding the new mouths of the office. My finances are still lousy but will get better soon—
indeed as soon as we finish the preliminary drawings for the Health Center which is
a difficult space per floor problem. Briefly the lot is so

[sketches with notes]

Dearest Anny:

I did receive your monumental letter of 10 pages and also to-day the one on Alberobello. Your sketches are so underplayed [full] of your genius for geometric form and topology. Those that don't have intermingled your errors [glow]. I show not great pride. I feel so dumb not able to show them all with pride and praise. What gets me about the Alberobello pictures is the incongruent facades. Were they redone or are the ones I mention thus which are copies just so old? I am referring to →

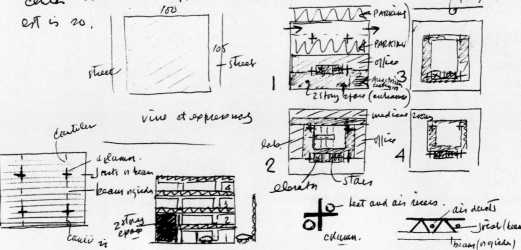

what this got to do with

I have a hunch [renovated] to have practical use. So ges! That they may have been

Your trip to Amalfi and places near gave me a twitch alright. Knowing what a fabulous place (romantically and picturesquely) it is. It's truly Italy of the [songs]. There can be no place like it. Your seeing those places thru the [eyes] of Alex is also delightful to read. With all my insecurity and apprehensions I assure you I love too and I am delighted with your bits about her as her mother. I am swamped with duties and the problems of leading this new month of the office. My finances are still lousy but will get better soon — indeed as soon as we finish the preliminary drawings for the Health center which is a difficult space problem. Briefly the ext is so.

As soon as we [figure] we get it approved we will be paid a good
sum for this stage [of] completion. I have been advanced $2000, [is] almost
spent but will be entitled to about $6 [000?] more when this stage is [finis].
Right now I am hanging on but [entered to be] helped (before the [Kresge?]
Center payments) by some [of the] work completed on the DeVore House maybe
worth $1500.00. I have submitted your time cards to [Alma] and I
believe in less than a week (10 [days]) I shall be able to deposit the amount [of pay]
you [earned] set in your account — By the time you get this
you may [easily] count on about 300 [.00] in your account. I
am really sorry to delay you even as [little] as so long. I just arrived
from Philadelphia at Yale it is almost 10 o'clock A.M., at [Timothy Dwight]
College. The boys have all arrived [in] their studies. The [monitors] are
[full of studies] young me hard at their assignments. Even my
first day I [realize] that it is not [for] me this life. I am most
grateful to be able to allow myself the independence from such
easy security. Teaching is wonderful [for] everyone — it is a duty
everyone owes to the younger person. The [college] I am convinced is
the wrong place to teach as it is set up now, with the professor
dishing it out and the student taking it in and with the
reaction to either process non active nor evident except as again
dishing it out and consuming it as regurgitating for exams! I
believe the architects have the best education since it does give
the opportunity to make the reaction & given in Talking (the personal
reaction) (30 reactions [for as many 30] pupils) a part of the process
of learning. I want to close now because it is late and because
[so] much desperately need the $20 I enclose. I will send more in
a few days [that] you will be able to draw from your account.
Please excuse this very dull letter but really I am in a hurry
myself [illegible] a kiss to you and Sky

180

As soon as we finish and get it approved we will be paid a good sum for this stage of completion. I have been advanced $2,000.00 almost spent but will be entitled to about $6,000.00 more when that stage is finished. Right now I am hanging on but intend to be helped (before the Health Center payment) by some of the work completed on the De Vore House maybe about $1,500.00. I have submitted your time cards to Alma and I believe in less than a week (a few days) I shall be able to deposit the amount for pay you would get in your account. By the time you get this you may easily count on about $300.00 in your account. I am really sorry to delay you even as little as so long. I just arrived from Philly at Yale. It is about 1 o'clock A.M. at Timothy Dwight College. The boys have all arrived for their studies. The movies are full of studious young men hard at their assignments. Even my first day I realize that it's not for me this life. I am most grateful to be able to allow myself the independence from such easy security. Teaching is wonderful for everyone—it is a duty everyone owes to the younger person. The college I am convinced is the wrong place to teach as it is set up now with the professor dishing it out and the student taking it in and with the reaction to either process non-active or evident except as again dishing it out, consuming it and regurgitating for exams. I believe the architects have the best education since it does give the opportunity to make the reaction, to giving and taking (the personal reaction) (30 reactions for as many 30 pupils) a part of the process of learning. I want to close now because it is late and because you must desperately need the $20 I enclose. I will send more in a few days though you will be able to draw from your account—Please excuse the very dull letter but really I am in a lousy mood.

All my love and kisses to you and Alex

Lou xxxxxxx

Dearest Anne

Your letter was most welcome especially to sense from it that we were received with grace and understanding. You must excuse my inexcusable delay in writing—you must sense that I am not over my depressed state of mind over us and the untangled financial difficulties— those due in great part to my own negligence. Alexandra making a hit does not surprise me. She is truly delightful and probably will grow up with more sense than both of us put together. Her interest in things around her and her ready laugh is irresistible. By now I hope you are more relaxed—I so felt your nervousness—though I must say I think you are marvelously controlled considering everything which is a very great deal indeed. Not until a few days ago I got nowhere with the Health Center—now we concocted a grid system of [sketch] which I believe is better than the cross beam construction because the forming is better and the effective strength is increased by the full depth of joists of 3'-0".

The deadlines we must meet are killing and we haven't really begun yet. The engineers being out of the office for this one makes it really much more difficult.

Please let this be only an acknowledgment of your welcome letter and I promise to follow up soon with all I can think of and send some drawings over for you to work on. I hope to sign the contract for the Trenton job which will put some money in my pocket to operate on. My very best to Mr. and Mrs. Tyng and all the relatives

With love to all and especially of course to you and Alex

> *Lou [sketches of hearts] those are valentines to all*

Dearest Anny: *Friday Night on the way to New Haven*

Yesterday I received photographs of the baby and you. They were wonderful to receive
but they were so little of you which I wanted so much to see too. I projected them and Alex
is most lovely and different. She sure is sturdy and seems to have no defects of the foot
which was so worrisome a thing. Of course I will save them like I have so far saved all your
letters and drawings where the writing was not too personal. I have pinned up your draw-
ings because they are truly great things. Our City Hall Building project drawings have been
widely published—so far I know of two recently published views on USA Tomorrow
(a new publication on building and planning—containing also some Mill Creek drawings)
and in L'Architecture d'Aujourdhui *(which I have not seen but was told about—shown in*
connection with experimental buildings of today) other views I have seen but don't
remember where—in new publications on art etc. I will send you all I can get a hold of
although I don't see too much interest it can hold for you since little is written on them. My
scribbling is due to the train's jiggle. I have to go to New Haven today Friday because the
New Jersey State Board requires prints of jobs to accompany registration application.
Had them printed in New Haven and am picking them up and returning back to Philly
immediately to mount photos. Terrible bother should really have my National registration
once and for all—and will do. The thought of returning to New Haven on Monday again
drives me nuts. On Sunday—in addition—I must attend a meeting with the Trenton
Community Center people to discuss contract. They will have no one else do the job but
me. They chose me because they felt by my submissions that I was the one man who
did not repeat himself in his work and therefore can expect a solution in keeping with
their problem. I think it an intelligent decision and a flattering one to me.

Anny honey you have no idea at all what I am still going thru on the financial side of my
existence. Though I have the Health Center resources to work with I have not yet produced
a satisfactory preliminary set. Melamed is a dear man but his mind is not so set about
what he needs and he worries us with changes and his extreme conscience about doing
the most commendable job in the world. Ordinarily I cannot be happier with such a good
client but now I cannot bill him and still satisfy the contract. In two weeks I believe
I will be able to see some light. I have managed to deposit $300.00 in your account and will
deposit the remaining $150.00 of your time cards in 2 weeks and if you send on some
more time cards I will take care of those at that time (in 2 weeks) too. The embarrassment
I have caused you has made me blue and old. I catch myself being a most uncharming
person. Unknowingly I am touchy about trivial things but constantly I cannot relax my
mind from your latest notes and that blast of Shakespeare I suppose written to make
me feel as dismal as possible had just that effect. That with "I hope you are all right"
even sharpened the guilty feeling I cannot escape and where I turn I want to turn away

183

from. I hope to God I can find a way to gather my wits and see everything in a bigger way but now my life is full of unsolved disconnected responsibilities [without] direction and little hope.

This season I went once to the football game with Sue. Penn is doing lousy. Harvard has a good team for Ivy league and can beat the ear off Penn. Penn so far played 5 games and lost 5. They played William and Mary and one sports commentator predicted that he did not believe that they will have to use William. He was right because the third team scored equally with ease. Harvard has played 5 and won 4 I believe and lost one very close 14–13 or something like that. Penn is also in the Ivy League strictly. So much for football which you mentioned with some resentment in one of your letters.

To be working with you again would be not only marvelous to feel again but good for buildings. Though the houses I am doing are interesting and I believe important, the Health Center is still rather dull. It is 3 dimensional only in a Samuely fashion but that is not its greatest fault or rather its greatest bid for dullness. It is me and my attitude and the chewed up time I make available to myself and the constant invasion of my time by people wanting Fullbrights, Guggenheims, Fellowships, scholarships, etc. etc. who like letters and help in framing their application, and the general unpreparedness of the conditions of the problem full of little specialized spaces no different than a house and demanding still future flexibility. Melamed has also injected little personal attitudes hard to group in their undamaging place in space.—But I should be satisfied when I recall the other day at the Art Alliance. At a reception 8 to 10 p.m. for Mrs. Andrade (arranged by Bendiner) to which I was invited and dropped in for near its end, I was greeted with much praiseful introducings by my architect confreres, being referred to as the "greatest" the "most outstanding" the "famous." It felt awful good and especially feeling sure that it was not ribbing but truly meant. What do they base it on—I believe the Gallery at Yale. The Homseys of Wilmington were there and they told me how they were prepared to dislike the building from the photos in P/A (they were terrible photos in a way more terrible in arrangement than in themselves bad) but when they saw it they immediately decided to place (it) among the world's best mind you world. It does have an effect on one. The dean (Sawyer) is so proud of it that he, when called to name who he would recommend for some new buildings in Ithaca U., he named me with Saarinen, Belluschi as the best to choose from. I did not hear from them as yet. The job in Central Africa is not yet ready to have given out, but it is not a dead thing at all—only recently I am speaking to Harbeson of H2L2 alerted me to some inquiries which were made around Philly on my behalf in this connection—the F.B.I. is investigating me. It is I believe a base involving quite a few buildings but I do not know for sure. What a job this would be for us to work on. (This train is completely impossible) and we are getting near New Haven. By next mail I will send you some money in the letter. Did you get my 2—$20 bills ($40) in my special delivery. I will write in a few days to keep up with your

184

The painter Edna Andrade

Alfred Bendiner, architect and artist

Victorine DuPont Homsey, architect, and her husband Samuel Homsey, landscape architect

H2L2, Philadelphia architecture firm of Harbeson, Hough, Livingston, and Larson, successor to Paul Cret's firm

faithful and much anticipated letters though they bring words not always cheerful.
But your words of encouragement I feel in all of them and for that I am deeply touched and
grateful and as the only real ray of hope for future laughter real deep laughter what
I haven't felt for so so long.

All my love to Alex and you

  Lou

30 November 1954

Dearest Anne:

I haven't written because of many reasons—but one is I had so little time trying to
get out of the woods with the Health Center. Melamed has given us dribbles of information
which blocked us (me) from getting at the spirit of the problem. I am writing this at the
Savarin Restaurant at the station in New York—have only about 20 min. before train time.
Just came from Yale on way to Philly and tomorrow I go to Tulane U. It couldn't be a worse
time for me to go with the Health Center in a miserable state and the Perspecta *article*
only dabbed at and little done. I sound mopey but don't get me wrong. As I wrote already
I see ways of overcoming this temporal difficulty. The financial problem of course won't
get better until I solve the H.C. then I am entitled to the preliminary fee which will get me
started again. I think I wrote you about me getting the job in Trenton this also is a good
job worth talking about. Did I write you about my having a breakfast meeting with
Belluschi. He wants me to come to M.I.T.—offers me the moon—$20,000 a year and the job
of setting up a design-construction graduate department. He will also throw an Art Gallery
(or art school) my way (Wellesley I believe)—I did not ask him about Africa but I am to
see him again very soon and then will be the best time for that. A contingent of the younger
profs from Penna also called on me—had dinner presented the idea (that since they heard
about the offer from M.I.T. from Sascha Nowicki) that I stay in Philadelphia, that my loss
would be Philly's loss. Sounds terribly important but I say "a plague on all their houses,"
because all I want is my independence which is after all what makes me click as me.
I believe I could be associated with M.I.T. without having to live in Boston and Philadelphia
takes me for granted anyway so I can't better that impression. Sam Feinstein is writing
about me in some Art Magazine. He says that I am the unrecognized prophet of
Philadelphia—why do they give synagogues to F. L. W. when I am around. (If you can
read this writing you're good). All the praise I know I don't deserve it mainly because it
pleases me so much but it does sadden me too. I'd rather not be made conscious of
praise on the outside. I heard another that should interest you. Willo Von Moltke came

Sascha Nowicki, professor
of architecture at the
University of Pennsylvania

*from Saarinen in Detroit. Eero's wife heard suddenly so much good about me that she is
coming to Phila to interview me for an article in* New York Times *magazine section.
This is what Willo brought back from Detroit. They had been discussing me all evening
at the Saarinens. Well well. I should have told them to see you who would have told them
about that long long time ago. I actually believe it is you who gave me my present confidence in my art. But that is really mutual because I think you the really unusual talent.
Please be patient Anny about money. I have so little that I had to borrow twice. But
now with Tulane U. trip (which I must not renege on) I can slip off a few bills and
send them to you and I also will cover the full amount of the first time cards in a few
days and if possible add some more soon after in any case positively when the Melamed
check is due. I must rush I have only a brief minute.*

All my love to you and Alex xxxxxxx

10 December 1954

186

Dearest Anne:

Again I had to postpone my letter which I intended to have follow the one with the
New York Times *sport page. I just came back from New Orleans after a week there—
returning to keep up with the demands of the Health Center which is still dragging in the
realm of mediocrity because the nature of the space is still unsettled. Today all day
I spent at the present health center interviewing doctors on the staff and I believe I can
get somewhere now. I am at least discovering what I have always suspected that the rooms
in general are all the same in dimension, which only last week (from Melamed) was not
possible. I am in such a lousy state of mind that I don't think it possible for me to create
anything worthwhile even though the spaces lent themselves now more readily to
construction. I don't feel proud of what I have done so far and therefore don't feel much
like sending copies to work over though I will do so in a week after I have returned again
from New Orleans where I shall be to finish my stay from the 11th to the 18th of Dec.
I am still unable to collect the preliminary fee on the Health Center because the scheme
is unsettled. I have borrowed wherever I could to continue the office but I cannot get
myself to submit what I do myself not feel satisfactory in order to receive the fee.
I hope to do this soon but with New Orleans in there betwixt and between I must wait
a little longer. I guess you already sense how happy I am. Your letters are the only things
that may cheer me but they don't especially the last ones. The demand on my time
is unbelievable. I am sure that everyone would be sore if I did not give some of it.
You know how much I love to give up the time and would think nothing of it. Now*

I resent it. I can't believe that I am that low in spirits. Maybe I sense too much trouble ahead maybe my world was never a real one but I sure don't know what is.

The trip from New Orleans was rough and we were grounded in Washington from where I took the train to Philadelphia. It took a long time to get to W. for flying but everyone was glad to get off the terra firma. On the train I met Kenneth Kassler and Vincent Kling. Since they were together I was friendly to both and we had a few drinks on the train which made my cold (I got in New Orleans taking the palm trees too seriously) feel a little better. I haven't had one since I got over the business of smoking but this makes up for the respite. Alma just called me to tell me that I don't have any money. She has the cheerful habit of giving me the bright news piece for piece, $1.38 for this and .78 for this and $502.04 for this and now it all adds up to 0 and then the question "what shall I do?" on the phone and it's all very accurate. I told her to refigure it and almost laughed about the whole damn thing.

In N. O. I stayed at the Pontchatrain Hotel and my relatives there discovered (from a news report) I was there, so—I was told the situation was unheard of and that I must stay with them. I was not really going to argue too much especially since my room cost $8.00 per day (arranged by the University of Tulane) and the last 4 days of the stay I was with them and when I go back I will continue to be with them. I have my own room and bath really very comfortable and the people very loving and cheerful. I saw quite a bit of the French Quarter and other historical areas which are very interesting and gay. I will try to write you from there next week. I found the boys very far behind those in other places—they have practically no work habits of value and the week so far I was able to soup them up a bit but I doubt it can have lasting value. This year I again received an invitation to Princeton to judge the thesis problem. The students as you know choose their 3 men as judges from the outside. I think that is a very good honor. Stop to think why I was not altogether given over to my work at Tulane—my relatives in N.O. when they discovered I was there and they insisted I stay with them I did nothing but be entertained and eat and ended up with a bad stomach and a cold. The New Jersey Board is taking its time to extend reciprocity. I called one on the board tonight and he told me that I must wait until January 15 to be called for an interview. I must not fall trap to the bait of signing contracts with the New Jersey clients before I receive my registration. This means that they can make it tough for you if they find out.

I am not going to pretend to be anything but blue and uninteresting to myself. My only hope is that everything and everybody I love will be happy together again in my mind and actually

Love Lou xxxxxxx

In January 1955, Robert Venturi drove Anne and Alexandra Tyng to Florence for Alexandra's baptism at the American Episcopal Church. On the same trip Tyng obtained a new passport that included Alex. Later, Venturi loaned Tyng $400 for the return trip to the United States.

25 January 1954

RADIOGRAM

S/S CONSTITUTION / KAEG

JANUARY, 25, 1955

4 WNY BF

NY 14 ANNE TYNG CONSTITUTION WNY

WILL MEET BOAT WHATEVER HOUR IT DOCKS

LOVE LOU

$$5 \times 3 - 9\tfrac{5}{8} = H.$$

$$\tfrac{9\tfrac{1}{2} - 9\tfrac{5}{8}}{}$$

$$3 \times 3 - 9\tfrac{5}{8} = H \text{ of Floor}$$

Dearest Anny   I must stop now since my eyes are ...
... about 2 A.M. (Tuesday 16th) and I must get up
... room what on Tuesdays happens the particular
... playing. I'm glad darling that any thing ...
... are happy and that you are not upset by by the
... if you cant listen. I sit at Yale ... must
... cheerful with the kids in your room and the ...
... philosophic attitude. I thought myself the
feelings.   with lots and lots of love   Lou

Return

Lou met Alex and me when our boat from Italy docked in New York on 25 January 1955. It was an emotionally charged, happy meeting and Lou stayed part of each night with us in New York, returning to Philadelphia very early each morning for several days. When Alex awoke on our first morning in New York, she (at ten months) popped her head up out of her carry-bed looking around and said clearly, "Daddy?" for the first time. I called long-time friends Barbara Crawford and Sam Feinstein in Philadelphia, who very generously let us stay with them until I could find my own place.

My arrival with my unexpected daughter was extremely difficult for my parents to accept; my father proposed that I put Alex up for adoption. Luckily, I was then thirty-four with a mind of my own, and there was no need for their financial help. I had earned my living for ten years and would continue to do so. In Rome I lived on some small savings, the fee as a principal consultant on the Mill Creek Redevelopment Plan, an IRS refund, and the money earned from Lou. Lou and I were lovers, but I was not his "mistress." I was uncomfortable with the idea of being "owned" that is often tied to being supported.

My mother was nonjudgmental, pragmatic, and had a sound, instinctive sense of connection to us, but Alex and I were the recipients of deeply negative projections from most of my family and others. I had to face the archaic attitude that women were totally accountable for the act of conceiving even if

*Kahn and Tyng with architect
Kenneth Welch, whom Tyng had met
while in Rome, at the office on
Twentieth and Walnut streets, 1955.*

The Trenton Bathhouse, completed in 1959, was the first project Kahn and Tyng worked on after her return from Rome.

they dealt responsibly and lovingly with the results. In contrast, men completely escaped both judgment and the responsibility of fathering.

The first job I worked on when I returned was the Trenton Bathhouse. Lou had started work with Tim Vreeland on a roofless rectangular scheme, but almost immediately I came up with the proposal of four symmetrically arranged squares with hipped roofs (later strengthened with tension rods) supported on 8-foot square occupiable hollow columns. The idea of using hollow columns as baffled entrances came from my memory of the bathhouses in China made of woven bamboo matting with only a system of baffles for privacy. It was a simple, straightforward concept, combining archetypal and innovative aspects, and Lou went for it. We developed a variety of other uses for the hollow columns—toilets, storage, a stair down to the chlorinating plant, and an office for the pool director.

Lou and I were working together at a drawing board for the first time in over a year. The Trenton Bathhouse design I developed with Lou included many suggestions I had sent to him from Rome for the Adler and De Vore houses. I was most enthusiastic about several concepts and sent sketches of them— using nondirectional structures for the nondirectional squares, shaping the square spaces with the triangulated structure of a hipped roof, and the concept of hollow columns as an extension of the concept of "servant" space used in the Yale Art Gallery ceiling. Lou had proposed flat roofs for both the

SECTION A·A

Section

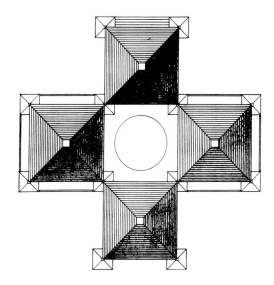

Roof plan

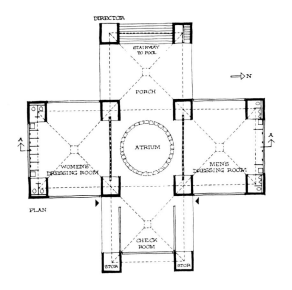

DIRECTOR

STAIRWAY
TO POOL

PORCH

⇒ N

ATRIUM

WOMEN'S
DRESSING ROOM

MEN'S
DRESSING ROOM

PLAN

CHECK
ROOM

STOR

STOR

Floor plan

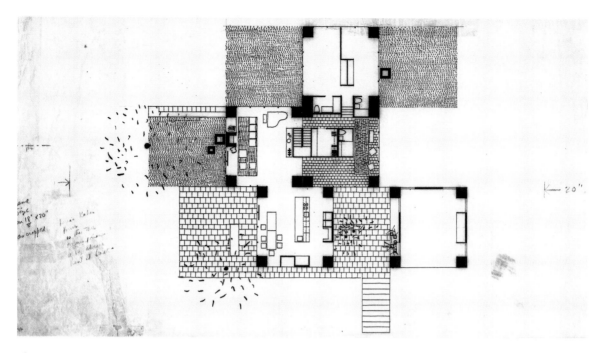

Plan, Dr. and Mrs. Francis H.
Adler house, Philadelphia,
1954–55 (unbuilt).

1 David G. De Long, *Louis
Kahn: In the Realm of
Architecture* (New York:
Rizzoli, 1991), p. 58.

2 Susan Brady, "The
Architectural Metaphysic
of Louis Kahn," *New York
Times Magazine* (15 November 1970), p. 86.

194

De Vore and Adler houses and in neither of those houses did Lou propose hollow columns; they were solid brick 1´4˝ x 1´4˝ or stone 3´6˝ x 3´6˝ piers. De Long's reference to Lou "exploring hipped roofs" may refer to the sketches I sent Lou.[1] But he did use my suggestion for a nondirectional structure of crisscrossed joists with metal connectors.

Later, in 1970, Lou was quoted as saying, "If the world discovered me after I designed the Richards Medical Research Building, I discovered myself after designing that little concrete block bathhouse in Trenton."[2] In 1973, on my nomination to Fellowship in the American Institute of Architects, Lou refused to check any of the standard categories for degrees of responsibility for work I had done in his office. Instead, on every project he wrote, "Anne Tyng reminded me of my own premises." They were premises that Lou and I shared and he often did forget them. The fact that we shared these basic ideas meant that I was able to anticipate the innovative and connective directions in which they might lead. Lou's capacity to start each project "from volume zero" with "the nature of the space" sometimes made him forget the non-specific but infinitely variable principles from which to begin. As in the Trenton Bathhouse, such premises might include new extensions of servant space concepts, organizing space into hierarchical clusters from individual human size to spaces for larger and larger groups, the hollowing out of structure, and shaping light with structure/space.

Lou had written to me in December 1953 about his theory of a three-phase creative process, "Nature of Space, Order, and Design."[3] Lou wrote that "order…is what makes the structure grow into a life of fiber enveloping the space so that its nature can be felt. *It is the seed. It is the integration from which design can work.*" What Lou called "the seed" correlates with the psychological archetype as described by Carl Jung: "Its form . . . might be compared to the axial system of a crystal . . . which, as it were, preforms the crystalline structure . . . although it has no material existence of its own. . . . The same is true of the archetype. In principle it can be named and has an invariable nucleus of meaning—but always in principle, never as regards its concrete manifestations."[4] Jung's statements here were not published in English until 1959, six years after Lou first wrote about the creative process. Lou had seen that the same geometric principle—seed or archetype—could "grow" my elementary school, my parents' house, the Yale Art Gallery ceiling, and our City Tower Project. The scales were different, the functions were different, and their total forms were different. It was a perception that informed his theory of the creative process. Lou included my independent work— my planning work, my proposed Bucks County Elementary School, and my parents' house on Maryland's Eastern Shore—in his lecture at the Baltimore Museum of Art in March 1954: "I spoke about planning, the Gallery, the 3-D structures [tower] . . . I showed your mother's house in [Eastern] shore and the 3-D of the Bucks County School. . . ."[5] Lou also included my work in his talk at Harvard: "[You] kept asking me about my talk at Harvard . . . It went over very big indeed. I showed much of your work."[6] The fact that he referred to my projects confirms the significant role those concepts played in his development.

I believe it was Robert Damora, photographer and former Yale architecture student, who proposed that our City Tower be included in a series of buildings he was photographing as advertisements for Atlas Cement/US Steel. We were to be paid the sum of eight hundred dollars to make drawings for the model. We wanted to make it taller than the earlier version published in *Perspecta 2* so that the rhythm of the undulations could be more dramatic. I worked out the movement from floor to floor and drew a section, elevation, and plans that were used in the Atlas brochure. Lou had given some thought to the design of a "hollow" capital where three tilted columns meet the floor structure: "I have thought recently that there could be an open star-like capital (as the Greek) which may be the shear head transition (capital is the shear head expression) to the column."[7] I thought Lou's concept was a highly original extension of the servant space premise: the "hollow capital" added to the Yale "hollow ceiling" and the "hollow column" at the Trenton Bathhouse.

3 Louis Kahn Letter to Anne Tyng, 18 December 1953.

4 C. G. Jung. *The Archetypes and the Collective Unconscious* (New York: Pantheon), 1959.

5 Louis Kahn Letter to Anne Tyng, 19 March 1954.

6 Louis Kahn Letter to Anne Tyng, 19 March 1954.

7 Louis Kahn Letter to Anne Tyng, 2 December 1953.

When I saw the number of drawings we were making, I began to feel frustrated and wondered how we could more effectively communicate our intent to the model-maker. Our plans and sections did not convey in two dimensions all the three-dimensional geometry between the floors. I tried to think like the model-maker and finally made a small rough model, discovering that the geometry of every structural level was identical to every other structural level, including the geometry at the edges. Once the choice was made consistently for the directions of movement from level to level, it would then follow the geometry to create the undulating effect. Armed with this surprisingly simple discovery, we decided I should go to the model-makers to rescue them from unnecessary complexity.

Our tower expressed a paradoxical new aesthetic: that structural strength and rigor based on an ordering principle can appear dramatically in motion with a life of its own. Primordial principles of form, the bonding of atoms and molecules out of which life grows, are resources for dynamic, innovative structures that can easily resist the forces of wind and earthquake. The naturally "grown" undulations anticipate such stresses—resistance is already built into their form, as the tree on the mountaintop grows its own shape in bends and gnarls to resist forces of the wind.

The fact that tetrahedron/octahedron geometry has a fundamental relation to orthogonal order is not realized by many architects. If close-packed cubes are sliced along their diagonals, close-packed tetrahedrons/octahedrons will result. Other consistent slicing will produce pentagonal symmetry. Helical and spiral forms can also be generated. The infinite variety of organic and inorganic matter results from such basic geometries. These forms are the essences of what is possible in three-dimensional space, a nonarbitrary resource independent of style, not belonging to anyone and available to everyone. They are ordering principles that have evolved over millenia—in the octet geometry that lightens the vast span of the vulture's wings, and in the octahedral form of a diamond that resists compression deep in the earth.

We explored Lou's and my premises in many projects, built and unbuilt. For the Wharton Esherick studio (1956) we developed hexagonal spaces with a hipped roof in three planes, its three sloping ridge members strengthened by a horizontal triangle of tension rods. The studio space was then free of columns, and the connected hexagonal spaces allowed for a flow of space between them to be expanded as a single space or divided into separate hexagons.

Page from Atlas Cement brochure on the City Tower project, at left. The drawing at top is by Tyng.

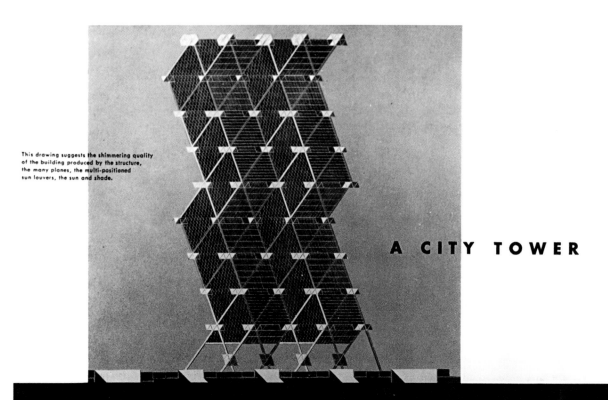

This drawing suggests the shimmering quality of the building produced by the structure, the many planes, the multi-positioned sun louvers, the sun and shade.

A CITY TOWER

a concept of natural growth

"*In Gothic times, architects built in solid stones. Now we can build with hollow stones. The spaces defined by the members of a structure are as important as the members. These spaces range in scale from the voids of an insulation panel, voids for air, lighting and heat to circulate, to spaces big enough to walk through or live in.*

The desire to express voids positively in the design of structure is evidenced by the growing interest and work in the development of space frames. The forms being experimented with come from a closer knowledge of nature and the outgrowth of the constant search for order. Design habits leading to the concealment of structure have no place in this implied order. Such habits retard the development of an art. I believe that in architecture, as in all art, the artist instinctively keeps the marks which reveal how a thing was done. The feeling that our present day architecture needs embellishment stems in part from our tendency to fair joints out of sight, to conceal how parts are put together. Structures should be devised which can harbor the mechanical needs of rooms and spaces. Ceilings with structure furred in tend to erase scale. If we were to train ourselves to draw as we build, from the bottom up, when we do, stopping our pencil to make a mark at the joints of pouring or erecting, ornament would grow out of our love for the expression of method. It would follow that the pasting over the construction of lighting and acoustical material, the burying of tortured unwanted ducts, conduits and pipe lines, would become intolerable. The desire to express how it is done would filter through the entire society of building, to architect, engineer, builder and craftsman."

Louis I. Kahn, architect and planner

Consultant to U.S. Housing Authority, Philadelphia Housing Authority, City Planning Commission and Redevelopment Authority. Chief of Design, Sesqui-Centennial Exposition. Co-designer, Hightstown, N.J. Organizer, architectural research group. Past President, American Society of Planners and Architects. Fellow, American Institute of Architects. Professor and Chief Architectural Critic, Yale University. Professor of Architecture, University of Pennsylvania. Visiting Albert F. Bemis Professor, M.I.T. Lecturer on architecture, Harvard, Princeton, Houston, Tulane, North Carolina.

Anne Griswold Tyng, architect associated

Master of Architecture, Harvard Graduate School of Design, 1944. Instructor, Architectural Design, Beaver College. Ten years associated in office of Louis I. Kahn, active with him in planning and redevelopment

Wharton Esherick studio, Paoli,
Pennsylvania, 1956.

198

In 1960 and 1961, as one of several proposals in the office for the General
Motors 1964 World's Fair exhibit, I explored the geometry of the tetrakaidecahedron, a fourteen-sided shape called the Kelvin Body in honor of
its discoverer Lord Kelvin. It is a shape formed by close-packed bubbles and
provides maximum volume with minimum surface. All its joints are in the
tetrahedral carbon bond, connecting eight warped hexagonal surfaces and six
square faces with bulging edges. The proposed semicircular cluster of tent
forms would be anchored to the ground with cables and supported by inflated
forms based on similar geometry. I made a model of it with slightly curved,
tempered steel rods and parachute silk. Putting it together was much easier
than I thought it would be. It was exciting to discover that the rods virtually
"wanted" to come together in that particular form.

One direction of exploration derived from the simpler geometry of the
seminal Trenton Bathhouse occurs in the Esherick studio with the geometry
of its roof structures and in the more complex geometry of the General
Motors exhibit building. Another direction of exploration occurs in the
Norma and Bernard Shapiro house (1962) and in the Elaine and Fred Clever
house (1962). In each, different expressions of the hollow column and central
open space evolve. In the Shapiro house the expression of the hollow column
is modified, occurring at the corners of square, gently hipped roofs as corner
closets, connecting halls, or entryways. The spaces act to brace the single
wood column against the outward thrust of the ridge beam at the corner,

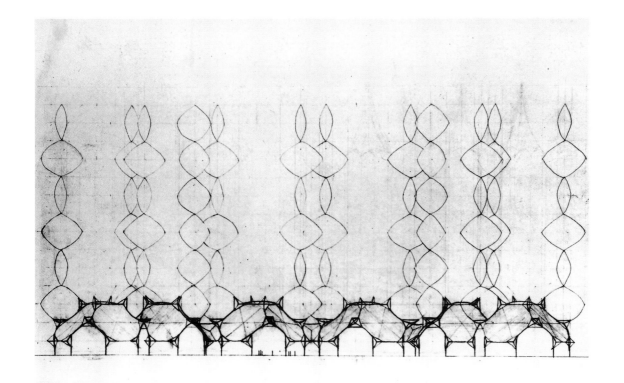

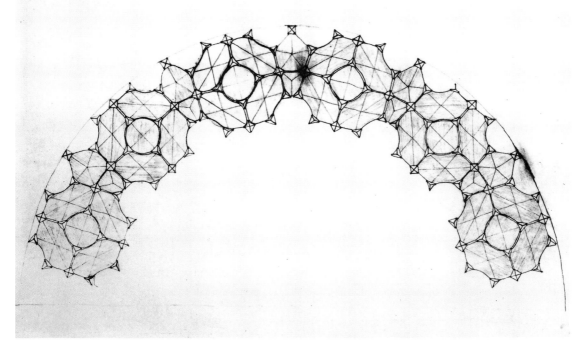

Tyng's proposed elevation and
plan, General Motors exhibit, 1964
World's Fair, New York
1960–61 (unbuilt).

Study model for the Elaine and Fred Clever house, Cherry Hill, New Jersey, completed 1962.

and are randomized by extending from the corner in either direction by at least the width of a door for access. On one side of the living and dining rooms, a wide joint is added to the overhangs to provide space for the kitchen, a stairway, a powder room, and on the lower level two baths and a laundry/utility room between three bedrooms and a study. At the time of Lou's death in March 1974, we were associated architects on the addition, which I then completed in 1975.

In the Elaine and Fred Clever house, the open atrium of the Trenton Bathhouse evolved into a two-story living room lit on four sides by generous triangular clerestories. Two steeply sloped roofs intersect to form a Greek cross in plan. Their roof planes are framed by triangles that project as shelter over the clerestory windows. The central space is surrounded by a cluster of low, gently sloped hipped roofs supported by columns that define eleven-foot squares with two-foot overhangs. The overhangs are used to expand the eleven-foot squares and, where two overhangs meet, they form bathrooms, a dressing room, and laundry and storage space. The dining room occupies a square, and the kitchen with informal dining occupies a square as well as the paired overhangs between it and the dining room. A two-story-high masonry square attached to a corner of the Greek cross contains the fireplace chimney and mechanical equipment. Additional randomness occurs with one high side of the living room open to the outdoors in addition to its view through the lower dining room space. Ten years later the Clevers asked me to design a garage/guest house, which I did, after first checking with Lou to see if he wanted to work together on it. But he was extremely busy at that time with a number of large projects including the Kimbell Art Museum and the Dacca government complex. My proposal relocated the drive to steer visitors to the front door and create privacy for the dining room. I proposed extending the concept of the existing house with open pavilions around an outdoor living room larger than their indoor living room. The pavilions would be open frames except where integrated with the two-car garage. The shallow and steep slopes of the garage/guest house correspond to the existing roof slopes on the house but are used to create different kinds of spaces.

ELAINE & FRED CLEVER GARAGE/GUEST HOUSE ¼"=1'-0"
SHERRY WAY   HUNT TRACT   OCT 22 '72
CHERRY HILL TOWNSHIP NEW JERSEY

ANNE GRISWOLD TYNG   ARCHITECT A I A

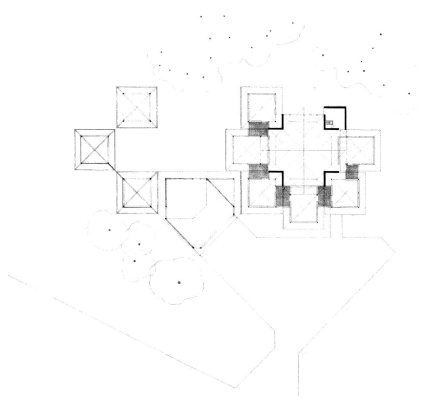

*Elevation and plan of Elaine
and Fred Clever house
with proposed addition by
Tyng, 1972.*

Reflections

The passion Lou and I shared for architecture survived many changes. When Lou wrote, "I am waiting anxiously for us to be together again in our own wonderful way of love and work . . . ," he was not thinking of change. But after Alex was born, I had to modify my total dedication to work to provide her with some degree of security. I felt that Lou's and my devotion to each other needed to make room for our shared love for Alex. When I applied for the Fulbright, breaking away from Lou would have been extremely difficult, and since we had Alex it would be far more difficult. My schedule involved working until Alex came home from school and working at night when she was in bed. At the same time I wanted her to continue to know her father. I believe Lou resented being deprived of some of the energy I had devoted to him, although it seemed to me that developing some degree of autonomy could in fact increase one's capacity to love, rather than be divisive or threatening.

In 1960, I suggested to Lou that our relationship should become platonic because I realized he was involved with someone else. This occurred not long before Lou's and my proposed City Tower was about to be in the Museum of Modern Art exhibit *Visionary Architecture*.[8] I did not get an invitation to the opening. When I asked our secretary about it, she said my name might not be on the credit label. I immediately asked Lou if my name was credited. He answered no, so I suggested it might be better if he called the museum than if I called. There was no Sturm und Drang; he simply called and my name was added. I was profoundly shocked that Lou would do such a thing, especially

8 The following year the City Tower was in another MoMA exhibit *Architecture and Engineering* in which we were both credited.

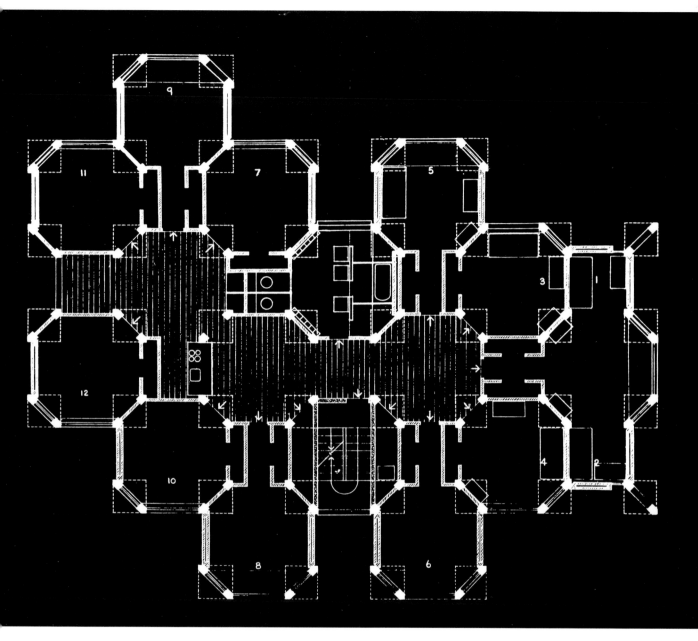

President Katherine McBride of Bryn
Mawr College called Tyng's proposal
for Kahn's Erdman Hall the
"molecular plan."

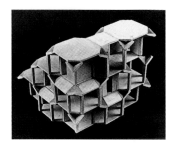

Study model for Erdman Hall "molecular plan."

since *Perspecta 2* (1953), *Progressive Architecture* (May 1954), and the Atlas Cement brochure on the Tower (1957) gave credit to both of us. I could not believe that his desire for recognition would erode his integrity, since sharing credit with me would not necessarily diminish his fame.

All of these problems, including my father's death from cancer and my own extremely severe six-week-long case of mumps, had an impact on the design process of Erdman Hall at Bryn Mawr (1965). It is clear, in retrospect, that from the very beginning Lou wanted me to produce ideas while at the same time rejecting ideas independent of their value for the design of the building. For my part, creativity toward a goal outside myself and outside our relationship was still a way of relating to Lou as well as a way of earning my living. I threw my energy into finding extensions of Lou's and my premises that might appeal to Lou and make a better building. Early in the design process I proposed a very rough sketch of three diagonally interlocking square spaces, but Lou did not respond favorably until it was revived much later in the design process. Lou hired David Polk, who had just graduated from architecture school at the University of Pennsylvania, and tended to work with him setting up a continuous competition of two schemes. Lou arranged with President Katherine McBride of Bryn Mawr that we would meet with her every Monday morning with two schemes until resolution was achieved. This went on for two or three months.

Tyng's sketches for Erdman Hall proposal

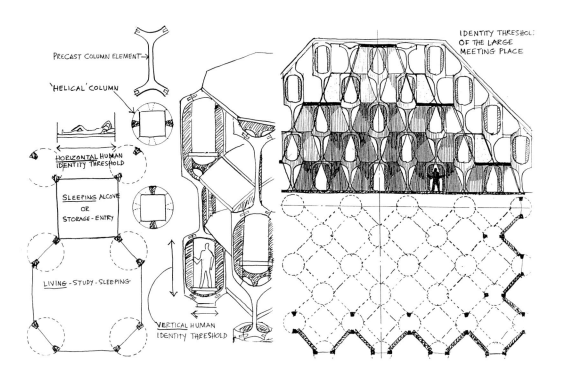

PRECAST COLUMN ELEMENT→

'HELICAL' COLUMN

HORIZONTAL HUMAN IDENTITY THRESHOLD

SLEEPING ALCOVE OR STORAGE - ENTRY

LIVING - STUDY - SLEEPING

VERTICAL HUMAN IDENTITY THRESHOLD

IDENTITY THRESHOLD OF THE LARGE MEETING PLACE

Two views of overall model of Tyng's proposal for Erdman Hall.

I developed a number of proposals, some combining eight-foot squares with irregular octagons of alternating eight-foot and five-foot sides, referred to as the "molecular" scheme by President McBride. In those patterns she saw potential for future adaptation to apartments for married students. For the structure of those spaces I was eager to try a cylindrical version of the hollow column with a five-foot diameter exterior and a three-foot-square interior. Its five-foot dimension matched the short sides of octagons framing windows and doors with the longer eight-foot sides of the octagons accommodating beds or the window seats requested by President McBride. Combined with the octagons were eight-foot squares that could be used as a sleeping/study alcove or entry/storage closets. On each level the cylinder would appear to be cut away to leave a "residual" pair of columns within its perimeter. At each level the paired "residual columns" turn at right angles to the pair above and below to support the alternating levels of squares and octagons. Although for the first model I had cut away arched openings also curved on the bottom, for the actual structure I proposed a precast concrete I-shaped column element to be poured in a horizontal position. Its curved surface would have been at the bottom of the "mold" form and the flat square interior surface leveled at the top of the form. Paired with itself, the I-shape formed a square interior and a circular perimeter when connected at right angles to pairs above and below (in plan a square in a circle). At floor levels, the paired columns were also connected by a tetrahedral joint within the cylinder.

Using the same column elements, octagons, and squares, I also developed a spanning system for the larger spaces (the large living room and dining room). Each octagon was to be corbelled as a unit with one of four short

205

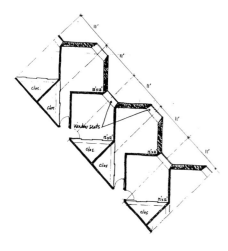

Detail plan of Tyng's proposal for Erdman Hall.

Kahn's Erdman Hall, completed in 1965.

sides to be cantilevered. The next level of octagons were also to be "corbelled" as a unit to form a large-scale corbelling system from level to level. The entire system met corbels coming from each of four directions, in a sense like a great faceted dome. All the columns were two stories high and continued in another level above the roof to form a three-dimensional flying buttress. I proposed a similar system, but an inverted one for the main entrance hall, with increasing spaces on the upper levels.

When the scheme returned to the parti of three diagonally interlocking squares that I had suggested in the very beginning, I proposed an interlocking arrangement of rooms in which they could all have window seats and at the same time save on the perimeter dimension of the three large squares in order to accommodate more rooms. The rooms, while only requiring a center-to-center dimension of eleven feet on the perimeter of the building, would have had more generous interior dimensions than ones that were built. The closets were larger and there were at least three walls where a bed could be placed. Most significantly, reflecting window-reveals framing the window seats would optimize natural light, and the two adjoining walls as extended reveals would have provided good light for a desk.

Another consideration was the play of diagonals in the overall plan. Within the three large diagonally connected squares, the counterpoint of the square clerestory towers would have been echoed in the squared orientation of the rooms and together formed the basis of an integrated overall structure. This orientation of the rooms along the main axis of the building may have

Kahn's model of Salk Institute meeting house, 1960–61 (unbuilt).

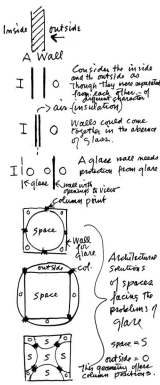

Kahn's sketches of square-in-circle and circle-in-square shading devices.

been less disorienting than the arrangement of rooms as built. Several people in the office tried to persuade Lou to use the diagonal room system. Although Lou may not have liked the diagonal walls of rooms on the exterior, I believe the flat planes of the windows would have been the dominant visual impact of the exterior wall. I was happy that we had wrapped the rooms around the large central spaces, but the rooms as built, and the fact that no direct outlook to the outdoors was provided from the living room, were serious disappointments for me. It was a long and difficult process of resolution but it bore fruit in the form of the many unbuilt ideas for later picking.

The "molecular" plan of irregular octagons and squares for Bryn Mawr was an extension of the regular octagons and squares proposed in 1955 for the unbuilt Community Building at Trenton. The four tilted hexagonal roofplanes of each octagon sloping up to a square are part of the Kelvin Body, the fourteen-sided tetrakaidecahedron that I proposed for the unbuilt General Motors exhibit building. I had proposed a variation of that geometry for the First Unitarian Church and School in Rochester (1969), but its proportions did not appeal to Lou. His return to a similar geometry for a modest octagonal synagogue built in Chappaqua, New York, late in his career (1972)—a building in which I was not involved—reveals geometry as a reconnective nurturing source in his work through a span of twenty years and affirms his recognition of the archetypal power of geometry.

Kahn's interior perspective sketch of Mikveh Israel Synagogue, Philadelphia, 1961–72 (unbuilt).

208

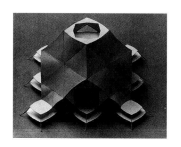

Model of Tyng's proposed scheme for the First Unitarian Church and School, Rochester, New York, completed 1969.

As far as I know, no cylindrical forms had been proposed in Lou's office for a *structural* column before I suggested one for Bryn Mawr. After my Bryn Mawr proposals, cylindrical forms were proposed for a number of projects in which I was not involved, but not as structural columns and at different scales. Square towers in cylinders and cylinders in square towers were proposed for the Salk Meeting House (1960) as shading devices. Lou also explored the idea of cylinders as shading devices for the U.S. Consulate in Luanda, Angola, in 1960 but later dropped the idea, squaring it off with a double roof arrangement. For the unbuilt chemistry building at the University of Virginia, six cylindrical towers were proposed around a hexagonal plan (1963). In the proposed plan of the Mikveh Israel Synagogue (1972), Lou explored cylindrical forms inside and out, cut away in arched forms right side up and upside down—somewhat similar to the shapes cut out of the cylinders in my Bryn Mawr proposal. Both Moshe Safdie (then in Lou's office) and I urged Lou to use the cylinders at Mikveh Israel as structural columns, but he saw them as light sources. At the great government complex at Dacca, Bangladesh, generously scaled cylinders occur in a kind of baroque monumentality with an array of arched and triangular openings. The ultimate legacy of the Trenton Bathhouse atrium reappears in both the mosque and the great central parliament space which are surrounded by clusters of smaller spaces.

Lou's projects and buildings expressed the premise of wrapping or clustering smaller spaces around a larger central space in many different ways. The open

Southwest section and schematic
plan for Kahn's Temple Beth-El
Synagogue, Chappaqua, New York,
completed 1972.

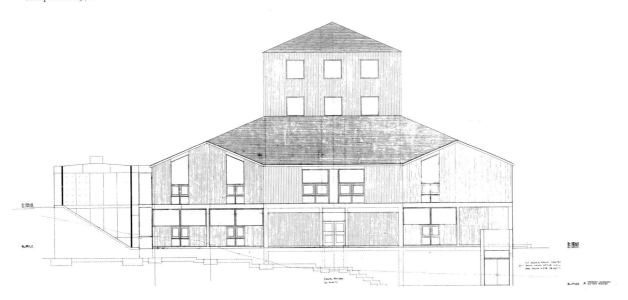

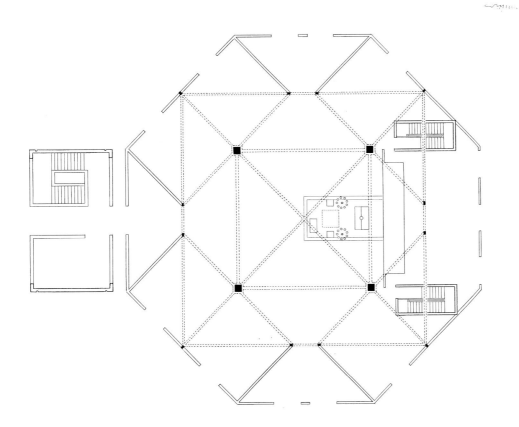

atrium surrounded by the hipped roofs of the Trenton Bathhouse, the two-story living room lit by clerestories and surrounded by low hipped roofs of the Elaine and Fred Clever house, and the large central spaces at Bryn Mawr lit by clerestory towers and wrapped around with dormitory rooms find a more transcendent expression in the First Unitarian Church in Rochester with its reflected clerestory light at its four corners surrounded by classrooms and other ancillary functions. The Exeter Library (1972) and the Hurvah Synagogue, in their great cubic masses with smaller spaces around a great central space, evoke the castle at Kahn's birthplace on Saaremaa.

During my work on the Elaine and Fred Clever house, the Norma and Bernard Shapiro house, and Erdman Hall at Bryn Mawr, David Wisdom said to me that I could "do a Louis Kahn better than Louis Kahn." Since Dave was not given to sarcasm, it might have been humor or praise. At the time I thought I might be overstepping some boundary like Icarus too near the sun. But in retrospect I see his comment as an affirmation of my ability and encouragement to start my own practice. In 1964, although Lou had plenty of work in the office, he "let me go" by simply not giving me work. Whether anger, resentment, or preoccupation with other relationships were the reason, it was a difficult time for me. I started my modest practice and received a Brunner grant that funded my 1964 exhibit *The Divine Proportion in the Platonic Solids* at Hayden Hall, the building then housing the Graduate School of Fine Arts of the University of Pennsylvania. In 1965, a Graham Foundation grant made it possible for me to go to Athens where I participated in a conference organized by Constantine Doxiadis and researched my theory of creative cycles in the history of architecture.[9] In 1968 I started teaching part-time at the Graduate School of Fine Arts of the University of Pennsylvania. Lou had had second thoughts and asked me to do part-time consultant work for him, such as reviewing his fairly well-developed projects and randomizing the geometry of the site plans of the government complex at Dacca in Bangladesh and at the Indian Institute of Management at Ahmedabad.

Several years after Lou's death I discovered how beautifully his three-phased process of creativity, "Nature of Space, Order, and Design," fit my four-phased theory of cycles. Since Lou was an introverted architect, he began the creative process with the "nature of the space." But in order to understand that difficult phase, two preceding phases should be included in the process—the all-important achievement of getting the commission and the next step of looking at precedents and history. From there many architects then make a quick, shallow return to the design phase. Lou's dissatisfaction with his students taking such an approach touched off his realization of the "nature of the space." That introverted phase requires a more profound probe beyond

9 My 1963 booklength proposal submitted to the Graham Foundation was the basis of my long article "Geometric Extensions of Consciousnes," *Zodiac 19* (Milan, 1969). In it I elaborated on the correlations between cycles in geometry, in natural forms, in psychology, in human creativity in individual cycles and in the collective cycles of history.

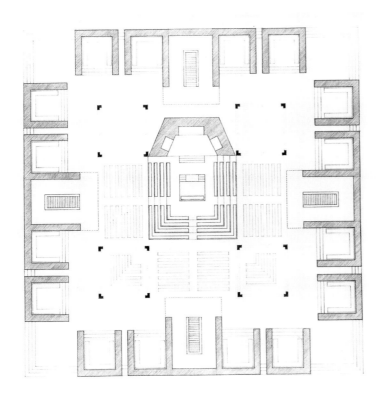

Kahn's plan for Hurva Synagogue, Jerusalem, in design 1967–74 (unbuilt).

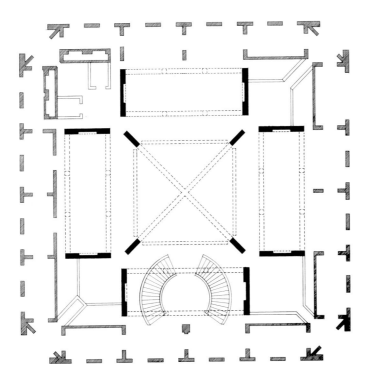

Kahn's plan for library at Phillips Exeter Academy, Exeter, New Hampshire, completed 1972.

history and *beyond memory* of any specific form, giving up some ego to ask what the space wants to be. The extroverted attitude of a superimposing "masculine" principle shifts to the introverted, receptive "feminine" principle—a genetic attitude that accepts all the complex multiple possibilities of time and space out of which the synthesis of a simple order may occur. This most difficult phase of creative breakthrough may never occur and cannot be forced. It has its own autonomous life force, a synchronous, spontaneous giving-birth to a conceptual order. The generative abstraction of order then evolves to complete the cycle in the extroverted design phase dealing with tangible, circumstantial requirements of site, structure, materials, specific program needs, and budget. This three-phase creative process (space, order, and design) fits meaningfully with the four-phase correlating cycles in my theory of geometry/nature/psyche/creativity, each of our concepts illuminating the other.

Lou Andreas-Salomé wrote, ". . . only when there is a twofold alternation between masculinity and femininity can two persons be more than one, no longer regarding each other as a goal (like miserable halves which need to be stuck together to form a whole) but rather *committed together to a goal outside themselves*. Only then are love and creation, natural fulfillment and cultural activity no longer opposites, but one."[10]

10 Lou Andreas-Salomé, *The Freud Journal of Lou Andreas Salomé*, trans. Stanley A. Leavy (New York: Basic Books, 1964).

212

Kahn's three-phase theory of creative process and Tyng's four-phase cycle of creativity.

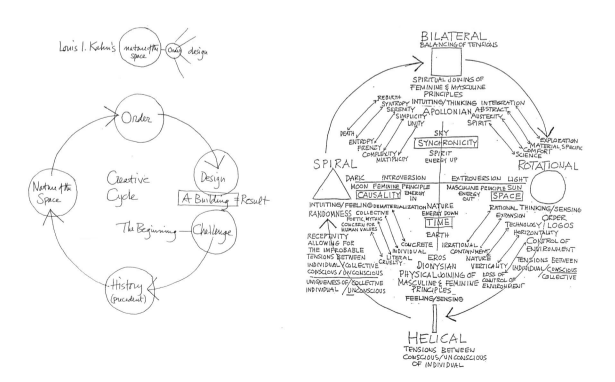

Self-portrait and portrait of
Tyng drawn by Kahn in 1946 and
inscribed December 27, 1972.

During the last two years of his life, Lou surprised me with gestures of affection on several of my visits to his office as consultant. Perhaps the passage of
time put our relationship in a more positive light for him. Lou had often said
that once you love someone you always love them. In the fall of 1973, Alex,
then in her junior year at Harvard, and I visited Lou's studio in the Furness
Building at the University of Pennsylvania in order to see him in action in his
role as teacher. Afterward he took us to the rare book room to show us drawings made by his own teachers. He also suggested I do a portrait of him and he
would do one of me for our National Academy of Design memberships. I did
not know until after he died on 17 March 1974, that, a little more than a year
before, he had inscribed to Jan Hochstim for his book a pair of drawings—
a self-portrait and a portrait he had made of me, both in 1946.[11] Surrounding
my portrait he wrote, "This is a portrait of Anne Tyng Architect who was the
geometry conceiver of the Philadelphia Tower. Well that is not exactly so
because I thought of the essence but she knew its geometry. To this day she
pursues the essence of constructive geometry, now teaches at the U. of P. and
other places like Harvard etc. We worked together on my projects from a
purely conception base. Dec 27, 1972." It was a public acknowledgment of
my role in our work together and, in a sense, Lou's last letter to me.

11 Jan Hochstim, *The*
Paintings and Sketches of
Louis I. Kahn (New York:
Rizzoli, 1991).

Index

Profound thanks to my extraordinary daughter Alex for giving me patient and wise advice, enthusiastic encouragement, and constructive suggestions and criticism in spite of her demanding schedule.

Continuing thanks to all at the Architectural Archives at the University of Pennsylvania for the esprit de corps that makes it a vital and stimulating place to work; special thanks for the generous spirit of my good friend and dynamic director of the Archives, Julia Converse, and for the invaluable help of Bill Whitaker, collections manager, who became an expert decipherer of Lou Kahn's handwriting. And warm thanks to Angie Geist for her cheerfulness in the face of continuous revisions.

Thanks to David Morton, senior editor at Rizzoli, for his calm guiding spirit and breadth of insight, to editor Megan McFarland and editorial assistant Ron Broadhurst, and to designers Brian Sisco and Susan Evans.

Finally, thank you to many friends who endured my preoccupation with this journey through the past and still remain friends.

Illustration Credits

Courtesy the Anne Griswold Tyng Collection: 9, 10, 11, 12, 13, 16, 19, 20, 21, 22, 23, 25, 26, 27, 29 (photo: Bachrach), 33, 35 bottom right (photo: Morton Weiss), 37 (photo: Morton Weiss), 38 (photo: Tana Hoban), 40–41 (photos: Edward Gallob), 42, 44, 47, 48, 49, 50, 51, 52–53 (photo: Jean Firth Tyng), 55, 58, 139, 146, 190, 198 (photo: John Ebstel), 199, 201, 203, 204, 205, 208 bottom, 212, 213

Courtesy the Louis I. Kahn Collection, University of Pennsylvania and Pennsylvania Historical and Museum Commission: 14, 32, 35 top (photo: John Ebstel), 35 bottom left, 36, 43, 54 (photo: Robert Damora), 56–57, 192, 193, 194, 197, 200, 206, 207, 208 top, 209, 211

Courtesy Yale University Press: 30, 46 (photo: Michael Bodycomb)